THE ADOLESCENT BRAIN

In recent years there have been tremendous advances in understanding how brain development underlies behavioural changes in adolescence. Based on the latest discoveries in the research field, Eveline A. Crone examines changes in learning, emotions, face processing and social relationships in relation to brain maturation, across the fascinating period of adolescent development.

This book covers new insights from brain research that help us to understand what happens when children turn into adolescents and then into young adults. Why do they show increases in sensation-seeking, risk-taking and sensitivity to opinions of friends? With the arrival of neuroimaging techniques, it is now possible to unravel what goes on in an individual's brain when completing cognitive tasks, when playing computer games, or when engaging in online social interactions. These findings help reveal how children learn, control thoughts and actions, plan activities, control emotions and think about intentions of others, offering a new perspective on behaviour and motivations of adolescents.

This is the first comprehensive book to cover the many domains of adolescent brain development, stretching from cognitive to affective to social development. It is valuable reading for students and researchers in the field of adolescent development and developmental cognitive neuroscience and those interested in how the developing brain affects behaviour in the teenage years.

Eveline A. Crone is Professor of Neurocognitive Developmental Psychology and is also Head of the Brain and Development Research Center at Leiden University, The Netherlands. Eveline's research includes the psychological and neural processes involved in cognitive control, self-regulation and social decision-making.

ESSAYS IN DEVELOPMENTAL PSYCHOLOGY

North American Editors:
Henry Wellman
University of Michigan at Ann Arbor

UK Editors:
Claire Hughes
University of Cambridge
Michelle Ellefson
University of Cambridge

Essays in Developmental Psychology is designed to meet the need for rapid publication of brief volumes in developmental psychology. The series defines developmental psychology in its broadest terms and covers such topics as social development, cognitive development, developmental neuropsychology and neuroscience, language development, learning difficulties, developmental psychopathology and applied issues. Each volume in the series will make a conceptual contribution to the topic by reviewing and synthesizing the existing research literature, by advancing theory in the area, or by some combination of these missions. The principal aim is that authors will provide an overview of their own highly successful research program in an area. It is also expected that volumes will, to some extent, include an assessment of current knowledge and identification of possible future trends in research. Each book will be a self-contained unit supplying the advanced reader with a well-structured review of the work described and evaluated.

PUBLISHED

Crone: *The Adolescent Brain*

Needham: *Learning About Objects in Infancy*

Hughes: *Social Understanding and Social Lives*

Sprenger-Charolles et al.: *Reading Acquisition and Developmental Dyslexia*

Barrett: *Children's Knowledge, Beliefs and Feelings about Nations and National Groups*

Hatano and Inagaki: *Young Children's Naïve Thinking about the Biological World*

Goldwin-Meadow: *The Resilience of Language*

Perez-Pereira and Conti-Ramsden: *Language Development and Social Interactions in Blind Children*

Bryne: *The Foundation of Literacy*

Meins: *Security of Attachment and Cognitive Development*

Siegal: *Knowing Children (2nd Edn.)*

Meadows: *Parenting Behavior and Children's Cognitive Development*

Langford: *The Development of Moral Reasoning*

Forrester: *The Development of Young Children's Social-Cognitive Skills*

Hobson: *Autism and the Development of Mind*

White: *The Understanding of Causation and the Production of Action*

Goswami: *Analogical Reasoning in Children*

Cox: *Children's Drawings of the Human Figure*

Harris: *Language Experience and Early Language Development*

Garton: *Social Interaction and the Development of Language and Cognition*

Bryant and Goswami: *Phonological Skills and Learning to Read*

Collins and Goodnow: *Development According to Parents*

For updated information about published and forthcoming titles in the *Essays in Developmental Psychology* series, please visit: **www.routledge.com/series/SE0532**

THE ADOLESCENT BRAIN

Changes in Learning, Decision-Making and Social Relations

Eveline A. Crone

Routledge
Taylor & Francis Group

LONDON AND NEW YORK

First published 2017
by Routledge
2 Park Square, Milton Park, Abingdon, Oxon OX14 4RN

and by Routledge
711 Third Avenue, New York, NY 10017

Routledge is an imprint of the Taylor & Francis Group, an informa business

British Library Cataloguing in Publication Data
A catalogue record for this book is available from the British Library

Library of Congress Cataloging in Publication Data
Names: Crone, Eveline, author.
Title: The adolescent brain : changes in learning, decision-making and
social relations in the unique developmental period of adolescence /
Eveline Crone.
Description: Abingdon, Oxon ; New York, NY : Routledge, 2017. |
Series: Essays in developmental psychology
Identifiers: LCCN 2016028559| ISBN 9781138855953 (hardback : alk. paper) |
ISBN 9781138855960 (pbk. : alk. paper) | ISBN 9781315720012 (ebook)
Subjects: LCSH: Adolescent psychology. | Adolescence. | Developmental
psychology.
Classification: LCC BF724 .C69 2017 | DDC 155.5 – dc23
LC record available at https://lccn.loc.gov/2016028559

ISBN: 978-1-138-85595-3 (hbk)
ISBN: 978-1-138-85596-0 (pbk)
ISBN: 978-1-315-72001-2 (ebk)

Typeset in Bembo and Stone Sans
by Florence Production Ltd, Stoodleigh, Devon, UK

Printed and bound by CPI Group (UK) Ltd, Croydon, CR0 4YY

CONTENTS

ACKNOWLEDGEMENTS

I am grateful to many people who supported me when writing this book. Zdena op de Macks read all the chapters carefully and provided valuable feedback. She also checked all the studies and added important literature sources. Sandra Arts-Binnendijk assisted me with translations and text editing. Sibel Altikulac made all the artwork.

I am also grateful to Mariette Huizinga and Lydia Krabbendam who hosted me at their department in the final stages of writing this book. I am very fortunate to work with amazing scientists at Leiden University, who always provide support and are inspiring at many levels.

Finally, I would like to thank the Netherlands Institute for Advanced Studies (NIAS) for providing the resources and facilities when writing this book.

1

INTRODUCTION

Imaging the adolescent brain

What is the matter with adolescents?

Why do adolescents always wake up so late? Why don't they plan their homework better? Why do they drive fast on motorcycles without helmets, or ride their skateboards on dangerous roads? Why do they come home much later than what they agreed upon with their parents when leaving the house? Why do they chat for hours with their friends on the phone or online, but don't take time to discuss their daily activities with their parents?

These are some of the many questions that parents and teachers wonder about when children grow up. For many parents it remains a mystery what goes on in their child's brain when entering adolescence; a new time period between childhood and adulthood and a natural time for exploration and trying new things.

This book will cover new insights from brain research that help us to understand what happens when children turn into adolescents, and from adolescents into young adults. With the arrival of neuroimaging techniques, it is now possible to unravel what goes on in an individual's brain when completing cognitive tasks, when playing computer games or when engaging in online social interactions. These findings inform us how children learn, control thoughts and actions, plan activities, control emotions and think about intentions of others. These findings offer a new perspective on behaviour and motivations of adolescents.

Neuroscience has taken large steps in the last decades, which has been a great source of new information that was not available 25 years ago. Methods have improved considerably in the last years, and studies have been developed with more targeted hypotheses and participant selections. At the same time, we need to be cautious not to take neuroscience findings as the golden standard too quickly, for example when the findings are quickly implemented in educational settings without a well-performed validation. In this book, I will present the newest findings in research on adolescent neuroscience with a broad focus on the different aspects that are important for cognitive, social and emotional development in adolescence.

What is adolescence?

Adolescence can be best described as the transition phase between childhood and adulthood. The word 'adolescence' comes from the Latin word *adolescere*, which means growing up. The age range for the start and the end of adolescence differs by culture, but generally it is agreed upon that adolescence is the period between ages 10 and 22 years (Steinberg, 2008).

Around 1900 the famous psychologist Stanley Hall described adolescence as a period of Storm and Stress (after the German Sturm und Drang movements) (Hall, 1904). According to Hall, there were three important aspects that characterized adolescence: conflicts with parents, mood swings and risky behaviour. This view of adolescence has for a long time been highly influential, and underscored that adolescence is a developmental period with its own problems and possibilities. Hall made a strong case for adapting the school requirements to the developmental phase of the adolescent, but it was not accepted at that time. Later, the idea of Storm and Stress was adapted, because it was documented that not all adolescents experience difficulties. Not all adolescents have conflicts with parents, and not all adolescents are risk takers. This adaptation to the Storm and Stress theory was important, because some researchers or theorists were so charmed by the Storm and Stress theory that they argued that Storm and Stress were necessary for healthy development, but this turned out not to be the case (Arnet, 1999). Nevertheless, more adolescents do, than do not experience Storm and Stress, and if Storm and Stress happens in a certain period of life, it is more likely to occur in adolescence than in another life period (Steinberg *et al.*, 2008).

Pubertal hormones

Puberty and adolescence are often intermixed, but puberty is only the starting point of adolescence, the period of hormonal change that results in sexual maturation (Shirtcliff, Dahl and Pollak, 2009). Puberty typically involves the period between ages 10 and 15 years, although there are marked individual differences, and in general puberty starts approximately 1 to 1.5 years earlier in girls than in boys (Braams, van Duijvenvoorde, Peper and Crone, 2015). The bodily changes that occur as a result of puberty are different for girls than for boys. Both girls and boys undergo the growth spurt and develop pubic hair, but in girls this goes together with changes such as breast growth and wider hips, and approximately 6 months after these bodily changes the menstrual cycle starts. In boys, puberty involves other changes such as lower voices and beard growth (Scherf, Behrmann and Dahl, 2012).

The start of these bodily changes is the result of the release of pubertal hormones that affect the pineal gland (Grumback and Styne, 2003). The pineal gland is connected – through the blood flow – to an important brain region, the hypothalamus.

The hypothalamus and pineal gland are constantly communicating with each other about the hormone levels that should be released. The hypothalamus regulates these levels and thereby controls the hormone levels that are released by the pineal gland. The start of puberty is characterized by the release of gonadotropin-releasing hormone (GnRH). GnRH is also released before puberty, but at a much lower level, and therefore has no influence yet on the sex-specific characteristics. The increase in both frequency and release of GnRH is what starts pubertal development. GnRH stimulates the pituitary, which releases luteinizing hormone (LH) and follicle stimulating hormone (FSH). LH causes the increase in oestrogen in girls and FSH causes the increase in testosterone in boys. This second phase of hormonal development (the first phase takes place in the uterus) contributes to sex-specific behaviour in both physical appearance and social behaviour (Scherf *et al.*, 2012).

Besides changes in bodily characteristics, hormones also influence how we feel and what we do. This is well illustrated by Sam, a 13-year-old boy who has felt quite insecure lately. He used to make friends easily, but now he feels awkward about looking different and he doesn't like that his voice and his skin are changing. Girls seem to make fun of him, which makes him feel uneasy. He doesn't understand where this is coming from, he never used to care about what girls were thinking, but now it makes him shy. He would prefer that everything would go back to how

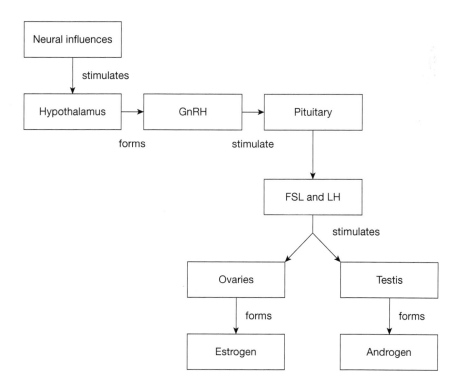

FIGURE 1.1 Neural influences and the development of pubertal hormones

it used to be, and he has decided to ignore girls altogether. Now, he mainly hangs out with his friends from the soccer team, which makes him feel least insecure.

Sam notices that not only his body is changing, but also his feelings are different. The influence of pubertal hormones works in two directions. First, the increase in hormone levels ensures that neurons in certain brain regions are temporarily activated. This occurs not only in puberty, but also in adulthood (Bos, Hermans, Ramsey and van Honk, 2012; van Honk et al., 2011). Hormone fluctuations can influence our moods, and this also occurs in puberty. Second, hormones also have an organizational influence on brain development, which is specific for puberty. During puberty brain organization changes and the presence or absence of certain hormones can have a long-term influence on brain function (Sisk and Foster, 2004; Sisk and Zehr, 2005). For example, in animal studies it was found that testosterone has direct effects on the development of the rat's brain (Melcangi et al., 2003; Pesaresi et al., 2015). Furthermore, in certain rare human childhood disorders, the release of GnRH is delayed, which causes a delay in the start of puberty (Grumback and Styne, 2003). This disorder can be overcome by hormone treatment, during which those hormones that are usually released naturally are externally given to the body. If the hormone treatment is started before or during the period in which puberty would usually start, this has no influence on intellectual capacities. However, when the hormone treatment is not given, or is started late, this can have consequences for certain cognitive abilities, such as spatial information processing (Linn and Petersen, 1985; Sisk and Zehr, 2005). Apparently, there is a constant communication between the brain and the pineal gland: they do not function well without each other. When the hypothalamus does not signal the pineal gland that GnRH should be released, then the absence of this hormone has again an influence on the development of the brain.

How do pubertal hormones influence brain and behaviour? It is well documented that hormones have a direct influence on bodily changes. This again has a large influence on how adolescents view themselves and others. Take the example of Sam. Because of the changes in the way he looks, he feels much more self-conscious and pays more attention to how his peers act. Given that the timing of puberty is different between boys and girls, and that the onset of puberty also varies within boys and girls, this causes large individual differences between adolescents. Where one 13-year-old girl can already be undergoing a growth spurt, developing breasts and wider hips, the other 13-year-old is much less advanced in puberty. Given that girls start puberty approximately 1.5 years earlier than boys, differences in pubertal development between boys and girls are especially apparent in the age range of 10–13 years. There are some indications that the onset of puberty has moved to younger ages. For example, large-scale studies have measured the onset of menarche and found a decline in the age of menarche since the 1800s (average age 17 years), until approximately 1940 (average age 13 years), after which it appears to have stabilized. These declines have been attributed to improved nutrition and health provision (Sorensen et al., 2012), although some have also argued that maladaptive environmental circumstances, such as good chemicals, may influence the onset of puberty (Parent et al., 2003). It remains debated if the age of puberty onset declined further after the 1940s (this seems to be the case for some, but not all puberty indices) (Euling *et al.*, 2008).

The timing of puberty can influence social identity (Brooks-Gunn and Warren, 1989). At a school party at Sam's school there were two groups of children who did not hang out together. The first group consisted of boys and girls who liked to act goofy and they were excited about their first school party. The second group consisted of the 'cool' boys and girls, who appeared much more mature than the first group. It was clear that they felt way too old to act goofy. Two boys from the 'cool' group secretly brought alcohol to the party, while the first group was happy to drink coke or sprite. Even though both groups were exactly the same age, the first group was less advanced in pubertal development than the second group. It has been documented in prior studies that while controlling for age, more advanced puberty is associated with more alcohol consumption (de Water, Braams, Crone and Peper, 2013).

Girls who are more advanced in puberty relative to their peers are more likely to develop depression and eating disorders (DeRose, Shiyko, Foster and Brooks-Gunn, 2011; Hamlat, Stange, Abramson and Alloy, 2014). The exact reason for this difference is not yet understood. The increase in depression rates in girls could be a direct consequence of hormones on the brain, but could also be due to the reaction from others and self on the bodily changes and physical appearance as a result of the hormonal effects on the body. The hormonal influences on the body generally cause the adolescent's physical appearance to change in such a way that it becomes more distanced from the ideal body image as displayed in the media. Especially in girls, the individual differences in the gain of body fat can make them feel insecure (McCabe, Ricciardelli and Banfield, 2001). Furthermore, dieting is often not successful, which causes feelings of failing. In boys, a maturer body is more accepted, leading to higher popularity and social dominance of those boys who are more advanced in puberty (Rowe, Maughan, Worthman, Costello and Angold, 2004).

Feeling jet lagged

Jim is 16 years old and he delivers the early morning newspaper in order to earn extra money to go on vacation with his friends to Spain. Even though he tries really hard to be on time, he has already overslept three times. The last time despite setting two alarms, he still failed to wake. The first two times that he overslept, his mother helped him: his boss called him at home and his mother drove him to work and helped him to deliver the papers, nearly delivering them on time. But the third time she did not feel like helping out anymore believing that as a 16-year-old, he should be responsible for waking himself up on time. It is not that he does not want to wake up, but it just seems impossible to get out of bed on time.

Going to bed late, having a hard time waking up, sleeping in on the weekends; these are all characteristics of the sleeping patterns of adolescents. During puberty, the release of the hormones changes to more adult-like patterns. This causes a huge change in the biorhythm of adolescents, and the related sleeping patterns (Crowley,

Acebo and Carskadon, 2007). Young children typically get tired earlier in the evening, which makes them fall asleep at a suitable time. In adolescents, the system that makes them feel tired gets delayed to later in the evening, which causes them to be awake until much later, not feeling tired until possibly 11 p.m. Yet, all the bodily changes associated with entering puberty take a lot of energy, which causes a difficult situation for adolescents – they cannot fall asleep until late in the evening but have a hard time waking up in the morning. It constantly feels like having a jet lag (Malone et al., 2015).

On average, young children need 10 hours of sleep per night, whereas adults feel rested when they sleep 8 hours a night. Adolescents need on average approximately 9–9.5 hours sleep to feel rested but they almost never get this amount of sleep (Dewald, Meijer, Oort, Kerkhof and Bogels, 2010; Mercer, Merritt and Cowell, 1998). There is a risk for a chronic feeling of sleep deprivation. Sleep quality is even more reduced under periods of stress, such as exam periods (Dewald, Meijer, Oort, Kerkhof and Bogels, 2014). This again influences their behaviour; with sleep deprivation it is much more difficult to store new information or to be creative (Landmann et al., 2015). Sleep deprivation can also cause mood swings, and in extreme circumstances it can lead to depression and affect the immune system (Dagys et al., 2012). Finally, recent studies have shown that sleep deprivation also has pronounced effects on brain structure development (Telzer, Goldenberg, Fuligni, Lieberman and Galvan, 2015), as well as on brain function. These studies show that sleep deprivation is related to reduced activity in brain regions that are important for behavioural regulation, specifically in the presence of rewards (Hasler et al., 2012; Telzer, Fuligni, Lieberman and Galvan, 2013).

Growing up to be a mature member of society

The developmental period between ages 10 and 22 is considered as the phase in development of attaining mature personal and social goals, such as being able to run a household, vote for political parties, being responsible in traffic and taking care of family members. Many changes in developing mature social goals occur during mid-adolescence (approximately ages 15–18 years) and late-adolescence (approximately ages 19–22 years).

Hester's parents don't have a specific religious background and they give her the freedom to develop her own ideas. When Hester is 16 years old, she watches a documentary on the Internet about a volunteer project set up by young people to help children who grow up in poor circumstances in Bolivia. This documentary makes a big impression on her, but because she is too young to take part in the project herself, she decides to join a humanistic youth society that helps children who grow up in poor circumstances. The society has specific ideas that appeal to Hester, and it gives her the feeling that they treat her as an adult and that she can contribute to issues that matter in society. It is the first time she feels that she is being treated as a person whose ideas matter, who can make a difference, not as a child. At home, she is very engaged in discussions and she talks about the importance of justice in societies. Her parents are surprised at this quick transition from a young girl who liked to play with her friends to a young woman with personal ideals about a better world.

Even though the start of adolescence is well defined by the hormonal changes that mark the onset of puberty, when adolescence ends is a more difficult question. For example, in the Netherlands youth can drink alcohol when they are 18 years old, but in the United States the legal drinking age is 21 years. In contrast, in the United States youth can drive a car when they are 16 years old, whereas this age is set to 18 years in the Netherlands. In some countries youth can vote for a political party when they are 18 years, but this used to be 21 years. Thus, it is not clear when adolescence ends and adulthood starts, and to some extent this end point is culturally defined (Schlegel and Barry, 1991). The end point of adolescence is also dependent on the domain that is being studied, for example, whether the domain is cognitive development or social-affective development.

One of the domains where changes occur during adolescence is in cognitive development, which largely refers to the way we learn new information and control thoughts and actions. This increase in cognitive abilities is often captured under the umbrella of the development of executive control functions. Executive functions encompass many different processes, such as the ability to keep information in working memory, to be able to switch flexibly between tasks, and to inhibit responses if the environment requires us to (Diamond, 2013). Together, these executive functions allow us to perform complex and goal-oriented behaviours. With age, executive functions improve considerably, which allows us to plan tasks and adapt to an ever-changing environment. However, the different subtypes of executive functions each develop at a different rate, and mature planning most likely is not yet in place until all subcomponents of executive functions work together well (Huizinga, Dolan and van der Molen, 2006). The brain regions that are important for the development of executive functions are described in Chapter 2.

Besides the development of cognitive abilities, adolescence is associated with changes in social-affective functions. Adolescents develop a different perspective on society. Additionally, the way they view themselves and others changes.

According to Loevinger's model (Loevinger, 1998; Westenberg, Drewes, Goedhart, Siebelink and Treffers, 2004), adolescents go through different stages of social-emotional development that all aid in the task of becoming an independent adult, with mature social goals. The first stage, the impulsive stage, is characterized by a combination of impulsive behaviour, dependence on others and obedience. Because of the impulsive character of this stage, children are likely to quickly act out aggressively, but also empathically. Children in this stage are mostly self-oriented, and expect others to fulfil their needs. They expect parents and teachers to set the rules, and this also means that impulsive behaviour can be easily corrected.

The next stage is the self-protective stage. Opportunistic relations characterize this stage. The dependent position in the impulsive stage is being replaced by a self-protective position, in which adolescents try to control their impulses and emotions. Feelings of being hurt or the experience of fear are often denied. This stage is characterized by hedonic goals, and friendships are formed based on self-benefit.

An important change occurs when switching from the second to the third stage, the conformist stage. This stage is characterized by equality, reciprocity and pro-social behaviour. In the impulsive stage children are mostly self-oriented, but in the conforming stage benefits of others are experienced as benefit for the self as well. Among friends it is important to be prosocial and there is a fear for rejection. Relations are reciprocal, that is, there needs to be mutual liking before participating in joint activities.

The final stage is the self-aware stage, which is characterized by a feeling of uniqueness, tolerance and personal relations. The adolescent in this stage is more aware of personal needs and goals, and also when these do not match the group goals. Being sincere and true to one's own needs is important, even when this can lead to rejection. Behaviour is more situation-dependent and flexible.

There are no clear age boundaries by which these stages occur, because the speed with which children go through these stages is different for each individual. Generally speaking one could say that the impulsive and self-protective stages occur mostly between ages 8 and 11 years. Between ages 12 and 14 years most adolescents switch from the self-protective to the conformist stage, which peaks around age 16 years, but still increases until approximately age 21 years. Between ages 21 and 25 years approximately 75 per cent of the adolescents are in the self-aware stage (Westenberg et al., 2004).

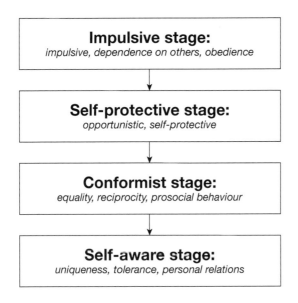

Impulsive stage:
impulsive, dependence on others, obedience

Self-protective stage:
opportunistic, self-protective

Conformist stage:
equality, reciprocity, prosocial behaviour

Self-aware stage:
uniqueness, tolerance, personal relations

FIGURE 1.2 Stadia of ego-development

While these cognitive and social-affective changes occur, there are massive changes in the structure and function of the developing brain, knowledge that has come available as a result of developmental neuroimaging research. Over the last 15–20 years, we have become able to describe these changes in relation to brain development. Before this time, we hardly had the tools to examine brain development in vivo, and even today the techniques for scanning the developing brains is advancing everyday. In the next chapters, we will go over these changes in brain development in more detail by examining the change in emotions and control of emotions (Chapters 3 and 4), and what makes adolescence a unique developmental period for developing social relations (Chapter 5–8). Before starting with exploring these exciting brain-behaviour relations, let's first go over the changes that occur in the structure of the brain in more detail.

Brain changes in adolescence

During adolescence there is a tremendous change in the organization of the brain, but not all brain regions develop at the same pace. It is thought that the pace with which a brain region develops is informative for the skills that children develop (Casey, Tottenham, Liston and Durston, 2005). For example, regions of the prefrontal cortex that develop most slowly are important for cognitive skills, such as planning, that also show protracted development (Gogtay et al., 2004; Mills and Tamnes, 2014).

Before these changes are described in more detail in the subsequent chapters, this chapter will first go over the basic building blocks of the brain. The description will be general. For more detailed descriptions of brain anatomy, readers are referred to the following handbooks: Scarabino and Salvolini, 2006; Standring, 2016.

Building a brain

The brain is an enormously complex organ. It consists of billions of neurons, which are all interconnected. The interesting aspect of these neurons and connections between them is that they form networks that communicate with each other.

The brain consists of both grey and white matter. The grey matter consists of cell bodies of neurons. These neurons generate action potentials (a wave of electrical power) and thereby send information to other cells. The neurons are being supported by glia cells (glia = glue), which make myelin (an isolating protection layer), which take care of the remaining structure of the cell and transporting waste. The white matter consists of axons (the strings of the neuron), which connect neurons over longer distances.

The brain has many subregions that are important for different psychological and behavioural functions. To understand these functions, it is important to learn more about the different subregions and how they are different from each other.

The cerebellum is the structure at the back of the brain that looks like a mushroom. The pons is a small brain region at the end of the spinal cord and is

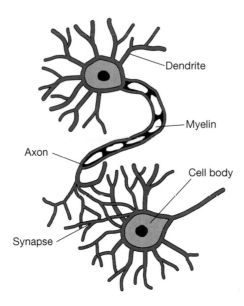

FIGURE 1.3 Neurons and their connections

evolutionary the oldest part of the brain. Even though the pons is a small region of the brain, its functions should not be underestimated. The pons is a crucial brain region for sending information to and from the cerebrum to the cerebellum. Above the pons, sits the mid-brain, and in front of the mid-brain the thalamus and hypothalamus are located. These structures are important for regulation of hormones and vital bodily functions, such as controlling body temperature.

More to the front and at the outer layers of the brain the cerebrum (also referred to as the cortex) is located. The cortex is the layered outer layer of the brain that is evolutionary relatively young. Because of the layered structure, the cortex encompasses a very large part of the brain. The cortex has the size of two hands folded like fists, but if it were to be completely unfolded it would have the size of a basketball.

The cortex can be subdivided into four subregions: the occipital lobe, the temporal lobe, the parietal lobe and the frontal lobe. As will become clear in the upcoming chapters, each of these lobes has different contributions to a wide range of complex social behaviours.

Because the cortices are so large, we often use indications that designate the location within the cortex. The first designation is superior/inferior, with superior meaning 'upper' and inferior meaning 'lower'. The second designation is ventral/dorsal, with ventral indicating 'belonging to the side of the stomach' and dorsal indicating 'situated at the side of the back'. The third designation is anterior/posterior, with anterior meaning 'towards the front' and posterior meaning 'towards the back'. And the final designation is medial/lateral, with medial referring to 'on the inner side' and lateral referring to 'on the outer side'.

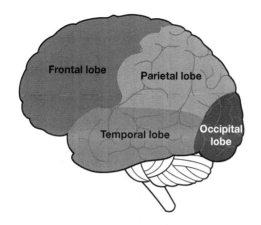

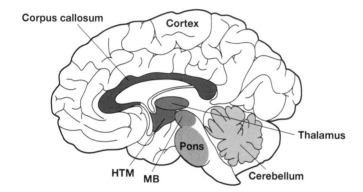

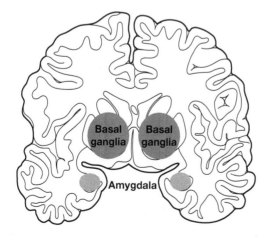

FIGURE 1.4 Brain regions from lateral and medial views. HTM= Hypothalamus, MB = Midbrain

Three structures located deep under the cortex are the basal ganglia, amygdala and hippocampus, which work closely together with the cortical regions.

Finally, the brain consists of two hemispheres (left and right), which are connected to each other through the corpus callosum, a structure in the middle of the brain that communicates signals quickly between the hemispheres. There are many speculations on the difference between left and right localized functions in the brain, but most of these hemispheric differences are not yet well understood. For most individuals, the language functions are left lateralized in the brain, but this is probably the best-documented function in terms of hemispheric differences. For many other functions, the left-right distinction is not yet clear, and researchers often report that both hemispheres are involved in a specific cognitive or social-affective function.

The developing brain

The development of the cortex is a very complicated process. The largest changes take place before an individual is born; in 9 months time a single cell is transformed into a complete complex organ with all its complexities. Before birth, approximately 6–18 weeks after conception, there is an enormous production of neurons (more than 200,000 a minute!) (Uylings, 2000). During this period, the brain is formed. Neurons travel from a neural tube to different locations and make connections between brain regions. The cortex is formed from the inside out. Some neurons already have a specific function when they are being developed and for these neurons it is important that they reach their final destination. But most neurons are very flexible and can fulfil different functions. They do not take on their specific function until they have reached their final destination, and by working together with the other local neurons they take on specific functions (Uylings, 2000).

The first brain region being developed is the brain stem, which is a region that is important for primary functions, such as controlling heart rate. The larger brain regions, including the cortex, develop later, but at approximately 4 months after conception the brain is basically formed. The only task it has to fulfil is growing and making connections. Much of this growth and making connections is taking place before a child is born.

Yet, after birth the cortex still develops with great speed, and the development of the different brain structures is accompanied by changes in behaviour. During development of the cortex, there is a large production of grey matter, which is followed by a decrease. This decrease in grey matter is often accompanied by better behavioural performance (use it or lose it). The overproduction potentially leads to less efficiency, and by decreasing the number of neurons the most effective ones are getting stronger and the ones that are inefficient are eliminated. This increase and decrease of grey matter take place at a different pace for different regions of the brain.

The peaks in grey matter for different brain regions take place approximately between ages 4 and 8 years, but the final stages are not reached until early adulthood (Gogtay *et al.*, 2004; Gogtay and Thompson, 2010). It was recently found that decrease in synaptic spine density in the prefrontal cortex continues even beyond adolescence, until the early thirties (Petanjek *et al.*, 2011). There is some evidence for gender differences in trajectories of brain development, especially in global brain volume, but if and how this relates to behavioural outcomes is not well understood (Koolschijn and Crone, 2013; Vijayakumar *et al.*, 2016).

The peak in grey matter occurs relatively early for primary sensory brain regions, such as the occipital lobe, but much later for the association cortices, such as the prefrontal cortex and the temporal-parietal lobes. Researchers believe that behaviour of children is influenced by the speed with which the grey matter peaks. These different developmental trajectories can potentially explain why children learn different skills at different ages. Some brain regions may not yet have reached maturity to perform certain tasks (Casey *et al.*, 2005).

Contrary to grey matter, which shows an increase and decrease, the white matter in the brain shows more general increases during childhood and adolescence (Ladouceur, Peper, Crone and Dahl, 2012), although a recent study also points out specific regional changes in white matter architecture between ages 4 and 11 years (Krogsrud *et al.*, 2016). The grey matter generates action potentials, which are being protected and transported by white matter. As such, the white matter is an important substance for communication between neurons. This information is being communicated by neurotransmitters, which can have an activating role, by which neurons start to work harder, or an inhibiting role, which makes neurons work less hard. The production of neurotransmitters also changes until approximately ages 15–16 years. A well-known neurotransmitter is dopamine, which has an important role in learning and motivation, and it has a particularly prominent role in adolescence (Telzer, 2016; Wahlstrom, White and Luciana, 2010).

Pubertal hormones influence brain development such that pubertal hormones can have a stimulating influence on grey and white matter development. Given that there is variation in the onset of puberty, it is possible to examine whether puberty influences brain development in children of the same age and the same socio-economic background. These studies demonstrated that children who are more advanced in puberty also have more mature white matter tracks in the brain (Peper, Hulshoff Pol, Crone and van Honk, 2011; Peper, Koolschijn and Crone, 2013). Even though puberty is expressed differently in boys and girls, there is not much evidence for gender differences in white matter development (Krogsrud *et al.*, 2016). Thus, it is likely that the developmental patterns for boys and girls are comparable, and that puberty affects brain development in both sexes.

Some brain regions have a period of increased sensitivity, or plasticity, which is a period during which brain development is extra flexible. These are time periods where damage and deprivation have a larger influence than during other stages in life. For example, if a child is exposed to alcohol or nicotine during pregnancy, this increases the likelihood of mental problems later in life (Gautam, Warner, Kan and Sowell, 2015). But also after birth there are periods when certain brain regions are additionally sensitive to environmental influences, such as the occipital lobe, which is highly sensitive to visual stimulation early in life. If this region is not stimulated in this specific period in development, it loses its function (Collignon *et al.*, 2015). In these sensitive periods the brain is highly equipped to fulfil a certain task and if connections are not made in this specific period, it becomes more difficult to make these connections later on because there is a lot of competition between neurons. For other brain regions, the sensitive period is less clear or takes much longer (Fuhrmann, Knoll and Blakemore, 2015). This is the case, for example, for brain regions that are important for learning new skills in school, such as algebra (Qin *et al.*, 2004).

Measuring the brain

The techniques that can be used to study structure and activity in the living brain have only been recently developed, but there is a longstanding interest in understanding how the brain works. Before the techniques were developed to study brain functions directly, researchers have gained their knowledge about brain functions from patients with brain damage by a tumour, a bullet or other types of brain damage. These types of brain damage, despite being devastating for the patients, have been a tremendous source of information about how the brain works. For example, neuropsychologists have made large steps in unravelling brain function during the Second World War, by studying the deficits of soldiers as a function of brain damage (Mecacci, 2005). These researchers examined which functions were intact and which ones were distorted, and after these patients died, their brain was dissected and the location of the deficit was determined. This allowed the researchers to unravel which brain damage caused which behavioural impairments.

This type of research is still conducted nowadays, with the exception that it is no longer necessary to wait until a patient has passed away until it is possible to determine the location of the damage. Using brain-imaging techniques, such as magnetic resonance imaging (MRI), the structure of the brain can be determined with great precision. When a patient has a specific behavioural impairment, such as face recognition deficit or verb generation deficit, and the damage is in a very specific location, it can be concluded that the brain region that is damaged is most likely important for that specific behaviour (Bechara, Damasio, Tranel and Damasio, 2005). But how can we determine which brain regions are important for performing certain tasks in healthy adults? Or in children and adolescents?

To answer this question, researchers have relied on two important techniques that can aid in answering these questions. In the 1930s the electroencephalograph (EEG) was developed. EEG works with electrodes that are placed on the outside of the skull and can detect small changes in brain activity. When a group of neurons fires together, this results in small electrical signals that are being picked up with EEG. A large advantage of this method is that it can determine with great precision *when* certain neural activity is taking place (it has good temporal resolution).

However, because activity is measured at the surface of the brain, that is, at the skull, we don't know yet *where* the activity is taking place (it has poor spatial resolution). Several excellent review papers have been written on the development of the brain based on EEG methods (Segalowitz, Santesso and Jetha, 2010; van Noordt and Segalowitz, 2012).

The location of brain activity can be measured in great detail with the second important brain imaging technique, which is MRI. The studies that are described in this book are mainly based on this method. MRI allows us to examine the structure of the brain, such as the grey matter and white matter. With functional MRI (or fMRI), it is possible to examine activity in the brain, that is to say, the brain in action (Huettell, Song and McCarthy, 2004). This works in the following way. Increased activity of neurons is associated with an increase in oxygen flow in the brain. This increase in oxygen can be picked up with fMRI. This technique measures the temporary increase in oxygen using magnetic sensitivity of oxygen parts. It can be summarized as follows: When a brain region works very hard (e.g. when we move our arms, motoric regions in the brain are activated), then blood flow to these areas increases. Blood contains red blood cells, which in turn contain a protein called haemoglobin. Haemoglobin can bind oxygen, and when it does, the magnetic properties of haemoglobin change. This change in magnetism is picked up with the MRI scanner, and referred to as the blood-oxygen-level dependent (BOLD) signal. In essence, the BOLD signal is an indirect measure of brain activity (Huettell *et al.*, 2004).

How does that work when someone is lying in an MRI scanner? This is where the behavioural scientists start to play an important role. When someone is in the MRI scanner, we can present computer tasks to the person in the scanner, using a projection screen outside of the scanner. Through a mirror system installed inside the MRI scanner and above the head of the person in the scanner, he or she can see the projection screen. With button boxes installed inside the scanner, the participant can make choices, such as for example responding to left or right pointing errors, or making judgements about emotional faces. While the participant performs the task, the MRI scanner makes hundreds of images of the brain, and this allows researchers to examine which brain region required a lot of oxygen when the participants sees an emotional face.

A large advantage of this technique is that it allows us to measure brain activity in a non-invasive way, without potentially harmful X-rays. Being inside an MRI scanner is quite comfortable. This makes MRI a very suitable technique to learn about brain development in children and adolescents. MRI research is even done in children as young as 4 years. With the arrival of MRI, the knowledge of how the brain develops has increased tremendously, but this is only the tip of the iceberg. If the developments continue at the same speed as over the last two decades, we can get ready for very exciting times ahead with many discoveries for scientists and anyone who is interested in the development of children and adolescents.

References

Arnet, J. J. (1999). Adolescent Storm and Stress, Reconsidered. *American Psychologist, 54*, 317–26.

Bechara, A., Damasio, H., Tranel, D. and Damasio, A. R. (2005). The Iowa Gambling Task and the somatic marker hypothesis: some questions and answers. *Trends Cogn Sci, 9*(4), 159–62; discussion 162–154. doi:10.1016/j.tics.2005.02.002

Bos, P. A., Hermans, E. J., Ramsey, N. F. and van Honk, J. (2012). The neural mechanisms by which testosterone acts on interpersonal trust. *NeuroImage, 61*(3), 730–737. doi:10.1016/j.neuroimage.2012.04.002

Braams, B. R., van Duijvenvoorde, A. C., Peper, J. S. and Crone, E. A. (2015). Longitudinal changes in adolescent risk-taking: a comprehensive study of neural responses to rewards, pubertal development, and risk-taking behavior. *J Neurosci, 35*(18), 7226–38. doi:10.1523/JNEUROSCI.4764-14.2015

Brooks-Gunn, J. and Warren, M. P. (1989). Biological and social contributions to negative affect in young adolescent girls. *Child Dev, 60*(1), 40–55. Retrieved from www.ncbi.nlm.nih.gov/pubmed/2702873

Casey, B. J., Tottenham, N., Liston, C. and Durston, S. (2005). Imaging the developing brain: what have we learned about cognitive development? *Trends Cogn Sci, 9*(3), 104–110. doi:10.1016/j.tics.2005.01.011

Collignon, O., Dormal, G., de Heering, A., Lepore, F., Lewis, T. and Maurer, D. (2015). A short period of visual deprivation at birth triggers long-lasting crossmodal reorganization of the occipital cortex in humans. *J Vis, 15*(12), 192. doi:10.1167/15.12.192

Crowley, S. J., Acebo, C. and Carskadon, M. A. (2007). Sleep, circadian rhythms, and delayed phase in adolescence. *Sleep Med, 8*(6), 602–612. doi:10.1016/j.sleep.2006.12.002

Dagys, N., McGlinchey, E. L., Talbot, L. S., Kaplan, K. A., Dahl, R. E. and Harvey, A. G. (2012). Double trouble? The effects of sleep deprivation and chronotype on adolescent affect. *J Child Psychol Psychiatry, 53*(6), 660–667. doi:10.1111/j.1469-7610.2011.02502.x

de Water, E., Braams, B. R., Crone, E. A. and Peper, J. S. (2013). Pubertal maturation and sex steroids are related to alcohol use in adolescents. *Horm Behav, 63*(2), 392–397. doi:10.1016/j.yhbeh.2012.11.018

DeRose, L. M., Shiyko, M. P., Foster, H. and Brooks-Gunn, J. (2011). Associations between menarcheal timing and behavioral developmental trajectories for girls from age 6 to age 15. *J Youth Adolesc, 40*(10), 1329–1342. doi:10.1007/s10964-010-9625-3

Dewald, J. F., Meijer, A. M., Oort, F. J., Kerkhof, G. A. and Bogels, S. M. (2010). The influence of sleep quality, sleep duration and sleepiness on school performance in children and adolescents: A meta-analytic review. *Sleep Med Rev, 14*(3), 179–189. doi:10.1016/j.smrv.2009.10.004

Dewald, J. F., Meijer, A. M., Oort, F. J., Kerkhof, G. A. and Bogels, S. M. (2014). Adolescents' sleep in low-stress and high-stress (exam) times: a prospective quasi-experiment. *Behav Sleep Med, 12*(6), 493–506. doi:10.1080/15402002.2012.670675

Diamond, A. (2013). Executive functions. *Annu Rev Psychol, 64*, 135–168. doi:10.1146/annurev-psych-113011-143750

Euling, S. Y., Herman-Giddens, M. E., Lee, P. A., Selevan, S. G., Juul, A., Sorensen, T. I., Dunkel, L., Himes, J. H., Teilmann, G. and Swan, S. H. (2008). Examination of US puberty-timing data from 1940 to 1994 for secular trends: panel findings. *Pediatrics, 121 Suppl 3*, S172–191. doi:10.1542/peds.2007-1813D

Fuhrmann, D., Knoll, L. J. and Blakemore, S. J. (2015). Adolescence as a sensitive period of brain development. *Trends Cogn Sci, 19*(10), 558–566. doi:10.1016/j.tics.2015.07.008

Gautam, P., Warner, T. D., Kan, E. C. and Sowell, E. R. (2015). Executive function and cortical thickness in youths prenatally exposed to cocaine, alcohol and tobacco. *Dev Cogn Neurosci*, *16*, 155–165.

Gogtay, N., Giedd, J. N., Lusk, L., Hayashi, K. M., Greenstein, D., Vaituzis, A. C., Nugent, T. F., 3rd, Herman, D.H., Clasen, L. S., Toga A. W., Rapoport, J. L. and Thompson, P. M. (2004). Dynamic mapping of human cortical development during childhood through early adulthood. *Proc Natl Acad Sci USA*, *101*(21), 8174–9. doi:10.1073/pnas.0402680101

Gogtay, N. and Thompson, P. M. (2010). Mapping gray matter development: implications for typical development and vulnerability to psychopathology. *Brain Cogn*, *72*(1), 6–15. doi:10.1016/j.bandc.2009.08.009

Grumback, M. M. and Styne, D. M. (2003). Puberty: Ontogeny, neuroencodrinology, physiology and disorders. In Larsen, P. R., Kronenberg, H. M., Melmed, S. and E. S. Polonsky (eds), *Williams Textbook of Endocrinology* (10th ed., pp. 115–1286). Philadelphia: WB Saunders/Elsevier Science.

Hall, G. S. (1904). *Adolescence: Its Psychology and its Relation to Physiology, Anthropology, Sociology, Sex, Crime, Religion, and Education*. Prentice-Hall, NJ: Englewoord Cliffs.

Hamlat, E. J., Stange, J. P., Abramson, L. Y. and Alloy, L. B. (2014). Early pubertal timing as a vulnerability to depression symptoms: differential effects of race and sex. *J Abnorm Child Psychol*, *42*(4), 527–538. doi:10.1007/s10802-013-9798-9

Hasler, B. P., Dahl, R. E., Holm, S. M., Jakubcak, J. L., Ryan, N. D., Silk, J. S., Phillips, M. L. and Forbes, E. E. (2012). Weekend-weekday advances in sleep timing are associated with altered reward-related brain function in healthy adolescents. *Biol Psychol*, *91*(3), 334–41. doi:10.1016/j.biopsycho.2012.08.008

Huettell, S. A., Song, A. W. and McCarthy, G. (2004). *Functional Magnetic Resonance Imaging, 3rd Edition*. Massachusetts USA: Sinauer Associates Inc.

Huizinga, M., Dolan, C. V. and van der Molen, M. W. (2006). Age-related change in executive function: developmental trends and a latent variable analysis. *Neuropsychologia*, *44*(11), 2017–2036. doi:10.1016/j.neuropsychologia.2006.01.010

Koolschijn, P. C. and Crone, E. A. (2013). Sex differences and structural brain maturation from childhood to early adulthood. *Dev Cogn Neurosci*, *5*, 106–18. doi:10.1016/j.dcn.2013.02.003

Krogsrud, S. K., Fjell, A. M., Tamnes, C. K., Grydeland, H., Mork, L., Due-Tonnessen, P., Bjørnerud, A., Sampaio-Baptistae, C., Anderssone, J., Johansen-Berge, H. and Walhovd, K. B. (2016). Changes in white matter microstructure in the developing brain– A longitudinal diffusion tensor imaging study of children from 4 to 11 years of age. *NeuroImage*, *124*(Pt A), 473–486. doi:10.1016/j.neuroimage.2015.09.017

Ladouceur, C. D., Peper, J. S., Crone, E. A. and Dahl, R. E. (2012). White matter development in adolescence: the influence of puberty and implications for affective disorders. *Dev Cogn Neurosci*, *2*(1), 36–54. doi:10.1016/j.dcn.2011.06.002

Landmann, N., Kuhn, M., Maier, J. G., Feige, B., Spiegelhalder, K., Riemann, D. and Nissen, C. (2015). Sleep strengthens but does not reorganize memory traces in a verbal creativity task. *Sleep*. Retrieved from www.ncbi.nlm.nih.gov/pubmed/26518596

Linn, M. C. and Petersen, A. C. (1985). Emergence and characterization of sex differences in spatial ability: a meta-analysis. *Child Dev*, *56*(6), 1479–1498. Retrieved from www.ncbi.nlm.nih.gov/pubmed/4075870

Loevinger, J. (1998). *Technical Foundations for Measuring Ego Development* Mahwah NJ: Lawrence Erlbaum.

Malone, S. K., Zemel, B., Compher, C., Souders, M., Chittams, J., Thompson, A. L. and Lipman, T. H. (2015). Characteristics associated with sleep duration, chronotype, and social jet lag in adolescents. *J Sch Nurs*. doi:10.1177/1059840515603454

McCabe, M. P., Ricciardelli, L. A. and Banfield, S. (2001). Body image, strategies to change muscles and weight, and puberty: do they impact on positive and negative affect among adolescent boys and girls? *Eat Behav*, *2*(2), 129–149. Retrieved from www.ncbi.nlm.nih.gov/pubmed/15001042

Mecacci, L. (2005). Luria: a unitary view of human brain and mind. *Cortex*, *41*(6), 816–822. Retrieved from www.ncbi.nlm.nih.gov/pubmed/16350662

Melcangi, R. C., Ballabio, M., Cavarretta, I., Gonzalez, L. C., Leonelli, E., Veiga, S., . . . Magnaghi, V. (2003). Effects of neuroactive steroids on myelin of peripheral nervous system. *J Steroid Biochem Mol Biol*, *85*(2–5), 323–327. Retrieved from www.ncbi.nlm.nih.gov/pubmed/12943718

Mercer, P. W., Merritt, S. L. and Cowell, J. M. (1998). Differences in reported sleep need among adolescents. *J Adolesc Health*, *23*(5), 259–263. Retrieved from www.ncbi.nlm.nih.gov/pubmed/9814385

Mills, K. L. and Tamnes, C. K. (2014). Methods and considerations for longitudinal structural brain imaging analysis across development. *Dev Cogn Neurosci*, *9*, 172–190. doi:10.1016/j.dcn.2014.04.004

Parent, A. S., Teilmann, G., Juul, A., Skakkebaek, N. E., Toppari, J. and Bourguignon, J. P. (2003). The timing of normal puberty and the age limits of sexual precocity: Variations around the world, secular trends, and changes after migration. *Endocr Rev*, *24*(5), 668–693. doi:10.1210/er.2002-0019

Peper, J. S., Hulshoff Pol, H. E., Crone, E. A. and van Honk, J. (2011). Sex steroids and brain structure in pubertal boys and girls: A mini-review of neuroimaging studies. *Neuroscience*, *191*, 28–37. doi:10.1016/j.neuroscience.2011.02.014

Peper, J. S., Koolschijn, P. C. and Crone, E. A. (2013). Development of risk taking: contributions from adolescent testosterone and the orbito-frontal cortex. *J Cogn Neurosci*, *25*(12), 2141–2150. doi:10.1162/jocn_a_00445

Pesaresi, M., Soon-Shiong, R., French, L., Kaplan, D. R., Miller, F. D. and Paus, T. (2015). Axon diameter and axonal transport: In vivo and in vitro effects of androgens. *NeuroImage*, *115*, 191–201. doi:10.1016/j.neuroimage.2015.04.048

Petanjek, Z., Judas, M., Simic, G., Rasin, M. R., Uylings, H. B., Rakic, P. and Kostovic, I. (2011). Extraordinary neoteny of synaptic spines in the human prefrontal cortex. *Proc Natl Acad Sci USA*, *108*(32), 13281–13286. doi:10.1073/pnas.1105108108

Qin, Y., Carter, C. S., Silk, E. M., Stenger, V. A., Fissell, K., Goode, A. and Anderson, J. R. (2004). The change of the brain activation patterns as children learn algebra equation solving. *Proc Natl Acad Sci USA*, *101*(15), 5686–5691. doi:10.1073/pnas.0401227101

Rowe, R., Maughan, B., Worthman, C. M., Costello, E. J. and Angold, A. (2004). Testosterone, antisocial behavior, and social dominance in boys: pubertal development and biosocial interaction. *Biol Psychiatry*, *55*(5), 546–552. doi:10.1016/j.biopsych.2003.10.010

Scarabino, T. and Salvolini, U. (2006). *Atlas of Morphology and Functional Anatomy of the Brain*. Berlin Heidelberg: Springer.

Scherf, K. S., Behrmann, M. and Dahl, R. E. (2012). Facing changes and changing faces in adolescence: a new model for investigating adolescent-specific interactions between pubertal, brain and behavioral development. *Dev Cogn Neurosci*, *2*(2), 199–219. doi:10.1016/j.dcn.2011.07.016

Schlegel, A. and Barry, H. (1991). *Adolescence: An Anthropological Inquiry*. Free Press.

Segalowitz, S. J., Santesso, D. L. and Jetha, M. K. (2010). Electrophysiological changes during adolescence: a review. *Brain Cogn*, *72*(1), 86–100. doi:10.1016/j.bandc.2009.10.003

Shirtcliff, E. A., Dahl, R. E. and Pollak, S. D. (2009). Pubertal development: correspondence between hormonal and physical development. *Child Dev*, *80*(2), 327–37. doi:10.1111/j.1467-8624.2009.01263.x

Sisk, C. L. and Foster, D. L. (2004). The neural basis of puberty and adolescence. *Nat Neurosci,* 7(10), 1040–7. doi:10.1038/nn1326

Sisk, C. L. and Zehr, J. L. (2005). Pubertal hormones organize the adolescent brain and behavior. *Front Neuroendocrinol, 26*(3–4), 163–174. doi:10.1016/j.yfrne.2005.10.003

Sorensen, K., Mouritsen, A., Aksglaede, L., Hagen, C. P., Mogensen, S. S. and Juul, A. (2012). Recent secular trends in pubertal timing: implications for evaluation and diagnosis of precocious puberty. *Horm Res Paediatr, 77*(3), 137–145. doi:10.1159/000336325

Standring, S. (2016). *Gray's Anatomy* (41st ed.). Canada: Elsevier.

Steinberg, L. (2008). A social neuroscience perspective on adolescent risk-taking. *Dev Rev, 28*(1), 78–106. doi:10.1016/j.dr.2007.08.002

Steinberg, L., Albert, D., Cauffman, E., Banich, M., Graham, S. and Woolard, J. (2008). Age differences in sensation seeking and impulsivity as indexed by behavior and self-report: evidence for a dual systems model. *Dev Psychol, 44*(6), 1764–1778. doi:10.1037/a0012955

Telzer, E. H. (2016). Dopaminergic reward sensitivity can promote adolescent health: A new perspective on the mechanism of ventral striatum activation. *Dev Cogn Neurosci, 17,* 57–67.

Telzer, E. H., Fuligni, A. J., Lieberman, M. D. and Galvan, A. (2013). The effects of poor quality sleep on brain function and risk taking in adolescence. *NeuroImage, 71,* 275–283. doi:10.1016/j.neuroimage.2013.01.025

Telzer, E. H., Goldenberg, D., Fuligni, A. J., Lieberman, M. D. and Galvan, A. (2015). Sleep variability in adolescence is associated with altered brain development. *Dev Cogn Neurosci, 14,* 16–22. doi:10.1016/j.dcn.2015.05.007

Uylings, H. B. (2000). Development of the cerebral cortex in rodents and man. *Eur J Morphol, 38*(5), 309–312. Retrieved from www.ncbi.nlm.nih.gov/pubmed/11151043

van Honk, J., Schutter, D. J., Bos, P. A., Kruijt, A. W., Lentjes, E. G. and Baron-Cohen, S. (2011). Testosterone administration impairs cognitive empathy in women depending on second-to-fourth digit ratio. *Proc Natl Acad Sci USA, 108*(8), 3448–52. doi:10.1073/pnas.1011891108

van Noordt, S. J. and Segalowitz, S. J. (2012). Performance monitoring and the medial prefrontal cortex: a review of individual differences and context effects as a window on self-regulation. *Front Hum Neurosci, 6,* 197. doi:10.3389/fnhum.2012.00197

Vijayakumar, N., Allen, N. B., Youssef, G., Dennison, M., Yucel, M., Simmons, J. G. and Whittle, S. (2016). Brain development during adolescence: A mixed-longitudinal investigation of cortical thickness, surface area, and volume. *Hum Brain Mapp.* doi:10.1002/hbm.23154

Wahlstrom, D., White, T. and Luciana, M. (2010). Neurobehavioral evidence for changes in dopamine system activity during adolescence. *Neurosci Biobehav Rev, 34*(5), 631–648. doi:10.1016/j.neubiorev.2009.12.007

Westenberg, P. M., Drewes, M. J., Goedhart, A. W., Siebelink, B. M. and Treffers, P. D. (2004). A developmental analysis of self-reported fears in late childhood through mid-adolescence: social-evaluative fears on the rise? *J Child Psychol Psychiatry, 45*(3), 481–495. Retrieved from www.ncbi.nlm.nih.gov/pubmed/15055368

2

THE LEARNING BRAIN

Executive functions

The rise of educational neuroscience

How do you tackle a difficult arithmetic problem? Why is it so easy for us to learn a second language while we're young, but harder once we get older? Why are some children brighter than others? Over the last few years, there has been increased attention for knowledge about the brain on the one hand and our expectations of adolescents in school on the other hand. This has led to an entirely new field of research called educational neuroscience (Byrnes and Vu, 2015). The beauty of this new trend is that it tries to combine the ideas of teachers, pupils, education experts and neuroscientists, in order to try and adapt the learning situation in schools to what is possible for the adolescent.

Suzanne is now attending high school and until last year, her grades were good. Unfortunately, over the past year her grades have dropped a bit. It's not that Suzanne doesn't want to move up to the next class, but when she gets home from school, there are often many other things vying for her attention. First she Whatsapps with one of her girlfriends, then she spends some time on Instagram, buys a new top at H&M and in the evening there's hockey practice. In between, there's little time to study for her physics test. And she completely forgot the English assignment that's not quite finished yet, not to mention tomorrow's history debate that needs preparing. When she focuses on one assignment at a time, there really isn't a problem, but having to deal with everything at once can sometimes be a little overwhelming. She can't manage to write it all down in her calendar, let alone remember what the scrawls and scribbles mean. Yet the school expects her to independently plan her schoolwork, as a way of practising the independence that will be expected of her once she moves on to further education. Suzanne is willing, but it seems like her brain isn't quite cooperating yet.

Researchers have discovered that exactly those areas of the brain that are important for planning have not reached their adult status during adolescence

(Gogtay *et al.*, 2004). These areas are still maturing and communication between the different areas of the brain involved is not yet optimal. So, when Suzanne is asked to plan her schoolwork independently, while simultaneously having to deal with all of the distractions outside of school, her brain is simply not able to cope with it all. In this chapter, I will discuss what is necessary for good planning skills, which areas of the brain are involved and how these areas of the brain mature.

The frontal cortex: regulator of executive functions

In order to be able to plan complicated tasks, you need a number of cognitive abilities or skills. These are the so-called executive functions that allow us to stay focused, achieve future goals and to engage in intelligent behaviour (Diamond, 2013). In order to understand what executive functions are and how they develop, this chapter will focus on the cortex – the outer, folded layer of the cerebrum (see Chapter 1).

Some areas of the brain have a single, specific function. In the case of the cortex, this is more complicated. Many of the functions managed by the cortex involve several sub-areas within the cortex, mainly because these functions are so complex. In order to plan future actions, you have to have command of all sorts of different skills. Let's go back to the example of Suzanne: it is clear now that she has to be able to do many different things at once in order to get all of her schoolwork done everyday. For one thing, she needs to make sure to write down clearly what is expected of her in her calendar. To do so, she needs to distil the most important information from potentially elaborately phrased instructions. It's important to not get distracted by something else that's happening in the classroom (fellow students talking, the school bell ringing), which could cause her to lose track of the instructions. In addition, she has to make sure to stay focused while doing her homework (concentration), and to ignore unimportant distractions (incoming text messages). Finally, she needs the flexibility to be able to switch between assignments. If she has homework assignments for five different subjects, she cannot afford to work on the first assignment until 11 p.m. All in all, this means that planning is quite a complex affair, for which you need to be able to consider several priorities and resist distractions in order to achieve your long-term goals, which is possibly why it involves a large number of brain areas.

For a large part, the frontal cortex manages planning, in collaboration with many connections with other cortical and subcortical regions (Casey, 2015; Diamond, 2013). This part of our brain is situated in the front of the skull and takes up about one-third of the cortex. So it's quite a large area, with many sub-areas and connections.

Within the frontal lobe, we discern three areas: the frontal motor cortex, the lateral frontal cortex and orbitofrontal cortex. These areas are situated in different locations and each has different functions. For example, the motor cortex is situated more towards the back, and is important for starting and performing motor functions (as indicated by its name). The lateral cortex is situated more to the front than the motor cortex, and is important for planning behaviour, applying rules and following instructions (Casey, 2015). The orbitofrontal cortex is situated under the lateral cortex. The orbitofrontal cortex is important for planning and purposeful actions, especially in the case of emotional decisions (Blakemore and Robbins, 2012) and social decisions (Blakemore, 2008).

Taken together, the frontal cortex contains a large number of functions that are important for planning. These planning functions are often clustered under the name *executive functions*. This term is an umbrella term for functions important for behaviour that is oriented towards future goals. For example, think of remembering a route or paying attention in class even when people behind you are talking. These are all skills that demand a certain measure of control and which are better executed by adults than by adolescents and children (Huizinga, Dolan and van der Molen, 2006). Our knowledge about the areas of the brain that are important for planning and control functions is based on different research methods, such as research in patients and brain-scanning techniques.

Planning after brain damage

Possibly due to ridges on the inside of the skull to the front of the head, the frontal cortex is the area of the brain that most often suffers brain damage. Logically, damage in this area has large consequences for everyday actions. However, the frontal cortex is large and heterogeneous, which is why damage to different areas within the frontal cortex still has different effects on behaviour, depending on the damage's location. As this chapter deals with the learning brain, I will mainly focus on the functions of the outer area of the frontal cortex (the lateral frontal cortex), because damage to this area of the brain has the most significant consequences for executive functions. What happens when there is damage to this area of the brain?

Based on research in patients, we know that the outer area of the frontal cortex, the lateral frontal cortex, is important for problem solving, retaining information in working memory and the ability to stop inappropriate behaviour in time (Szczepanski and Knight, 2014). Because these functions are difficult for patients with damage to the frontal cortex, they often make inappropriate remarks, simply because they lack the inhibition to hold them back (Kramer *et al.*, 2013). They also have difficulty understanding jokes with a punchline, but do laugh about simple slapstick humour (Docking, Murdoch and Jordan, 2000). The former requires information about several situations to be combined, whereas this is not required for slapstick humour.

Patients with damage to the frontal cortex experience difficulty with adjustments especially (Barcelo and Knight, 2002). They are used to performing actions the way they normally do them and find it hard to switch to different, unexpected behaviour. For example, when a frontal cortex patient is asked to hit a nail into the wall using the back of a hairbrush, this may cause more difficulty for the patient than expected, despite the simple instructions. The patient will understand the instruction, but will feel the inclination to brush his hair as soon as he gets hold of the hairbrush. This is because the action of using a brush to comb your hair is so automatized that it is hard for the patient to suppress (Besnard *et al.*, 2010).

As we can see below, behavioural adjustment is a skill that is still strongly developing during adolescence, too, which is important when considering the importance of direction and feedback in a school environment.

A glimpse into the human brain during planning

The way the frontal cortex works in healthy individuals has been extensively mapped using neuroimaging techniques such as functional magnetic resonance imaging (fMRI). This research has mainly led to the discovery that different areas in the frontal cortex have different functions, a discovery that was hard to determine based on patient research.

The studies using neuroimaging techniques have mainly been important to investigate the abilities of children and adolescents, and which areas of the brain are involved in these abilities. For example, we know that in some parts of the frontal cortex, the number of brain cells (i.e., grey matter) changes more slowly than in other areas (Casey, 2015). This structural change has large consequences for the way children retain or plan information. We only recently discovered how the areas of the brain important for planning and performing a certain task actually *function* during childhood and adolescence. In this chapter, a number of these (cognitive) skills are described in relation to the developing brain.

As we will see in this chapter, most of the basic executive function skills develop between the ages of 4 and 12 years of age (Diamond, 2013). This is reflected in children's working memory and inhibitory skills, which improve hugely during their school years. However, many complex cognitive skills continue to mature into adolescence, such as planning and flexibility (Huizinga *et al.*, 2006). This is not surprising considering we know the frontal cortex continues to develop, only reaching its full potential when we reach the age of 20–25 (Casey, 2015; Petanjek *et al.*, 2011). We have come to know more and more about the areas of the brain that are important for the development of these skills, and how they work together.

There are a few points we should keep in mind. The early fMRI studies used relatively small sample sizes, with 15–25 participants per age group. More recent studies used larger samples and have therefore more power to detect developmental trajectories. Furthermore, researchers try to select these participants so that they form a good reflection of the population, but in small samples, that is a lot harder than when 100 or 200 children are tested. In addition, it can be difficult sometimes to translate the tasks used in the lab to the complex planning demanded in daily life. For example, in the case of lab tasks, there is often a specific instruction, participants are highly motivated to perform well and there are very few external distractions. Keeping that in mind, we have come to learn a lot about how the adolescent brain is involved in different types of executive control functions. Below, these are described by function.

Working memory: out of sight, out of mind?

When an 18-month-old infant is asked to get a doll or toy car, which has just been hidden under one of two boxes, the infant will be able to indicate the right location fairly accurately. But when the time between hiding and being allowed to search is extended, for example to 10 or 20 seconds, the infant will no longer know where the toy is hidden (Diamond, 2013). This is because the infant's working memory has not yet properly developed. The largest changes in working memory occur during early childhood. Contrary to the traditional assumption that working memory is fully developed around 10 years of age, researchers now know that the working memory continues to be improved during adolescence. The extent of the changes during adolescence depends on the level of difficulty of the working memory's task (Diamond, 2013; Huizinga et al., 2006).

One way of measuring working memory is by varying the amount of time between stimulus presentations and retrieving information, as is done in the study with infants we mentioned earlier. For example, such a task will show three locations on a screen in succession, and the participant is asked to point to these three locations in the same order, after a delay of 5, 10 or 15 seconds. Everyone, both adults and children, has more difficulty performing this task after a delay of 15 seconds compared to 5 seconds. However, comparatively speaking, young children have more difficulty with the 15-seconds-task than adults, while performing equally well on the 5-seconds-task (Diamond, 2013). Based on these findings, it is concluded that the capacity of young children's working memory is smaller. By the time children reach the age of 12 years or thereabouts, they can perform this task just as well as adults.

A second way to investigate working memory is by varying not the duration, but the amount of information someone needs to remember. An example: You are taking part in a quiz show and you are being shown four objects, which then disappear behind a screen. Next, you're asked to name these objects from memory. That is not such a difficult task, but when the number of objects increases to eight or ten, the task becomes more complicated. After all, your working memory now needs to remember eight objects instead of four. The same goes for a working memory task in the lab. If you're asked to remember the order of four locations on a computer screen, this is not very hard to do, but once the number of locations increases, the task becomes a lot more difficult. This can also be the case when asked to remember ten random words or pictures of objects. Here, too, we observe that people find it difficult to remember several locations, words or pictures, but children make more mistakes compared to adults as the number of locations, words or pictures increases (Diamond, 2013). For this reason, young children have difficulty remembering several assignments at once, or a long shopping list. In the two working memory tasks above (in which either the time between the objects and retrieval, or the number of objects was varied), researchers have found age-related changes until the age of 15 years. Although the changes became smaller between the ages of 12 and 15 years, during this period of adolescence, the participants still had not reached adult levels (Klingberg, 2006). After the age of 14–15 years, adolescents usually perform at adult level (Brahmbhatt, McAuley and Barch, 2008).

Age differences become even larger when participants are asked to reorganize the information in the working memory. This type of working memory is measured by the so-called manipulation task. This can be done by asking someone to remember a random string of letters, such as P-B-F-N, for 6 seconds, and subsequently to repeat them back out loud. This is a little tricky, but will not take a great deal of effort. However, if you ask the person to repeat the letters after 6 seconds and in alphabetical order, this will be significantly harder. Another example of a complicated manipulation task concerns the n-back task, during which a consecutive list of letters is presented (or in the spatial version a dot moves around in a grid), and the participants need to press a button if the letter, or the spatial location, is the same as what was presented two or three trials earlier.

This type of working memory, in which you need to *work* with the information in your mind, is a lot more difficult for children and adolescents than it is for adults (Diamond, 2013). This most likely has to do with the functioning of several sub-areas in the frontal cortex, which need to become attuned to each other and need to learn how to communicate. Therefore, the skill to manipulate information within your own mind, or to work with it in your thoughts, continues to develop far into adolescence (Kwon, Reiss and Menon, 2002).

This type of working memory plays an important part in several skills at school. Just picture a difficult math problem that requires numbers to be manipulated. Or picture outlining a working schedule, taking into account the starting and finishing times of class periods, time to eat lunch and being on time for football practice in the afternoon. Such planning puts a high demand on the working memory, especially on the manipulation of information in the working memory. Indeed, prior studies observed that working memory performance is correlated to school tasks such as math and language abilities (Libertus, Brannon and Pelphrey, 2009). Furthermore, not only behavioural measures of working memory, but also brain activity during a working memory task turned out to be a predictor of future school outcomes, specifically for arithmetics (Dumontheil and Klingberg, 2012).

The lateral prefrontal cortex, together with the parietal cortex, is important for successfully performing a working memory task. Several studies have shown that activity in these areas of the brain increases whenever information needs to be held in memory for a longer period of time, or when the number of locations or pictures to be remembered increases (D'Esposito and Postle, 2015; Smith and Jonides, 1999). Performance on a working memory task is directly related to the degree of activity in the lateral prefrontal cortex. That is to say, individuals in whom this area of the brain works harder, perform better in the working memory task (Finn, Sheridan, Kam, Hinshaw and D'Esposito, 2010; Huang, Klein and Leung, 2015; Klingberg, 2006). So, we have fairly strong indications that this area is responsible for a solid working memory.

It appears that the type of information does not make much of a difference; the lateral prefrontal cortex is active when retaining information about locations as well as pictures, numbers and objects (Brahmbhatt *et al.*, 2008; Thomason *et al.*, 2009). However, the type of working memory that is drawn upon does appear to make a difference, that is, whether you only need to remember information, or whether you actually need to *work* with this information. If information only needs to be retained (you do not need to do anything with the information except for remembering it), activation is observed in the ventral and superior lateral prefrontal cortex (D'Esposito and Postle, 2015).

Several researchers have shown that activity in the lateral prefrontal cortex and parietal cortex during working memory maintenance increases childhood and adulthood (Klingberg, Forssberg and Westerberg, 2002; O'Hare, Lu, Houston, Bookheimer and Sowell, 2008). Others have shown that in children activity is more diffusely active across different regions of the brain, whereas in adolescence it starts to specialize towards the specific neural regions that are also active in adults (Ciesielski, Lesnik, Savoy, Grant and Ahlfors, 2006; Geier, Garver, Terwilliger and Luna, 2009; Libertus *et al.*, 2009; Scherf, Sweeney and Luna, 2006).

Consistent with this finding, two prior studies have observed a decrease in activity in the hippocampus with increasing age while performing a working memory task (Finn *et al.*, 2010; von Allmen, Wurmitzer and Klaver, 2014), suggesting that younger individuals may rely on different neural regions when performing a working memory task.

Possibly children are more easily distracted during the delay period of a working memory task; it was previously found that children show stronger frontal cortex activity than adults during the delay period when distractors are presented (Olesen, Macoveanu, Tegner and Klingberg, 2007). However, other studies have found increased activity in lateral prefrontal cortex in children across ages 8–14 years when they had to ignore distracting information during a working memory task (Wendelken, Baym, Gazzaley and Bunge, 2011), so the exact way in which distractors work is not yet well understood.

In the prior section, studies were discussed that examined working memory maintenance, which relies on the ventral lateral prefrontal cortex. However, when the information needs to be *worked within the mind* (such as being alphabetized), we observe activation in the mid-dorsal (upper) lateral prefrontal cortex (D'Esposito and Postle, 2015). This distinction is important, since we know that the structural maturation of the brain takes place earlier for the ventral and superior area than for the mid-dorsal area. That is why we have investigated which areas of the brain are active in children when they are asked to remember pictures of objects (such as a clock, a house, a shoe or a dog) for 6 seconds. We compared this to the brain activity when asked to reproduce the pictures in inverted order. Children below the age of 12 had more trouble with the manipulation task, and their dorsal-lateral prefrontal cortex was less active than that of 15- and 16-year-olds and adults (Crone, Wendelken, Donohue, van Leijenhorst and Bunge, 2006; Jolles, Kleibeuker, Rombouts and Crone, 2011). Similar results were obtained when researchers presented this task in a visuospatial n-back version. In this task it was found that both activity in the lateral prefrontal cortex and the parietal cortex increased linearly across ages 7–22 years (Kwon *et al.*, 2002; Spencer-Smith *et al.*, 2013), possibly related to adults being better able to activate these regions over a sustained period of time (Brahmbhatt, White and Barch, 2010).

Importantly, in a large sample of 951 participants between ages 8 and 22 years, it was found that activity in the lateral prefrontal cortex and parietal cortex mediated the age-related increases in working memory performance, accounting for 38 per cent of the variance (Satterthwaite *et al.*, 2013). Therefore, we believe that adolescents mainly have more difficulty with working memory *manipulation*, because the dorsal area of the lateral frontal cortex shows protracted development.

In a laboratory in Sweden, Torkel Klingberg and his colleagues have been studying the relationship between the increase in working memory capacity in

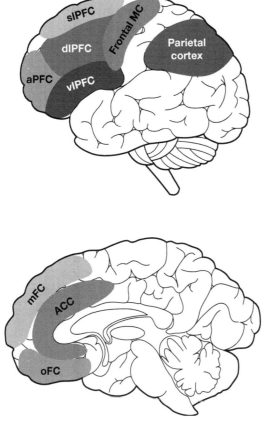

FIGURE 2.1 Brain regions from lateral and medial views. slPFC = superior lateral prefrontal cortex; dlPFC = dorsal-lateral prefrontal cortex; vlPFC = ventral lateral prefrontal cortex; aPFC = anterior prefrontal cortex; ACC = anterior cingulate cortex; oFC = orbitofrontal cortex; mFC = medial frontal cortex

children and the development of the brain, cross-sectionally and longitudinally. They mainly use tasks in which participants have to remember the location of pictures on the computer screen, and they compare performance on this task with brain activity in children, adolescents and adults aged 6–22 years. These studies showed that the areas of the brain that are important for location-related working memory in adults (the lateral prefrontal cortex, in collaboration with the parietal cortex) become more and more active as children get older (Dumontheil *et al.*, 2011). Using advanced measuring methods, they also investigated whether the paths between these areas of the brain were important for the performance of the task. And indeed: the stronger the white matter connections between these areas of the brain, the better the working memory performance (Darki and Klingberg, 2015). Moreover, brain structure in regions outside the typical working memory network (basal ganglia and thalamus) was predictive for future cognitive outcomes, over and above the cognitive tests that were administered at baseline (Ullman, Almeida and Klingberg, 2014). Together, these findings implicate that both functional activity, as well as structural measures such as white-matter connectivity and grey-matter volume, in regions within and outside of the frontal-parietal network, are important for understanding age-related changes in working memory capacity.

Inhibition: stopping in time

You're cycling to work or school in a hurry, so you rush to cross the road – but suddenly the traffic light changes to yellow. You have to brake quickly, before the light turns red.

Or you're visiting your neighbour and the phone that lies on the table rings. You move to answer it, but just in time you realize you're not in your own home.

All of the above are examples of inhibition, that is to say, restraining or stopping your behaviour. Being able to restrain our behaviour in time is of crucial importance to safe and socially adjusted behaviour, but is mainly difficult when you suddenly have to deviate from what you are used to doing (such as not picking up the phone) or when you are halfway into performing an action (such as crossing the road when the light changes).

The game 'Simon says' is a good example to demonstrate that children have more difficulty restraining or stopping their behaviour than adults. For this game, the children are instructed to perform an action, but only when the instruction is preceded by the words 'Simon says'. For example, when the instruction is: 'Simon says: clap your hands', everybody claps his/her hands. When the instruction is: 'Simon says: stamp your feet', everybody stamps his/her feet. However, when the instruction is 'Shake your head', you're not supposed to do anything, because it was not preceded by 'Simon says'. It is difficult not to carry out this instruction, because you are so used to doing what is said that the movement has already been started, as it were, before you realize that this time, you're not supposed to act. This is especially difficult for children.

Inhibition has been abundantly researched in development psychology. Researchers often use computer tasks for this, because they want to measure very precisely when it is possible for children and adults to inhibit their behaviour. For the 'go/no-go' task, a participant is asked to press a red button if a certain picture is shown, a red dog, for example. The dog is shown again and again in quick succession, so the button has to be pressed again and again, too. But if the dog is blue, the button may not be pressed. Sometimes children manage not to press the button for the blue dog, but often, they fail. This is especially hard for preschoolers (Diamond, 2013), but children up to the age of 12 or so also have more trouble restraining their behaviour than adults (Casey, 2015; Schel and Crone, 2013).

The go/no-go task measures inhibition ability (the ability to restrain yourself) in a simple way. Researchers have looked for more advanced ways of measuring inhibition, with the development of the 'stop-signal' task. The reason for developing this was because researchers wanted to know more precisely how long it takes for someone to be able to stop. But how can you measure the speed of stopping if no buttons are being pressed? Researchers found a smart way around this. For the stop-signal task, the participant is asked to respond to green arrows pointing left or right, by pressing a left or right button with their index fingers. This has to happen very quickly, so the response becomes automatic. But when the arrow turns red, the participant is not allowed to respond (as in the case of a traffic light). That is easy when the arrow turns red right away, but it becomes much harder when the arrow remains green for a while first, and only turns red when you are about to press the button. This can be compared to a traffic light turning yellow when you're still some distance from the crossing, or a traffic light turning yellow when you've just started to cross. By varying the time between showing the arrow and turning the arrow red, researchers can determine how much time someone needs in order to be able to stop successfully. This time is called the stop signal reaction time (SSRT). Between the ages of 3 and 6, the SSRT is slow (Lee, Lo, Li, Sung and Juan, 2015). However, the SSRT does not reach adult levels until the ages of 12–14 at least (van den Wildenberg and van der Molen, 2004). Until that age, children and adolescents have more difficulty stopping than adults (Schel, Scheres and Crone, 2014).

When someone has damage to the right ventral area of the lateral prefrontal cortex (in an area slightly below the area that is important for retaining information in working memory), this also leads to great difficulty with stopping (Aron, Robbins and Poldrack, 2004). Healthy adults show activity in this area when performing a go/no-go task or a stop-signal task (Aron *et al.*, 2004; Aron, Robbins and Poldrack, 2014).

A number of researchers have investigated the development of this inhibition area between the ages of 8 and 12, and the ages of 18 and 25 using go/no-go task or stop signal tasks. The most important finding was that when 8- to 12-year-olds perform a go/no-go task during an fMRI-scan, they show less activity in the right ventral part of the lateral prefrontal cortex than the 18- to 25-year-olds (Bunge, Dudukovic, Thomason, Vaidya and Gabrieli, 2002; Durston *et al.*, 2006; Rubia et al., 2006; Tamm, Menon and Reiss, 2002). This probably means that this area of the brain is not yet fully developed in children. Interestingly, these children often show activity in a different area of the prefrontal cortex, such as the dorsal area of the prefrontal cortex (Booth et al., 2003; Durston et al., 2006). Similar results have been obtained for the stop-signal task (Rubia et al., 2013; Rubia, Smith, Taylor and Brammer, 2007), especially for proactive inhibition (Vink et al., 2014). So, possibly children have to call upon other brain areas, because the area important for inhibition has not yet fully matured or shows a shift from diffuse to localized activity.

During adolescence (between the ages of 12 and 18), this child-like utilization of brain capacity changes into adult-like brain activity, especially because the ventrolateral part of the prefrontal cortex continues to mature. When the same children are tested a few years later, the ventrolateral frontal cortex worked better for the go/no-go task (Durston et al., 2006). It seems that the inhibition area starts working better and better as children grow older, which is possibly why they become better at inhibiting their behaviour over the years (Cohen et al., 2010a). Increased activity in the ventral part of the prefrontal cortex during a go/no-go task is also associated with more safe driving, suggesting that brain activity not only explains task performance but also other aspects or real-world behaviour that relies upon the ability to stop possibly dangerous actions (Cascio et al., 2015).

It is important to keep in mind that these developmental trajectories differ between individuals and are possibly also related to environmental circumstances. One study looked into this by following boys and girls across multiple sessions who came from lower or average social economic status (SES) backgrounds. They found that especially girls from low SES environments showed deviant development of response inhibition and reduced communication between important brain regions for behavioural control in prefrontal cortex (the dorsolateral prefrontal cortex and the anterior cingulate cortex, the latter region will be discussed in more detail below) (Spielberg et al., 2015). Therefore, in future research it will be important

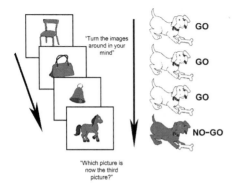

FIGURE 2.2 Examples of working memory and inhibition go/no-go tasks

to perform more longitudinal studies in which it is possible to examine general maturational trends as well as individual differences in background variables.

Resisting interference

Earlier, we discussed outside distractions that needed to be ignored. But sometimes, the distraction is contained within the assignment itself, leading to part of the assignment needing to be suppressed. The reading inhibition task is a good example of an assignment that contains the distraction. Reading words can be done very quickly, in fact making it an automatic process. That is why it's difficult to ignore the *meaning* of these words. This is what characterizes the famous Stroop task, named after American psychologist John Ridley Stroop, who developed this task in 1935 (Stroop, 1935). The purpose of this task is to read out the colour of a word. The twist is in this difficulty: the word being presented is also a colour. For example, the words RED or GREEN are presented in the corresponding colour (e.g., RED in red ink) or in a different colour (e.g., GREEN in yellow ink). When required to name the colour, but with the word stating something else, it is very hard to not read what the word says. This is because reading is an automated process; we are so used to reading that we cannot suppress it.

This process is called *interference* and continually goes on all around us. For example, a slip of the tongue is often due to interference. This often happens when we mix up two family members or call a new love by our ex-lover's name. Patients with damage to the frontal cortex, but also children, find it very difficult to suppress the reading response in the Stroop task (Cipolotti *et al.*, 2015). For this task, researchers have measured how the brains of children and adolescents work when performing this task.

The areas of the brain important for successfully performing the Stroop task in adults (the dorsal-lateral frontal cortex) keep changing until far into adolescence; changes are visible until the age of 20. One study conducted in 7- to 25-year-olds looked at the relationship between the age and the degree of activity in the lateral frontal cortex during the interference word pairs (e.g., the word BLUE printed in the colour green, for which the colour green needed to be named). Results showed that there was a linear increase in the degree of activity in this area of the brain until the age of 22 (Adleman *et al.*, 2002). So, the older the adolescent, the better he or she can suppress irrelevant information, because there is more activity in the lateral frontal cortex. These changes were strongest on the left side of the brain, probably because this task calls on language processes that are situated on the left side. These changes in brain activity were also present between adolescents of 18–19 years and young adults of 23–25 years, suggesting that this task calls upon late maturing processes (Veroude, Jolles, Croiset and Krabbendam, 2013).

So, although adolescents are quite good at restraining their actions at the age of 12–14 years (as in the traffic light example), they still have a lot of difficulty suppressing interference. For example, Suzanne will find it hard to remember French vocabulary when the radio is on while she studies. Although adolescents seem to excel at *multitasking* (making phone calls, sending text messages and doing home-work at the same time), these studies show that the adolescent brain is hindered more by *interference* (Mills, Dumontheil, Speekenbrink and Blakemore, 2015).

Flexibility and planning: fast adaptation to a changing environment

Flexibility is probably the most important control function. After all, we often have to adjust our plans because something unexpected happens, suddenly demanding our attention. For example, you've just decided to go out for some groceries when the phone rings. We have to make a flexible switch from our first plan (leaving) to the second plan (picking up the phone), and after that remembering what our initial goal was. We need this flexibility when learning all kinds of new skills such as mathematics or a new computer program. To do so, we make continuous use of feedback about our own behaviour. We perceive what was and what wasn't right, and adjust what we were doing based on that information. That's why feedback learning is incredibly important to the learning process in school. Flexibility is especially challenged when the action you need to perform is different from what you are used to.

The role of flexibility has largely been much investigated with experiments in which participants are required to apply rules (e.g., respond to a colour) and are given feedback about this (correct or incorrect). Once a participant has responded according to the colour rule for a certain period, the rule will change without warning. The participant is supposed to use the 'feedback' in order to find the new rule. For example, the test leader will provide negative feedback when participants respond to the colour of a picture (namely, he will say the answer is incorrect), but positive feedback when they respond to its shape (saying the answer is correct). The original version of this task – developed in 1948 – is called the *Wisconsin Card Sorting Task* (Milner, 1963). However, many new and adjusted versions of this task have been developed, which are used to try and measure different types of flexibility. One such task requires participants to sort cards according to one of three differ-ent rules: colour, shape or number. The rules are not given beforehand but the participant needs to use positive and negative feedback based on their sorting behaviour to find out what the correct rule is. However, unbeknown to the partici-pant, after a number of correct sorts, the rule changes and the participant needs to find out the new rule based on feedback. Patients with damage to the lateral pre-frontal cortex have more difficulty with inhibition responding according to the old rule (referred to as perseveration) and they have more difficulty updating infor-mation to find the new rule (distraction errors) (Barcelo and Knight, 2002). They will remain 'stuck' in the old behaviour and are unable to switch in a flexible way.

Interestingly, they can explain to the test leader what the new rule should be. It seems that their actions do not incorporate the knowledge they have about the task. This may be due to the fact that the knowledge about the task is represented in a different area of the brain from the demanded actions.

In their behaviour, young children resemble patients with damage to the frontal cortex, as they too have difficulty flexibly switching between tasks. For example, when a 3-year-old is told to sort pictures by shape (flowers in the flower pile, trucks in the truck pile), this task will be performed fairly well. As it happens, some of the pictures are red and some are blue, but they don't need to pay attention to that. Now the assignment changes and the 3-year-old is asked to disregard the flowers and trucks from now on and to pay attention to the colour of the picture instead. The red pictures are to go in the red pile, blue pictures in the blue pile. The 3-year-old is quite able to understand this change in the rules, and can explain it to the test leader ('I will now pay attention to the colour, red with red and blue with blue'). However, when it is time to perform the task, they will continue to sort based on the previously learned rule (flowers with flowers, trucks with trucks) (Doebel and Zelazo, 2013; Zelazo, 2006). This is remarkable because they do understand the new rule. As it were, there is a division between knowing and doing, just like there is in patients with damage to the frontal cortex. Four- and 5-year-old children are much better at performing this task. This means that an important change in flexibility takes place during early childhood. And yet it appears that complete flexibility will not have fully developed until the age of at least 15 years (Crone, Ridderinkhof, Worm, Somsen and van der Molen, 2004; Diamond, 2013; Huizinga *et al.*, 2006). The differences between 15-year-olds and adults are much smaller than the differences between 3-year-olds and adults, but still it is more frequent for adolescents to get 'stuck' in the rule that was previously correct.

In the lab at Leiden University in the Netherlands, we have taken a closer look at the areas of the brain important for flexibility. Based on fMRI findings, we know that two areas of the brain in the frontal cortex are important when adults learn from feedback about their own behaviour. But how do these develop, and how do they communicate?

We investigated how 8- to 11-year-old children, 14- to 15-year-old adolescents and young adults (ages 18 to 25-years) learned from feedback about their own behaviour when they had to flexibly switch between rules (Crone, Zanolie, Van Leijenhorst, Westenberg and Rombouts, 2008). Feedback that indicated the preceding behaviour was incorrect activated the two brain areas in the frontal cortex connected to purposeful behaviour. Namely, the dorsal-lateral prefrontal cortex, and an area in the middle of the frontal cortex, called the anterior cingulate cortex. The latter area is also called the alarm system of the brain, because it becomes active when people make mistakes (Ridderinkhof, Ullsperger, Crone and Nieuwenhuis, 2004). Importantly, a number of areas involved in the task reached an adult level early on. However, the dorsal-lateral prefrontal cortex and the anterior cingulate cortex had not yet reached adult levels in 14- to 15-year olds. This means that the areas important for purposeful behaviour in adults are still developing in young people until late adolescence. This result was followed up in a study that included 268 participants between ages 8 and 25 years. Also in this study it was found that with increasing age, adolescents recruit lateral prefrontal cortex and parietal cortex more when they received negative performance feedback (Peters, Braams,

Raijmakers, Koolschijn and Crone, 2014), and the more they recruited these regions, the more they learned to adapt their behaviour to the task demands (Peters, Koolschijn, Crone, Van Duijvenvoorde and Raijmakers, 2014). Similar results were found in a study that focused specifically on error-processing in a simple anti-saccade task. The task involves an eye movement to a dedicated location and participants monitor their own behaviour during the course of the task. This study involved a longitudinal assessment of 123 participants across a large age range spanning ages 9–26 years and found that the anterior cingulate cortex was increasingly engaged following errors when participants were older (Ordaz, Foran, Velanova and Luna, 2013).

There is a bright side: although adolescents showed less brain activity after receiving negative feedback, it turned out they showed more brain activity in lateral prefrontal cortex and parietal cortex than adults after receiving positive feedback (Peters, Braams, *et al.*, 2014; van den Bos, Guroglu, van den Bulk, Rombouts and Crone, 2009; van Duijvenvoorde, Zanolie, Rombouts, Raijmakers and Crone, 2008). It appears that adolescents' brains are more attuned to encouragement and confirmation, and less well equipped to deal with punishment and rejection. There is even evidence for a heightened activity in a specific region of the brain, the striatum, that is specific for adolescents when they receive feedback that positively differs from their expectations or positive prediction errors (Cohen et al., 2010b). In addition, there is heightened activity in adolescence relative to adults in the insula when they receive feedback that negatively differs from their expectations, or negative predictor errors (Hauser, Iannaccone, Walitza, Brandeis and Brem, 2015). In the next chapters, we will investigate in more detail whether reward or rejection feelings are more pronounced in adolescents than in children and adults.

Creativity in adolescence

There is another bright sight to adolescence when it comes to another type of cognitive abilities, which is creativity. Creativity refers to those cognitive skills that allow us to generate ideas, insights and solutions that are both original and feasible. Creative cognition can be achieved through a flexible and divergent way of thinking, as well as a persistent and systematic way of thinking. Creative outcomes are probably achieved by a combination of both ways of thinking, with different contributions depending on the task and on individual differences (De Dreu, Baas and Nijstad, 2008).

Interestingly, it was previously found that different types of creative processes mature with different developmental trajectories. For example, insight developed gradually and linearly between childhood and adulthood. In contrast, divergent thinking, which is referred to as cognitive processes that aim to find a solution for open-ended problems, followed a different developmental time course. Especially spatial divergent thinking increased between childhood and adolescence and was most efficient at ages 15–16 years, after which it declines again somewhat in early adulthood (Kleibeuker, De Dreu and Crone, 2013).

Given that adolescent brain development follows non-linear developmental trajectories (Gogtay *et al.*, 2004), and given that executive control functions develop at different rates (Huizinga *et al.*, 2006), possibly adolescence is a period in life when creativity flourishes most. This question was addressed in an fMRI study in which 15- to 17-year-old adolescents and adults between ages 25 and 30 years completed a spatial divergent thinking task. Participants were asked to find solutions for Match Stick problems, a task that previously was found to rely on dorsolateral prefrontal cortex (Goel and Vartanian, 2005). Both adolescents and adults showed activation in the dorsal-lateral prefrontal cortex when solving these open-ended problems, but adolescents recruited this region of the brain more strongly than adults. They also showed slightly better performance than adults (Kleibeuker, Koolschijn, Jolles, Schel, *et al.*, 2013).

It should be noted that this finding could not be generalized to the verbal domain. For verbal divergent thinking, the dorsal-lateral prefrontal was also related to divergent thinking performance (in this case: think of as many possible ways in which you can use a brick, or an umbrella, for example). However, adults found more original solutions and showed stronger activity in the dorsal-lateral prefrontal cortex than adolescents (Kleibeuker, Koolschijn, Jolles, De Dreu and Crone, 2013). This is possibly related to adults having more life experience and a larger verbal knowledge domain.

The theory of interactive specialization

The findings described in this chapter highlight the potential flexibility of the prefrontal cortex. A large set of studies shows that children and adolescents recruit core regions for executive functions less for specific tasks such as working memory and inhibition. But they use sometimes other regions to perform these tasks, more strongly than adults. Possibly these regions are compensatory regions, or possibly children and adolescents use different strategies to perform a specific task compared to adults. A second set of studies shows that for tasks where it might be useful to abandon using strict rules (such as divergent thinking, which requires participants to think out of the box), adolescents show stronger recruitment of prefrontal cortex than adults.

This shift from a more diffuse way of thinking to a more structured way of thinking is captured in the interactive specialization theory of Mark Johnson (Johnson, 2011). According to this theory, at an early age, children use regions in the prefrontal cortex for a wide range of functions, whereas later in adolescence and adulthood these functions become more localized and specialized in specific networks. In other words, the theory suggests that in early childhood there is less differentiation between functions and modalities, whereas specialization emerges over the course of adolescence and adulthood. Increased specialization results in many gains (such as faster information processing and more focused learning) but may also result in losses (such as reduced creativity).

The theory challenges the traditionally assumed maturational viewpoint, which in a strict sense assumes that brain regions are 'salient' early in development and come online later in development. Even though appealing for its simplicity, this viewpoint doesn't seem to capture the dynamic changes in brain recruitment over the course of childhood and adolescence. The interactive specialization theory on the other hand is based on the assumptions that cortical regions begin with a broad functionality, and as a process of activity-dependent interaction and competition acquire their role in new computational abilities. Furthermore, interactive specialization involves the process of organization of interregional interactions. That is to say, young children will show activity over several regions and networks, while this becomes more specialized during childhood and adolescence. As such, it provides a more comprehensive explanation of the dynamic changes that are observed over the course of development. The theory of interactive specialization provides an elegant description of the changes in executive functions, but is also applied to other domains such as face processing and social learning.

The idea behind interactive specialization provides a new perspective on adolescence by not only seeing adolescence as a period of cognitive restrictions or 'deficits' (as would be predicted by the maturational viewpoint), but also as a time of unique opportunities. One possible reason is that it is important for adolescents to be able to think of creative solutions in this important transition period in life (Crone and Dahl, 2012).

Training the brain

One of the questions that remain unanswered by research on brain maturation is the controversy between maturation and practice. We presume that children don't use particular areas of the brain very well yet because the neurons aren't yet working efficiently enough or because the connections have not yet been made. On the other hand, it's possible that children have simply had less practice than adults. Would it be possible to have children perform as well as adults with a great deal of practice? These questions are difficult to answer, but in turn raise exciting questions about the flexibility of the brain (i.e., plasticity). Just as an athlete trains his body, it may also be possible to train your brain and become superior in working memory or flexibility (Diamond and Ling, 2016).

There is much evidence from research in adults that it is possible to train cognitive functions. Most of these studies have focused on working memory and showed that increased working-memory performance after a period of training is associated with increased activity in the lateral prefrontal and parietal cortex (Klingberg, 2010), as well as other regions such as the striatum (Dahlin, Neely, Larsson, Backman and Nyberg, 2008). Some studies have also reported decreases for simple working-memory tasks and increases for challenging tasks, suggesting that training of simple tasks mainly leads to automatization (Jolles, Grol, Van Buchem, Rombouts and Crone, 2010).

If it is possible to train your working memory and if there is an optimal period for training working memory, that could be very beneficial, because working memory is important to almost all academic skills. Preliminary evidence for the potential of training effects comes from a small fMRI training study that showed that children recruited prefrontal cortex more after a 6-week-period of training (Jolles, van Buchem, Rombouts and Crone, 2012). At the same time, we know we cannot turn everybody into a Mozart and transfer effects are often limited, so we won't find out which areas of the brain can and cannot be trained until sometime in the future. The transfer effects of working memory training are still debated, and probably depend on a variety of factors such as task demands (simple versus challenging) and whether training involves a single task or multiple tasks (Diamond and Ling, 2016).

In this chapter, I have tried to explain what we know about the developing adolescent brain, and how we can relate this information to what we can expect of adolescents in the classroom. In the future, it will be important to communicate these results clearly to teachers, because unfortunately, the rise of *educational neuroscience* has also given rise to so-called neuro-myths (Howard-Jones, 2014). A *neuro-myth* is based on wrongly interpreted findings from brain research. An example is the so-called training programs for the brain aimed at making the brain better and faster, but which have no scientific basis whatsoever.

This chapter only touches upon cognitive functioning in a controlled, laboratory setting. It should be noted that in our daily lives, our decisions are influenced or even controlled by our emotions and/or our social environment (i.e., our family and friends). These influences are very important during adolescence and can be traced back to changes in the brain, which is why the emotional brain is the focus of the next chapter.

References

Adleman, N. E., Menon, V., Blasey, C. M., White, C. D., Warsofsky, I. S., Glover, G. H. and Reiss, A. L. (2002). A developmental fMRI study of the Stroop color-word task. *NeuroImage*, *16*(1), 61–75. doi:10.1006/nimg.2001.1046

Aron, A. R., Robbins, T. W. and Poldrack, R. A. (2004). Inhibition and the right inferior frontal cortex. *Trends Cogn Sci*, *8*(4), 170–177. doi:10.1016/j.tics.2004.02.010

Aron, A. R., Robbins, T. W. and Poldrack, R. A. (2014). Inhibition and the right inferior frontal cortex: one decade on. *Trends Cogn Sci*, *18*(4), 177–185. doi:10.1016/j.tics.2013.12.003

Barcelo, F. and Knight, R. T. (2002). Both random and perseverative errors underlie WCST deficits in prefrontal patients. *Neuropsychologia*, *40*(3), 349–356. Retrieved from www.ncbi.nlm.nih.gov/pubmed/11684168

Besnard, J., Allain, P., Aubin, G., Osiurak, F., Chauvire, V., Etcharry-Bouyx, F. and D, L. E. G. (2010). Utilization behavior: clinical and theoretical approaches. *J Int Neuropsychol Soc*, *16*(3), 453–462. doi:10.1017/S1355617709991469

Blakemore, S. J. (2008). The social brain in adolescence. *Nat Rev Neurosci*, *9*(4), 267–277. doi:10.1038/nrn2353

Blakemore, S. J. and Robbins, T. W. (2012). Decision-making in the adolescent brain. *Nat Neurosci*, *15*(9), 1184–1191. doi:10.1038/nn.3177

Booth, J. R., Burman, D. D., Meyer, J. R., Lei, Z., Trommer, B. L., Davenport, N. D., Li, W., Parrish, T. B., Gitelman, D. R. and Mesulam, M. M. (2003). Neural development of selective attention and response inhibition. *NeuroImage*, 20(2), 737–751. doi:10.1016/S1053-8119(03)00404-X

Brahmbhatt, S. B., McAuley, T. and Barch, D. M. (2008). Functional developmental similarities and differences in the neural correlates of verbal and nonverbal working memory tasks. *Neuropsychologia*, 46(4), 1020–1031. doi:10.1016/j.neuropsychologia.2007.11.010

Brahmbhatt, S. B., White, D. A. and Barch, D. M. (2010). Developmental differences in sustained and transient activity underlying working memory. *Brain Res*, 1354, 140–151. doi:10.1016/j.brainres.2010.07.055

Bunge, S. A., Dudukovic, N. M., Thomason, M. E., Vaidya, C. J. and Gabrieli, J. D. (2002). Immature frontal lobe contributions to cognitive control in children: evidence from fMRI. *Neuron*, 33(2), 301–311. Retrieved from www.ncbi.nlm.nih.gov/pubmed/11804576

Byrnes, J. P. and Vu, L. T. (2015). Educational neuroscience: definitional, methodological and interpretive issues. *Wiley Interdiscip Rev Cogn Sci*, 6(3), 221–234. doi:10.1002/wcs.1345

Cascio, C. N., Carp, J., O'Donnell, M. B., Tinney, F. J., Jr., Bingham, C. R., Shope, J. T., Ouimet, M, C., Pradhan, A, K., Simons-Morton, B. G. and Falk, E. B. (2015). Buffering social influence: neural correlates of response inhibition predict driving safety in the presence of a peer. *J Cogn Neurosci*, 27(1), 83–95. doi:10.1162/jocn_a_00693

Casey, B. J. (2015). Beyond simple models of self-control to circuit-based accounts of adolescent behavior. *Annu Rev Psychol*, 66, 295–319. doi:10.1146/annurev-psych-010814-015156

Ciesielski, K. T., Lesnik, P. G., Savoy, R. L., Grant, E. P. and Ahlfors, S. P. (2006). Developmental neural networks in children performing a Categorical N-Back Task. *NeuroImage*, 33(3), 980–990. doi:10.1016/j.neuroimage.2006.07.028

Cipolotti, L., Healy, C., Chan, E., MacPherson, S. E., White, M., Woollett, K., Turner, M., Robinson, G., Spanò, B., Bozzali, M. and Shallice, T. (2015). The effect of age on cognitive performance of frontal patients. *Neuropsychologia*, 75, 233–241. doi:10.1016/j.neuropsychologia.2015.06.011

Cohen, J. R., Asarnow, R. F., Sabb, F. W., Bilder, R. M., Bookheimer, S. Y., Knowlton, B. J. and Poldrack, R. A. (2010a). Decoding developmental differences and individual variability in response inhibition through predictive analyses across individuals. *Front Hum Neurosci*, 4, 47. doi:10.3389/fnhum.2010.00047

Cohen, J. R., Asarnow, R. F., Sabb, F. W., Bilder, R. M., Bookheimer, S. Y., Knowlton, B. J. and Poldrack, R. A. (2010b). A unique adolescent response to reward prediction errors. *Nat Neurosci*, 13(6), 669–671. doi:10.1038/nn.2558

Crone, E. A. and Dahl, R. E. (2012). Understanding adolescence as a period of social-affective engagement and goal flexibility. *Nat Rev Neurosci*, 13(9), 636–650. doi:10.1038/nrn3313

Crone, E. A., Ridderinkhof, K. R., Worm, M., Somsen, R. J. and van der Molen, M. W. (2004). Switching between spatial stimulus-response mappings: a developmental study of cognitive flexibility. *Dev Sci*, 7(4), 443–455. Retrieved from www.ncbi.nlm.nih.gov/pubmed/15484593

Crone, E. A., Wendelken, C., Donohue, S., van Leijenhorst, L. and Bunge, S. A. (2006). Neurocognitive development of the ability to manipulate information in working memory. *Proc Natl Acad Sci U S A*, 103(24), 9315–9320. doi:10.1073/pnas.0510088103

Crone, E. A., Zanolie, K., Van Leijenhorst, L., Westenberg, P. M. and Rombouts, S. A. (2008). Neural mechanisms supporting flexible performance adjustment during development. *Cogn Affect Behav Neurosci*, 8(2), 165–177. Retrieved from www.ncbi.nlm.nih.gov/pubmed/18589507

D'Esposito, M. and Postle, B. R. (2015). The cognitive neuroscience of working memory. *Annu Rev Psychol, 66*, 115–142. doi:10.1146/annurev-psych-010814-015031

Dahlin, E., Neely, A. S., Larsson, A., Backman, L. and Nyberg, L. (2008). Transfer of learning after updating training mediated by the striatum. *Science, 320*(5882), 1510–1512. doi:10.1126/science.1155466

Darki, F. and Klingberg, T. (2015). The role of fronto-parietal and fronto-striatal networks in the development of working memory: a longitudinal study. *Cereb Cortex, 25*(6), 1587–1595. doi:10.1093/cercor/bht352

De Dreu, C. K. W., Baas, M. and Nijstad, B. A. (2008). Hedonic tone and activation level in the mood-creativity link: toward a dual pathway to creativity model. *Journal of Personality and Social Psychology, 94*(5), 739–756.

Diamond, A. (2013). Executive functions. *Annu Rev Psychol, 64*, 135–168. doi:10.1146/annurev-psych-113011-143750

Diamond, A. and Ling, D. S. (2016). Conclusions about interventions, programs, and approaches for improving executive functions that appear justified and those that, despite much hype, do not. *Dev Cogn Neurosci, 18*, 34-48. doi: 10.1016/j.dcn.2015.11.005

Docking, K., Murdoch, B. E. and Jordan, F. M. (2000). Interpretation and comprehension of linguistic humour by adolescents with head injury: a group analysis. *Brain Inj, 14*(1), 89–108. Retrieved from www.ncbi.nlm.nih.gov/pubmed/10670664

Doebel, S. and Zelazo, P. D. (2013). Bottom-up and top-down dynamics in young children's executive function: labels aid 3-year-olds' performance on the Dimensional Change Card Sort. *Cogn Dev, 28*(3), 222–232. doi:10.1016/j.cogdev.2012.12.001

Dumontheil, I. and Klingberg, T. (2012). Brain activity during a visuospatial working memory task predicts arithmetical performance 2 years later. *Cereb Cortex, 22*(5), 1078–1085. doi:10.1093/cercor/bhr175

Dumontheil, I., Roggeman, C., Ziermans, T., Peyrard-Janvid, M., Matsson, H., Kere, J. and Klingberg, T. (2011). Influence of the COMT genotype on working memory and brain activity changes during development. *Biol Psychiatry, 70*(3), 222–229. doi:10.1016/j.biopsych.2011.02.027

Durston, S., Davidson, M. C., Tottenham, N., Galvan, A., Spicer, J., Fossella, J. A. and Casey, B. J. (2006). A shift from diffuse to focal cortical activity with development. *Dev Sci, 9*(1), 1–8. doi:10.1111/j.1467–7687.2005.00454.x

Finn, A. S., Sheridan, M. A., Kam, C. L., Hinshaw, S. and D'Esposito, M. (2010). Longitudinal evidence for functional specialization of the neural circuit supporting working memory in the human brain. *J Neurosci, 30*(33), 11062–11067. doi:10.1523/JNEUROSCI.6266-09.2010

Geier, C. F., Garver, K., Terwilliger, R. and Luna, B. (2009). Development of working memory maintenance. *J Neurophysiol, 101*(1), 84–99. doi:10.1152/jn.90562.2008

Goel, V. and Vartanian, O. (2005). Dissociating the roles of right ventral lateral and dorsal lateral prefrontal cortex in generation and maintenance of hypotheses in set-shift problems. *Cereb Cortex, 15*(8), 1170–1177. doi:10.1093/cercor/bhh217

Gogtay, N., Giedd, J. N., Lusk, L., Hayashi, K. M., Greenstein, D., Vaituzis, A. C., Nugent, T. F. 3rd., Herman, D. H., Clasen, L. S., Toga, A. W., Rapoport, J. L. and Thompson, P. M. (2004). Dynamic mapping of human cortical development during childhood through early adulthood. *Proc Natl Acad Sci U S A, 101*(21), 8174–8179. doi:10.1073/pnas.0402680101

Hauser, T. U., Iannaccone, R., Walitza, S., Brandeis, D. and Brem, S. (2015). Cognitive flexibility in adolescence: neural and behavioral mechanisms of reward prediction error processing in adaptive decision making during development. *NeuroImage, 104*, 347–354. doi:10.1016/j.neuroimage.2014.09.018

Howard-Jones, P. A. (2014). Neuroscience and education: myths and messages. *Nat Rev Neurosci*, *15*(12), 817–824. doi:10.1038/nrn3817

Huang, A. S., Klein, D. N. and Leung, H. C. (2015). Load-related brain activation predicts spatial working memory performance in youth aged 9–12 and is associated with executive function at earlier ages. *Dev Cogn Neurosci*, *17*, 1–9. doi:10.1016/j.dcn.2015.10.007

Huizinga, M., Dolan, C. V. and van der Molen, M. W. (2006). Age-related change in executive function: developmental trends and a latent variable analysis. *Neuropsychologia*, *44*(11), 2017–2036. doi:10.1016/j.neuropsychologia.2006.01.010

Johnson, M. H. (2011). Interactive specialization: a domain-general framework for human functional brain development? *Dev Cogn Neurosci*, *1*(1), 7–21. doi:10.1016/j.dcn.2010.07.003

Jolles, D. D., Grol, M. J., Van Buchem, M. A., Rombouts, S. A. and Crone, E. A. (2010). Practice effects in the brain: changes in cerebral activation after working memory practice depend on task demands. *NeuroImage*, *52*(2), 658–668. doi:10.1016/j.neuroimage.2010.04.028

Jolles, D. D., Kleibeuker, S. W., Rombouts, S. A. and Crone, E. A. (2011). Developmental differences in prefrontal activation during working memory maintenance and manipulation for different memory loads. *Dev Sci*, *14*(4), 713–724. doi:10.1111/j.1467-7687.2010.01016.x

Jolles, D. D., van Buchem, M. A., Rombouts, S. A. and Crone, E. A. (2012). Practice effects in the developing brain: a pilot study. *Dev Cogn Neurosci*, *2*(Suppl 1), S180–191. doi:10.1016/j.dcn.2011.09.001

Kleibeuker, S. W., De Dreu, C. K. and Crone, E. A. (2013). The development of creative cognition across adolescence: distinct trajectories for insight and divergent thinking. *Dev Sci*, *16*(1), 2–12. doi:10.1111/j.1467-7687.2012.01176.x

Kleibeuker, S. W., Koolschijn, P. C., Jolles, D. D., De Dreu, C. K. and Crone, E. A. (2013). The neural coding of creative idea generation across adolescence and early adulthood. *Front Hum Neurosci*, *7*, 905. doi:10.3389/fnhum.2013.00905

Kleibeuker, S. W., Koolschijn, P. C., Jolles, D. D., Schel, M. A., De Dreu, C. K. and Crone, E. A. (2013). Prefrontal cortex involvement in creative problem solving in middle adolescence and adulthood. *Dev Cogn Neurosci*, *5*, 197–206. doi:10.1016/j.dcn.2013.03.003

Klingberg, T. (2006). Development of a superior frontal-intraparietal network for visuo-spatial working memory. *Neuropsychologia*, *44*(11), 2171–2177. doi:10.1016/j.neuropsychologia.2005.11.019

Klingberg, T. (2010). Training and plasticity of working memory. *Trends Cogn Sci*, *14*(7), 317–324. doi:10.1016/j.tics.2010.05.002

Klingberg, T., Forssberg, H. and Westerberg, H. (2002). Increased brain activity in frontal and parietal cortex underlies the development of visuospatial working memory capacity during childhood. *J Cogn Neurosci*, *14*(1), 1–10. doi:10.1162/089892902317205276

Kramer, U. M., Solbakk, A. K., Funderud, I., Lovstad, M., Endestad, T. and Knight, R. T. (2013). The role of the lateral prefrontal cortex in inhibitory motor control. *Cortex*, *49*(3), 837–849. doi:10.1016/j.cortex.2012.05.003

Kwon, H., Reiss, A. L. and Menon, V. (2002). Neural basis of protracted developmental changes in visuo-spatial working memory. *Proc Natl Acad Sci U S A*, *99*(20), 13336–13341. doi:10.1073/pnas.162486399

Lee, H. W., Lo, Y. H., Li, K. H., Sung, W. S. and Juan, C. H. (2015). The relationship between the development of response inhibition and intelligence in preschool children. *Front Psychol*, *6*, 802. doi:10.3389/fpsyg.2015.00802

Libertus, M. E., Brannon, E. M. and Pelphrey, K. A. (2009). Developmental changes in category-specific brain responses to numbers and letters in a working memory task. *NeuroImage*, *44*(4), 1404–1414. doi:10.1016/j.neuroimage.2008.10.027

Mills, K. L., Dumontheil, I., Speekenbrink, M. and Blakemore, S. J. (2015). Multitasking during social interactions in adolescence and early adulthood. *R Soc Open Sci*, *2*(11), 150117. doi:10.1098/rsos.150117

Milner, B. (1963). Effects of different brain lesions on card sorting. *Archives of Neurology*, *9*, 100–110.

O'Hare, E. D., Lu, L. H., Houston, S. M., Bookheimer, S. Y. and Sowell, E. R. (2008). Neurodevelopmental changes in verbal working memory load-dependency: an fMRI investigation. *NeuroImage*, *42*(4), 1678–1685. doi:10.1016/j.neuroimage.2008.05.057

Olesen, P. J., Macoveanu, J., Tegner, J. and Klingberg, T. (2007). Brain activity related to working memory and distraction in children and adults. *Cereb Cortex*, *17*(5), 1047–1054. doi:10.1093/cercor/bhl014

Ordaz, S. J., Foran, W., Velanova, K. and Luna, B. (2013). Longitudinal growth curves of brain function underlying inhibitory control through adolescence. *J Neurosci*, *33*(46), 18109–18124. doi:10.1523/JNEUROSCI.1741-13.2013

Petanjek, Z., Judas, M., Simic, G., Rasin, M. R., Uylings, H. B., Rakic, P. and Kostovic, I. (2011). Extraordinary neoteny of synaptic spines in the human prefrontal cortex. *Proc Natl Acad Sci U S A*, *108*(32), 13281–13286. doi:10.1073/pnas.1105108108

Peters, S., Braams, B. R., Raijmakers, M. E., Koolschijn, P. C. and Crone, E. A. (2014). The neural coding of feedback learning across child and adolescent development. *J Cogn Neurosci*, *26*(8), 1705–1720. doi:10.1162/jocn_a_00594

Peters, S., Koolschijn, P. C., Crone, E. A., Van Duijvenvoorde, A. C. and Raijmakers, M. E. (2014). Strategies influence neural activity for feedback learning across child and adolescent development. *Neuropsychologia*, *62*, 365–374. doi:10.1016/j.neuropsychologia.2014.07.006

Ridderinkhof, K. R., Ullsperger, M., Crone, E. A. and Nieuwenhuis, S. (2004). The role of the medial frontal cortex in cognitive control. *Science*, *306*(5695), 443–447. doi:10.1126/science.1100301

Rubia, K., Lim, L., Ecker, C., Halari, R., Giampietro, V., Simmons, A., Brammer, M. and Smith, A. (2013). Effects of age and gender on neural networks of motor response inhibition: from adolescence to mid-adulthood. *NeuroImage*, *83*, 690–703. doi:10.1016/j.neuroimage.2013.06.078

Rubia, K., Smith, A. B., Taylor, E. and Brammer, M. (2007). Linear age-correlated functional development of right inferior fronto-striato-cerebellar networks during response inhibition and anterior cingulate during error-related processes. *Hum Brain Mapp*, *28*(11), 1163–1177. doi:10.1002/hbm.20347

Rubia, K., Smith, A. B., Woolley, J., Nosarti, C., Heyman, I., Taylor, E. and Brammer, M. (2006). Progressive increase of frontostriatal brain activation from childhood to adulthood during event-related tasks of cognitive control. *Hum Brain Mapp*, *27*(12), 973–993. doi:10.1002/hbm.20237

Satterthwaite, T. D., Wolf, D. H., Erus, G., Ruparel, K., Elliott, M. A., Gennatas, E. D., Hopson, R., Jackson, C., Prabhakaran, K., Bilker, W. B., Calkins, M. E., Loughead, J., Smithm, A., Roalf, D. R., Hakonarson, H., Verma, R., Davatzikos, C. and Gur, R. E. (2013). Functional maturation of the executive system during adolescence. *J Neurosci*, *33*(41), 16249–16261. doi:10.1523/JNEUROSCI.2345-13.2013

Schel, M. A. and Crone, E. A. (2013). Development of response inhibition in the context of relevant versus irrelevant emotions. *Front Psychol*, *4*, 383. doi:10.3389/fpsyg.2013.00383

Schel, M. A., Scheres, A. and Crone, E. A. (2014). New perspectives on self-control development: highlighting the role of intentional inhibition. *Neuropsychologia*, *65*, 236–246. doi:10.1016/j.neuropsychologia.2014.08.022

Scherf, K. S., Sweeney, J. A. and Luna, B. (2006). Brain basis of developmental change in visuospatial working memory. *J Cogn Neurosci*, *18*(7), 1045–1058. doi:10.1162/jocn.2006. 18.7.1045

Smith, E. E. and Jonides, J. (1999). Storage and executive processes in the frontal lobes. *Science*, *283*(5408), 1657–1661. Retrieved from www.ncbi.nlm.nih.gov/pubmed/10073923

Spencer-Smith, M., Ritter, B. C., Murner-Lavanchy, I., El-Koussy, M., Steinlin, M. and Everts, R. (2013). Age, sex and performance influence the visuospatial working memory network in childhood. *Dev Neuropsychol*, *38*(4), 236–255. doi:10.1080/87565641.2013. 784321

Spielberg, J. M., Galarce, E. M., Ladouceur, C. D., McMakin, D. L., Olino, T. M., Forbes, E. E., Silk, J. S., Ryan, N. D. and Dahl, R. E. (2015). Adolescent development of inhibition as a function of SES and gender: converging evidence from behavior and fMRI. *Hum Brain Mapp*, *36*(8), 3194–3203. doi:10.1002/hbm.22838

Stroop, J. R. (1935). Studies of interference in serial verbal reactions. *Journal of Experimental Psychology*, *18*, 643–662.

Szczepanski, S. M. and Knight, R. T. (2014). Insights into human behavior from lesions to the prefrontal cortex. *Neuron*, *83*(5), 1002–1018. doi:10.1016/j.neuron.2014.08.011

Tamm, L., Menon, V. and Reiss, A. L. (2002). Maturation of brain function associated with response inhibition. *J Am Acad Child Adolesc Psychiatry*, *41*(10), 1231–1238. doi:10.1097/ 00004583-200210000-00013

Thomason, M. E., Race, E., Burrows, B., Whitfield-Gabrieli, S., Glover, G. H. and Gabrieli, J. D. (2009). Development of spatial and verbal working memory capacity in the human brain. *J Cogn Neurosci*, *21*(2), 316–332. doi:10.1162/jocn.2008.21028

Ullman, H., Almeida, R. and Klingberg, T. (2014). Structural maturation and brain activity predict future working memory capacity during childhood development. *J Neurosci*, *34*(5), 1592–1598. doi:10.1523/JNEUROSCI.0842–13.2014

van den Bos, W., Guroglu, B., van den Bulk, B. G., Rombouts, S. A. and Crone, E. A. (2009). Better than expected or as bad as you thought? The neurocognitive development of probabilistic feedback processing. *Front Hum Neurosci*, *3*, 52. doi:10.3389/neuro.09.052. 2009

van den Wildenberg, W. P. and van der Molen, M. W. (2004). Developmental trends in simple and selective inhibition of compatible and incompatible responses. *J Exp Child Psychol*, *87*(3), 201–220. doi:10.1016/j.jecp.2003.11.003

van Duijvenvoorde, A. C., Zanolie, K., Rombouts, S. A., Raijmakers, M. E. and Crone, E. A. (2008). Evaluating the negative or valuing the positive? Neural mechanisms supporting feedback-based learning across development. *J Neurosci*, *28*(38), 9495–9503. doi:10.1523/JNEUROSCI.1485-08.2008

Veroude, K., Jolles, J., Croiset, G. and Krabbendam, L. (2013). Changes in neural mechanisms of cognitive control during the transition from late adolescence to young adulthood. *Dev Cogn Neurosci*, *5*, 63–70. doi:10.1016/j.dcn.2012.12.002

Vink, M., Zandbelt, B. B., Gladwin, T., Hillegers, M., Hoogendam, J. M., van den Wildenberg, W. P., Du Plessis, S., Kahn, R. S. (2014). Frontostriatal activity and connectivity increase during proactive inhibition across adolescence and early adulthood. *Hum Brain Mapp*, *35*(9), 4415–4427. doi:10.1002/hbm.22483

von Allmen, D. Y., Wurmitzer, K. and Klaver, P. (2014). Hippocampal and posterior parietal contributions to developmental increases in visual short-term memory capacity. *Cortex*, *59*, 95–102. doi:10.1016/j.cortex.2014.07.010

Wendelken, C., Baym, C. L., Gazzaley, A. and Bunge, S. A. (2011). Neural indices of improved attentional modulation over middle childhood. *Dev Cogn Neurosci*, 1(2), 175–186. doi:10.1016/j.dcn.2010.11.001

Zelazo, P. D. (2006). The Dimensional Change Card Sort (DCCS): a method of assessing executive function in children. *Nat Protoc*, 1(1), 297–301. doi:10.1038/nprot.2006.46

3

COMPLEX DECISIONS AND RISKY CHOICES

Yesterday, Suzanne was invited to a birthday party and she's looking forward to it. All her friends are going and it will be a real happening. She bought a new outfit just for the party, and she'll also get to see that friend who moved away and who she's been missing a lot. But that afternoon, she gets an unexpected phone call: her cousin had a nasty fall down the stairs and has just left the emergency room with a sprained wrist. As this has left him a little clumsy, he asks her if she can cook him dinner that evening. He is her favourite cousin and always ready to lend a helping hand. Suzanne would love to help him, but that would also mean she can't go to the party . . .

What should Suzanne do in a situation like this? She's experiencing all kinds of emotions. On the one hand, she really wants to go to the party, and she thinks she can maybe tell her cousin she has another important engagement. On the other hand, she would feel guilty about not being there for her cousin, because only recently, he totally helped her out when her bicycle had a flat tyre and he came and picked her up in his car. And didn't he cancel a football match for that too?

In our daily lives, we are often confronted with similar, emotionally complex decisions. And yet, we are capable of making a choice quite quickly. Actually, it's impossible to make such a decision based on a cost-benefit analysis – we don't make a list of pros and cons to weigh against each other for every decision. That would take too much time, and moreover, it's hard to compare the importance of the pros and cons. So how *do* we make these decisions?

According to the well-known neuropsychologist Antonio Damasio, in these cases, we use our feelings, like our gut feeling (Damasio, 1994). Damasio argues that our brains are formed in such a way that we develop a feeling for what is right and wrong in the event of a difficult decision. That way, it could be the case that Suzanne experiences an elated feeling when thinking of the party, but an unpleasant feeling when thinking about letting her cousin down. As such, the one feeling can triumph over the other feeling. Feelings provide us with the possibility to weigh short- and long-term decisions against each other (short-term feeling: going to a nice party; long-term feeling: a continued good relationship with her family when skipping the party). This immediately illustrates the great change that takes place during adolescence: we only develop the skill of knowing what is better in the long term at quite a late stage in development (Smith, Xiao and Bechara, 2012).

Studies have shown that this has to do with the development of a system in the brain, which links certain feelings to short- and long-term results. The concept of feelings may sound complicated. To throw some more light on this, we are focusing on research in patients with damage to a specific area of the brain, the orbitofrontal cortex, an area that appears to be crucial for the link between feelings and actions (Bechara, Damasio, Tranel and Damasio, 2005).

Patients with decision-making problems

The orbitofrontal cortex takes up the nethermost region of the frontal cortex, the area just behind your eyes. This area of the brain has a special function, as it has pathways linking it to a number of other areas that are important for emotional decisions. First, it has connections to the limbic system (O'Doherty, 2011; Peper et al., 2013). This area is situated very deep in the brain (below the cortex). It responds immediately to being rewarded and punished, and regulates emotions in both humans and animals (Haber and Knutson, 2010). We will learn more about the limbic system when we discuss risk behaviour further on in this chapter. In addition to connections to the limbic system, the orbitofrontal cortex also has connections to the somatosensory cortex (Bechara et al., 2005). This is the area of the brain in which our body is represented, for example the sensation we have in our legs, stomach or chest. Finally, the orbitofrontal cortex has connections with the lateral frontal cortex (Longe, Senior and Rippon, 2009; O'Doherty, 2011), which was extensively discussed in Chapter 2. This area of the brain is important for planning and remembering choices. So, the orbitofrontal cortex has the unique location for weighing emotional decisions, because it is in this area that emotions, physical sensations and planning skills come together (Bechara et al., 2005). Research in patients with damage to the orbitofrontal cortex shows that this area is crucial for making the right choices. For the most famous example, we have to go back to 13 September 1848, to the story of Phineas Gage.

Phineas Gage was a building contractor in Vermont, who was working on the construction of a railway. Because he was in charge of the railway team, he had a lot of responsibilities – a job he managed easily, as he was reputed to be a reliable man. He was quiet and friendly and got along well with his workers. While they were working on the new railway, something terrible happened: an explosion caused a large steel rod to fly through the air and pierce Gage's skull. The rod entered his head near his left eye and exited at the top of his skull. Onlookers had no idea of what to do, and thought this must be the end of Gage. Much to everyone's surprise, Gage only lost consciousness for a short time and quickly came to consciousness. He knew where he was, could say his name and move normally, while a large part of his left hemisphere had been damaged. Gage was immediately taken to a doctor, who dressed his wounds, and 10 weeks later he was allowed to go home. After a few months, Gage even felt he had recovered enough to go back to work. Does this mean he didn't need the front part of his brain for anything? Not quite.

Despite being physically capable of performing his job, his employers did not want to hire him again. Although he had been a capable man who made conscious decisions before, now, he was easily vexed, aggressive, impulsive and unreliable. Something unusual had happened to Gage: as a result of his brain damage, his *personality* had changed (Damasio, 1994). As far as we know, Gage never again held an executive position and neither did he manage to keep the same job anywhere for long. He worked in three different horse stables, but when his health declined in 1859, he went to live with his mother. Gage died in 1860. No post-mortem examination of his brain was done at the time, but in 1867, his skull was examined by the doctor who treated him after the accident. The doctor established the extent and location of the brain damage. Eventually, he donated the skull and the steel rod to the museum of the Harvard Medical School library, where they can still be viewed.

The damage to Gage's brain was extensive. As reported by the doctors in 1848 and 1867, a large area of the frontal cortex and the surrounding skull had been damaged. In 1994, Antonio and Hanna Damasio studied the damage using more advanced methods and they showed that the damage had mainly affected the orbitofrontal cortex (Damasio, Grabowski, Frank, Galaburda and Damasio, 1994). Indeed, it appears that the area on the interface of emotions and cognition leads to a change in personality when damaged.

It was only a few years ago that an actual explanation for this change in behaviour was given. In his work as a neuropsychologist, Damasio regularly dealt with patients with damage to the orbitofrontal cortex. However, it was always difficult to capture their problems in a test. These patients did not have any trouble with memory tests, motor skills or language processing. Their intelligence remained intact and they were able to solve abstract problems without difficulty (Bechara, Damasio, Tranel and Anderson, 1998). Yet, these patients – like Gage – had major difficulties in their daily lives. After the brain damage occurred, these patients turned into risk-taking, impulsive individuals, who often had trouble holding down a job or keeping their marriage together. Their behaviour was regularly described as 'childlike', because they made choices that were rewarding in the short term, but ill-considered in the long run (Bechara *et al.*, 2005).

Damasio and his colleagues concluded that these people's behaviour is based on short-term satisfaction and that they are unable to look ahead. This is not because these patients do not understand a situation, but because they do not *feel* what the right decision is. Damasio developed a theory, which he called the somatic marker theory (Damasio, 1994). According to this theory, we are all continually making choices in our daily lives for which it is impossible to weigh all pros and cons.

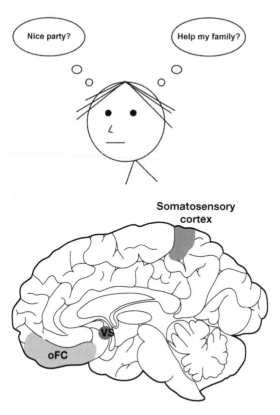

FIGURE 3.1 Deliberating between short- and long- term outcomes. oFC = orbitofrontal cortex; VS = ventral striatum

After all, we habitually make split-second decisions, simply because we don't have enough time to deliberately consider every choice. Our system is so efficient, that we are able to make the right choices very quickly. This type of decision is often made based on a feeling, which tells us whether what we are doing is right or wrong. A previous situation has been 'marked' with a pleasant or unpleasant feeling and these feelings are now influencing the new situation (Bechara *et al.*, 2005). For example, if you argued with a colleague or a classmate last month and felt bad about it, you were left with an unpleasant feeling. Possibly, your heart rate increased and you started perspiring, because grim words were exchanged. Subsequently, when you are in a new situation and you think back to this person or situation, you may experience these changes in your heart rate and perspiration all over again. The pathways in your mind between a situation and the feeling accompanying it can be created very quickly. When you have to make a decision for which you have to consider several alternatives, all these pathways are activated and the dominant feeling will be followed. This means it is very important to trust your feelings in order to make the right decisions.

Gambling in the laboratory

In the laboratory, the complex decision situation that humans continually experience was mimicked by a card game, called the Iowa Gambling Task (IGT) (Bechara *et al.*, 2005). For participants, the aim of the IGT is to learn which of the stacks of cards will yield the most money. In the game, four stacks of cards are presented: Stacks A, B, C and D. Whenever the participant draws a card from Stacks A or B, he receives 100 dollars. Whenever he draws a card from Stacks C or D, he gets 50 dollars. So, at first sight, it seems better to draw a card from Stacks A or B, because these yield more money. However, sometimes the participant does not receive a reward, but has money taken away from him. This doesn't happen every time he draws a card, but only once in a while, and the amount of money lost changes every time, too. That makes it very hard to find out which stacks are the best to choose from. As the participant continues to choose cards from different stacks, he will find that Stacks A and B will eventually lose him money, because overall the losses are greater than the gains for those stacks. Stacks C and D are eventually profitable, because overall the losses are smaller than the gains. So, to perform well on the IGT, the participant has to learn that the choices that are best in the short term (A and B) will result in a loss in the long term.

When healthy adults carry out this task, they learn to switch strategies while performing the task and they will switch from choices A and B to choices C and D. What is interesting is that they will draw cards from the profitable stacks before being able to use their experience to indicate which choices are better in the long term (Bechara, Damasio, Tranel and Damasio, 1997). It seems they feel what the right choices are before their knowledge about the task tells them. This is also indicated by the changes in their physical reactions. When they choose the disadvantageous Stacks A and B during the task, they exhibit an increased sweating reaction, whereas this increase is not noticeable when they choose Stacks C and D. It is as if the body indicates that these stacks are dangerous by means of this sweating reaction (Crone, Somsen, Van Beek and Van Der Molen, 2004). When patients with damage to the orbitofrontal cortex perform this task, they continue to choose Stacks A and B, and do not learn to switch to the stacks that are better in the long term. Neither do these patients develop a sweating reaction previous to drawing from the dangerous stacks. However, when they have to take a large loss, they do exhibit a sweating reaction, so it is not the case that they do not experience emotions (Bechara, Tranel and Damasio, 2000). Specifically, the warning emotions prior to risky or dangerous choices are affected. According to the somatic marker hypothesis, patients with damage to the orbitofrontal cortex make many impulsive, unthinking choices in daily life, because they do not experience the physical warnings that guide the behaviour of healthy people. Studies performed by other research groups have demonstrated that patients with orbitofrontal damage have specific difficulties with reversal learning, or the ability to switch away from an alternative that previously seemed advantageous (Fellows and Farah, 2005).

Somatic marking in development

Feelings and emotions play an important part in the daily lives of adolescents. But it's questionable if these experiences are always used well in order to guide choices, as it is typical of adolescents to often make short-term choices. Researchers have tried to find out if this is possibly connected to changes in somatic signals. The absence of somatic marking has been proven to be typical of adolescents' choices as well (Smith *et al.*, 2012). The development of somatic markers appears to be a complex process because changes can be detected until after puberty, that is to say, until the age of 18. Research has shown that adolescents aged 16 to 18 show the first signs of somatic marking, but this marking does not work as well in them as it does in adults (Crone and van der Molen, 2007). Possibly, the areas of the brain responsible for somatic marking mature slowly.

In the studies in our own lab, we asked participants aged between 6 and 25 to make choices in a computer task based on the IGT, but the design had been changed in such a way that the task could also be grasped easily by the youngest participants. In the task, participants were asked to collect apples for a hungry donkey. The more apples they collected, the more points they were given at the end of the experiment. The apples could be won by choosing from among four doors, which were shown next to each other on the screen. Whenever a choice was made, the door was opened and the number of apples won or lost was shown. Here, too, Doors A and B led to great gains, but on occasion, a large number of apples were taken way, so that these doors led to a loss in the long run. Doors C and D yielded fewer apples, but the losses were smaller, too, so that these doors eventually led to the biggest gains (Crone and van der Molen, 2004).

Children aged 6 to 10 mainly chose Doors A and B; so they only chose the short-term gains and were blind to the long-term consequences. In that sense, the children's choice pattern resembles that of patients with damage to the orbitofrontal cortex. This choice pattern changes during adolescence, when teenagers are learning to make long-term choices, but even in 16- to18-year-olds, the choice pattern is not quite as targeted on the long term as it is in adults aged 20 to 25 (Cauffman *et al.*, 2010; Crone and van der Molen, 2004; Hooper, Luciana, Conklin and Yarger, 2004). For adolescents, it is possibly still hard to understand the consequences of their behaviour and the option to make a quick profit beats the safer, long-term choices.

In order to investigate whether these changes are linked to changes in physical signals, we also measured the sweating reaction and changes in heart rate in these participants. As it turns out, the first indication of a warning signal preceding a dangerous choice was only found in 16-year-olds and even then, the warning signal wasn't as strong in this age group as it was in 20- to 25-year-olds (Crone *et al.*, 2004; Crone and van der Molen, 2007). However, when the participants sustained a great loss, a sweating reaction and change in heart rate were noticeable from a young age. That means the participants did indeed find it unpleasant to lose (just like all patients with damage to the orbitofrontal cortex), but they did not anticipate the possible bad outcome. The warning signals are still 'under construction', which sometimes leads to ill-considered decisions. Adolescents may be quite capable of identifying which situations are dangerous and which are not, but it seems they don't *feel* it. So if Suzanne decides to go to the party after all instead of helping her cousin, she may realize that this is not a very nice thing to do, but the unpleasant feeling of letting her cousin down does not yet beat the exciting feeling of the prospective party.

Risks and dangerous choices

Ever since the first descriptions of adolescence, risky behaviour has been indicated as the most important feature of this period. Adolescents do things that (most) adults would never do, such as skateboarding on a bridge railing or tuning up their mopeds. Research using questionnaires has indicated that adolescents have more need for dangerous events and experiences than young children and that they are not fully capable of assessing dangerous situations yet (Steinberg *et al.*, 2008). How can it be that they experience risky situations differently compared to adults?

First, it's important to know that adolescents do not assess all risky situations differently compared to adults. When they are shown a vase containing four red balls and two blue ones and told to guess which ball will be drawn, they have no problems indicating the odds of winning or losing. If subsequently they are told they can win 5 points with a blue ball and 1 with a red one, they will bet on the blue ball a little more often, but still this is no different from adults, who do the same thing (Schlottmann and Anderson, 1994; Van Leijenhorst, Westenberg and Crone, 2008). Rationally, adolescents are perfectly capable of assessing this type of situation. Where they differ from adults is in the emotions they experience when they have the prospect of the reward, or actually experience the reward or loss. Researchers have shown that on laboratory tasks adolescents show more risk-taking behaviour compared to children and adults when taking the risk is emotionally arousing (Braams, van Duijvenvoorde, Peper and Crone, 2015; Burnett, Bault, Coricelli and Blakemore, 2010; Figner, Mackinlay, Wilkening and Weber, 2009; Gardner and Steinberg, 2005), but not when taking risks in an emotionally 'cold' or 'rational' context (Figner *et al.*, 2009; Van Leijenhorst *et al.*, 2008). To understand how this works, we will take a more extensive look at a new brain structure that has been briefly discussed earlier: the subcortical (situated deep inside the brain) basal ganglia and the reward centre inside it, the ventral striatum and nucleus accumbens.

The role of the basal ganglia in winning and losing

The basal ganglia are made up of a number of nuclei situated deep within the brain, which are mainly known for their important role in initiating movement (Jahanshahi, Obeso, Rothwell and Obeso, 2015). However, that most certainly is not the basal ganglia's only function. These nuclei in the brain have important pathways to the frontal cortex and to areas of the brain important for processing emotions (Haber and Knutson, 2010; van den Bos, Rodriguez, Schweitzer and McClure, 2014). A specific part of the basal ganglia, the nucleus accumbens (which literally means: adjacent core), predominantly has a lot of pathways to emotional areas in the frontal cortex (Haber and Knutson, 2010). The nucleus accumbens is often described as the pleasure centre of the brain, because it is so sensitive to reward. We know this from the following experiment. When an electrode is placed in this area of a rat's brain, allowing it to stimulate this area whenever the rat presses a lever, the rat will press the lever ever more frequently and even forego food for this self-stimulation (Kokarovtseva, Jaciw-Zurakiwsky, Mendizabal Arbocco, Frantseva and Perez Velazquez, 2009). This is probably the case because this area of the brain produces a certain chemical substance, called dopamine, which causes a pleasurable feeling (Schultz, 1998). A second reason for considering the nucleus accumbens as the pleasure centre is that it plays such a large role in addiction behaviour. It is assumed that this area is highly susceptible to addictive substances, such as cocaine (Jasinska, Stein, Kaiser, Naumer and Yalachkov, 2014). Improved or decreased functioning of this area will therefore be connected to increased or decreased sensitivity to addiction. So, the nucleus accumbens can be considered the pleasure centre of the brain in animals. Some researchers have extended this to the ventral striatum, so below I will refer to the reward centre of the brain as the ventral striatum/nucleus accumbens.

Several studies have shown that in healthy adults, the nucleus accumbens is highly susceptible to reward, too (Haber and Knutson, 2010). But it is not just the reward that creates activity in the nucleus accumbens, even a sign indicating there could *possibly* be a reward forthcoming already creates activity in this area. In a pioneering study by Adriana Galvan, participants were asked to press a button every time a

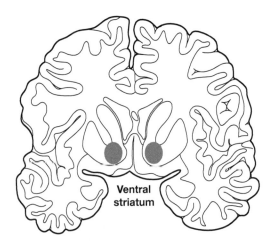

FIGURE 3.2 Display of ventral striatum

small pirate appeared on the screen. A few seconds later, the participants were shown a reward. There were three types of pirates and while performing the task it became clear that these predicted the magnitude of the reward. For example, the pirate with the sword was always followed by a small reward, but the pirate with the dagger was always followed by a large reward, and the third pirate yielded a medium-sized reward. Analysis of activity in the brain during this task showed that only seeing the pirate associated with the large reward in itself led to an increase in activity in the nucleus accumbens (Galvan et al., 2005). So these results show that the nucleus accumbens responds to just the *expectation* of a reward. That is why this area of the brain is very important for risk assessment too, in which the expected reward can sometimes beat the analysis of potential risk.

Interestingly, the ventral striatum/nucleus accumbens is highly sensitive to hormonal changes. For example, researchers have shown that the hormone testosterone is related to how much risks people take in the laboratory (Peper, Koolschijn and Crone, 2013). Furthermore, men typically take more risks in gambling studies than women (Van Leijenhorst et al., 2008). Evidently, this means that the emotional areas of the brain are strongly influenced by the onset of puberty (Op de Macks et al., 2011; Peper and Dahl, 2013).

Hyperactive emotion system during adolescence

Researchers have further investigated reward sensitivity in the brain of adolescents in a lab situation, in which adolescents were asked to play simple reward games. In the first study, the three pirates-task was offered to participants ages 7–10 (prepuberty), 13–17 (puberty and adolescence) and 23–29 (adult). The participants had to press the button every time they saw a pirate, and learned that some pirates yielded more rewards than others while working on the task. All participants showed increased activity in the nucleus accumbens (the pleasure area) when they saw a pirate that signalled a bigger reward. But in adolescents, this increase was much larger than in children and adults. It appears that this area is hypersensitive during this age. In addition, all participants also showed activity in the orbitofrontal cortex, the area of the brain important for forming emotional pathways and connections. However, here too the activity changed from one age group to the next. Both young children and adolescents showed more activity in this area of the brain than adults. As such, the adolescent group was unique in showing an increased reaction to a potential reward in both those areas of the brain indicating the pleasure of being rewarded, and those areas of the brain that steer behaviour towards being rewarded (Galvan et al., 2006).

A study in our own lab investigated whether these age-related changes were connected to the prediction or the outcome of a reward. Participants aged 11–12 (early puberty), 14–15 (middle adolescence) and 18–24 years (end of adolescence, early adulthood) were exposed to a casino situation. The participants were shown three successive gambling machines. In every gambling machine, a picture of a piece of fruit appeared. Only if all three gambling machines displayed the same picture, they would receive a reward. This set-up could lead to three possible outcomes. If the order of appearance on the gambling machine would be, for example, an apple, followed by an orange and then a grape, the participant would know from the second picture onwards that there would be no reward (because the apple and orange are already not the same). But when an apple appeared, followed by another apple, things got exciting, because there was a chance that they might win something. Part of the time, this came true and they were shown a third apple: a big reward. But a number of times, this did not happen and the two apples were followed by some other kind of fruit, such as a grape or a cherry. Analysis of the brain areas that were active during this task revealed important differences between the age groups. Not just receiving a reward, but also the anticipation of a possible reward resulted in increased activity in the nucleus accumbens. The anticipation reaction was magnified for both the young adolescents (11–12 years old) and the middle-adolescents (14–15 years old) compared to the oldest age group. These findings show that in adolescence, it is not only the prospect of a reward (as in the pirates signalling a reward) that results in hyperactivity of the pleasure area, but also the prospect of a *potential* reward (as when two apples are visible) (Van Leijenhorst et al., 2010). In another study, it was found that increased activity in the ventral striatum/nucleus accumbens can even predict if adolescents will subsequently make a risky choice in a driving task (Kahn, Peake, Dishion, Stormshak and Pfeifer, 2015), showing that it also has real-life predictive value.

A longitudinal study in our laboratory that examined reward sensitivity made use of a heads or tails gambling task. In this study, 249 participants between ages 8 and 25 years made guesses about whether the computer would pick heads or tails. In case their choice matched the choice of the computer, they won money, but if it didn't match they lost money. They played this game not only for themselves, but also for their best friend and someone they didn't like. When they played the game for themselves and for their best friend, the nucleus accumbens was more active when winning versus losing money, but this was not the case when they won for someone they disliked (in fact, in this condition it was

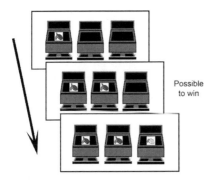

Possible
to win

FIGURE 3.3 Example of a gambling task with slot machines

reversed; participants activated the nucleus accumbens more when they lost money for someone they disliked). However, only for the self-condition, there was heightened activity in the nucleus accumbens for adolescents. This peak was observed around the age of 16–17 years, suggesting that this is the time when adolescents are most sensitive to rewards (Braams, Peters, Peper, Guroglu and Crone, 2014). In a subsequent study, this peak in nucleus accumbens activity was also observed when the same individuals were followed longitudinally (Braams *et al.*, 2015), suggesting that there is robust evidence for a peak in reward activity in mid-adolescence.

Some controversies also exist however. A well-known and validated task that is used to examine reward sensitivity is the monetary incentive delay (MID) task, and developmental neural activity patterns on this task look quite different. In the MID task, participants are presented cues that signal potential reward, but only if they respond within a certain time window. So the reward is not a sure outcome, similar to risks we take in everyday life. Therefore, the period between the cue and the outcome is seen as an index of *potential* reward anticipation. Intriguingly, it is consistently observed that activity in the nucleus accumbens and ventral striatum in this anticipation period is stronger in adults than in adolescents (Bjork, Smith, Chen and Hommer, 2010; Hoogendam, Kahn, Hillegers, van Buuren and Vink, 2013; Lamm *et al.*, 2014). Thus, possibly adolescents only show heightened nucleus accumbens activity when they anticipate a relatively sure reward.

This has led several researchers to examine the relation between reward anticipation and reward delivery in more detail. First of all, a study using the MID task replicated the reduced ventral striatum activity in adolescence when anticipating outcomes, but found that the same adolescents showed increased ventral striatum activity relative to adults when receiving rewards (Hoogendam *et al.*, 2013). Second, Beatriz Luna and colleagues examined reward anticipation and reward delivery in an anti-saccade task, which is a relatively simple eye-movement paradigm. They observed also that ventral striatum activity was attenuated in adolescents relative to adults when processing the cue, but activity in the ventral striatum to rewards was heightened when preparing for a response and when receiving the reward, specifically in mid-adolescence (Geier, Terwilliger, Teslovich, Velanova and Luna, 2010; Padmanabhan, Geier, Ordaz, Teslovich and Luna, 2011; Paulsen, Hallquist, Geier and Luna, 2015).

Together, the findings from these studies indicate that the specifics of reward anticipation sensitivity are dependent on specific task demands (Richards, Plate and Ernst, 2013), but that there is robust evidence for a stronger reward response in adolescence. This stronger reward response was also further supported by a meta-analysis (Silverman, Jedd and Luciana, 2015). This hyperactivity in the brain could also explain why adolescents seek out thrilling situations. Because it so happens that thrilling situations are often linked to a potential attractive outcome; it may be thrilling to jump off a low wall on your skateboard, but you wouldn't jump off a tall block of flats, as the chances of that ending well are far too small. Or, for example, consider young people driving their mopeds home after school. One of them will come up with the idea of tearing down a footpath and having a slalom along the street posts. At that moment, you might be worried about falling, or hitting someone. But you may also think about the fun you'll be having with your friends. Based on brain research, it seems that in adolescents, just the possibility of this 'rewarding' feeling in itself is enough to ignite the pleasure centre in the brain. Indeed, prior studies that looked at the relation between nucleus-accumbens activity and real-life reward seeking and risk-taking behaviour showed that more risk and reward-seeking adolescents in real life showed stronger nucleus-accumbens activity to rewards (Braams et al., 2015; Galvan, Hare, Voss, Glover and Casey, 2007).

Taking risks

Let's take an in-depth look at these choices. In the studies described above, we did lab research to investigate which areas of the brain are active in anticipating a potential reward. But how exactly are choices made? How do adolescents choose between a dangerous and a safe situation?

In order to investigate this, Monique Ernst and colleagues used a wheel-of-fortune task in the lab – another task that has a lot of similarities to risky situations of the type we see in the casino. When playing wheel of fortune in this study, there was a small chance of large winnings (an amount of money) and a large chance of small winnings. Participants were allowed to indicate whether they wanted to play for the large or small winnings. In this study, the adolescents – when compared to the adults – more often opted for the small chance to win big. They also indicated they were happier with their winnings than adults, however, they were less affected by losses than adults. Once more, they were mainly focused on the advantages of risky behaviour, while not paying much attention to the disadvantages (losing money) (Ernst et al., 2005).

In addition, during the task the adolescents showed more activity in the nucleus accumbens (brain area that reacts to rewards), whereas adults had more activity in the amygdala (emotion area that reacts to dangerous situations) and the prefrontal cortex (control area important for understanding the long-term consequences of behaviour) (Ernst et al., 2005; Eshel, Nelson, Blair, Pine and Ernst, 2007).

In our lab in Leiden we used a similar wheel-of-fortune task that was presented in a child-friendly format, so that we were sure that younger children would also understand the task. The wheel of fortune was now presented as a cake with different pieces which could have chocolate or strawberry flavour (referred to as the cake-gambling task). Participants were instructed to make a guess of whether someone with his eyes closed would pick chocolate or strawberry. When there were five pieces of strawberry and one piece of chocolate this choice was easy, but when there were three pieces of strawberry and three pieces of chocolate this choice was more difficult. On each trial, participants could make gambles that were associated with small or large rewards. When examining neural activity, the ventral striatum tracked, as expected, the value of the rewards (showing stronger activity when rewards were larger). In addition, for reward trials activity in the ventral striatum peaked in early (12–14 years) to mid-adolescence (16–17 years), relative to childhood (8–10 years) and adulthood (18–25 years). Thus, the peak in reward activity was consistently observed, also in this more active gambling task (Van Leijenhorst *et al.*, 2010).

In the studies we described, money is used to vary the reward, but the same areas sensitive to a monetary reward prove to be sensitive to other pleasurable yields as well, such as chocolate, attractive faces, friendship and cooperation (Lieberman and Eisenberger, 2009). This means that adolescents' behaviour can be influenced by all these 'rewarding' situations. In fact, a prior study showed that adolescents also show more ventral-striatum activity when they receive feedback that is not pleasurable (a bad-tasting liquid) (Galvan and McGlennen, 2013), which may indicate that adolescents respond more strongly to important emotional events in general, or that they experienced the aversive event as exciting.

Does reward help or hinder?

An important question is whether the heightened neural activity in the ventral striatum is only hindering adolescents (which is for example the case when they take excessive risks) or is also potentially helpful, for example when they are more focused on a task or need to learn from an ever-changing environment. Interestingly, there are several studies that showed that individuals perform better when they are rewarded, and that this benefit is larger for adolescents (Geier *et al.*, 2010; Smith, Halari, Giampetro, Brammer and Rubia, 2011). A large study that tested 304 participants between ages 8–22 years found that the ventral striatum is more active following correctly performed working-memory trials, and that this response peaked in mid-adolescence (Satterthwaite *et al.*, 2012). Interestingly, a prior study showed that under high-reward trials, adolescents show stronger activity in the lateral prefrontal cortex, which suggests that the reward helps them to perform better and use more cognitive control resources (Teslovich *et al.*, 2014).

The studies described in the section above all present conditions where reward can be successfully used to perform better. But what if there is a conflict between rewarding situations? For this question we have to turn to the connection between the nucleus accumbens/ventral striatum and the prefrontal cortex.

Now versus later

The nucleus accumbens works together with the prefrontal cortex in situations in which profit, reward or risk play a large role. As we have seen earlier, the nucleus accumbens is very sensitive to stimuli in the environment that represent a reward, even before these stimuli have been reacted to. The orbitofrontal cortex in particular plays an important role in controlling responses to reward stimuli

(O'Doherty, 2011), as we have also seen earlier in neuropsychologist Damasio's research, but which was confirmed in white matter tract studies in healthy adults (Peper *et al.*, 2013; van den Bos *et al.*, 2014). Other areas that play roles in risk assessment are the lateral frontal areas, which are of considerable importance for keeping track of long-term goals (Casey, 2015). For example, when a choice has to be made between an immediate, quick reward or a possible, larger reward on the long term, the emotion-related areas of the brain are active when the quick reward is chosen, whereas the lateral frontal cortex areas are active when the long-term alternatives are chosen (McClure, Laibson, Loewenstein and Cohen, 2004).

A well-known task that measures these types of decisions in the laboratory is the delay of gratification task (also known as temporal discounting task). This task asks participants to choose between a smaller immediate reward (for example 5 euros today) or a larger delayed reward (for example 8 euros in 2 weeks). The more impulsive individuals typically choose more for the immediate reward. It is often found that children make more impulsive choices and the ability to delay gratification (or make long-term choices) increases over the course of adolescence (Achterberg, Peper, Van Duijvenvoorde, Mandl and Crone, 2016; Banich *et al.*, 2013; Steinbeis, Haushofer, Fehr and Singer, 2016). Interestingly, when adolescents make immediate choices, they show stronger activity in the ventral striatum/nucleus accumbens than adults (Christakou, Brammer and Rubia, 2011). Overcoming responses to immediate reward is associated with strong functional coupling between the regulating dorsolateral prefrontal cortex and the reward-valuing ventromedial frontal cortex, a connection that becomes stronger with increasing age (Steinbeis *et al.*, 2016).

Moreover, studies that have looked at white matter tracts between the striatum and the frontal cortex have shown that the stronger these connections, the less impulsive people are. This tract becomes stronger between childhood and adulthood and explains, at least partly, the developmental changes in delay of gratification (Achterberg *et al.*, 2016; Olson *et al.*, 2009; van den Bos, Rodriguez, Schweitzer and McClure, 2015). A carefully conducted study that examined how adolescents and adults track the value of a reward demonstrated that the increased neural response in the ventral striatum in adolescents is not simply the result of them having less money to spend in daily life, but demonstrated that this is the result of adolescents assigning more value to the rewards (Barkley-Levenson and Galvan, 2014).

That means that at the time a decision needs to be made ('Will I drive carefully and keep to the rules I needed to learn to get my license, or will I join in?'), the prospect of the immediate kick may already gain the upper hand, winning out over the rational thoughts that indicate long-term outcomes. This struggle between different areas of the brain indicates once more why adolescents sometimes do and sometimes don't make sensible choices and decisions. For parents and teachers, this can lead to situations that are hard to predict. So when an adolescent's choice leads you to wonder: 'What on earth did you think you were doing, why would

you do a thing like that? Were you not thinking?' – the answer will probably be
'Er . . . no, I just went ahead and did it . . .'

The dual processing model of adolescent risk taking

What have we learned so far about the dynamic relationship between the prefrontal
cortex and limbic areas? The differential developmental trajectories of these brain
regions, where some regions may mature faster than others, may cause a period of
risk in adolescence, as is described in detail in the dual systems model (Shulman
et al., 2016) and the circuit-based imbalance model (Casey, 2015). These models
presume, based on numerous fMRI studies on cognitive control, that in young,
prepubescent children, the frontal cortex does not regulate behaviour as well as in
older children yet, but their nucleus accumbens also still keeps a low profile. This
is probably why they are less inclined to *seek out* risky situations. In addition, children
still look to their parents when wondering which behaviour is appropriate and which
is not. At the start of puberty, this system is thrown off balance. Influenced by
increasing hormone levels, the emotional areas of the brain are additionally
stimulated and become extra sensitive. However, the regulating frontal cortex is
by no means fully mature yet. So the emotional system is hypersensitive, while
the regulation system is not yet capable of keeping this sensitivity under control.
Not until we reach adulthood will we be capable of getting these two systems in
tune. On a side note, the exact dimensions of the dual systems model, or circuit-
based imbalance model, are currently the focus of lots of discussion between
scientists, see for example Pfeifer and Allen, 2012 and Strang, Chein and Steinberg,
2013). Future studies will need to sort out the specifics of the models. Nonetheless,
these models have provided an intriguing starting point for understanding the
interplay between cortical and subcortical brain regions.

The implications of this model for adolescent behaviour are that adolescents
may be more prone towards exploring (dangerous) activities, while not being able
yet to control their actions (Steinberg *et al.*, 2008). Combining the insights from
behavioural studies with neuroscience findings, we come to the following
conclusion: when adolescents find themselves in a non-emotionally stimulating
environment, they are perfectly capable of assessing risks and reasoning about possible
outcomes (for example having a serious conversation with their parents at the kitchen
table about an upcoming holiday to Spain with friends). However, as soon as there
is a prospect of a feeling of reward (in the broadest sense of the word), the emotion
centres become hyperactive (for example, once they find themselves in a nightclub
in Spain). This explains why adolescents often seek out new, challenging situations:
a necessary step towards adult social functioning. When adolescents are asked what
they think about dangerous situations, it immediately becomes apparent that they
do not experience the warning feeling that adults do experience. This warning
system matures slowly and doesn't get going until late-adolescence.

Interestingly, feeling what is right or wrong also has important consequences
for social relationships, but that is the subject of the next chapters.

References

Achterberg, M., Peper, J. S., Van Duijvenvoorde, A. C., Mandl, R. C. and Crone, E. A. (2016). Fronto-striatal white matter integrity predicts development in delay of gratification: a longitudinal study. *Journal of Neuroscience, 36*(6), 1954–1961.

Banich, M. T., De La Vega, A., Andrews-Hanna, J. R., Mackiewicz Seghete, K., Du, Y. and Claus, E. D. (2013). Developmental trends and individual differences in brain systems involved in intertemporal choice during adolescence. *Psychol Addict Behav, 27*(2), 416–430. doi:10.1037/a0031991

Barkley-Levenson, E. and Galvan, A. (2014). Neural representation of expected value in the adolescent brain. *Proc Natl Acad Sci USA, 111*(4), 1646–1651. doi:10.1073/pnas.1319762111

Bechara, A., Damasio, H., Tranel, D. and Anderson, S. W. (1998). Dissociation of working memory from decision making within the human prefrontal cortex. *J Neurosci, 18*(1), 428–437. Retrieved from www.ncbi.nlm.nih.gov/pubmed/9412519

Bechara, A., Damasio, H., Tranel, D. and Damasio, A. R. (1997). Deciding advantageously before knowing the advantageous strategy. *Science, 275*(5304), 1293–1295. Retrieved from www.ncbi.nlm.nih.gov/pubmed/9036851

Bechara, A., Damasio, H., Tranel, D. and Damasio, A. R. (2005). The Iowa Gambling Task and the somatic marker hypothesis: some questions and answers. *Trends Cogn Sci, 9*(4), 159–162; discussion 162–154. doi:10.1016/j.tics.2005.02.002

Bechara, A., Tranel, D. and Damasio, H. (2000). Characterization of the decision-making deficit of patients with ventromedial prefrontal cortex lesions. *Brain, 123*(Pt 11), 2189–2202. Retrieved from www.ncbi.nlm.nih.gov/pubmed/11050020

Bjork, J. M., Smith, A. R., Chen, G. and Hommer, D. W. (2010). Adolescents, adults and rewards: comparing motivational neurocircuitry recruitment using fMRI. *PLOS One, 5*(7), e11440. doi:10.1371/journal.pone.0011440

Braams, B. R., Peters, S., Peper, J. S., Guroglu, B. and Crone, E. A. (2014). Gambling for self, friends, and antagonists: differential contributions of affective and social brain regions on adolescent reward processing. *NeuroImage, 100*, 281–289. doi:10.1016/j.neuroimage.2014.06.020

Braams, B. R., van Duijvenvoorde, A. C., Peper, J. S. and Crone, E. A. (2015). Longitudinal changes in adolescent risk-taking: a comprehensive study of neural responses to rewards, pubertal development, and risk-taking behavior. *J Neurosci, 35*(18), 7226–7238. doi:10.1523/JNEUROSCI.4764-14.2015

Burnett, S., Bault, N., Coricelli, G. and Blakemore, S. J. (2010). Adolescents' heightened risk-seeking in a probabilistic gambling task. *Cogn Dev, 25*(2), 183–196. doi:10.1016/j.cogdev.2009.11.003

Casey, B. J. (2015). Beyond simple models of self-control to circuit-based accounts of adolescent behavior. *Annu Rev Psychol, 66*, 295–319. doi:10.1146/annurev-psych-010814-015156

Cauffman, E., Shulman, E. P., Steinberg, L., Claus, E., Banich, M. T., Graham, S. and Woolard, J. (2010). Age differences in affective decision making as indexed by performance on the Iowa Gambling Task. *Dev Psychol, 46*(1), 193–207. doi:10.1037/a0016128

Christakou, A., Brammer, M. and Rubia, K. (2011). Maturation of limbic corticostriatal activation and connectivity associated with developmental changes in temporal discounting. *NeuroImage, 54*(2), 1344–1354. doi:10.1016/j.neuroimage.2010.08.067

Crone, E. A., Somsen, R. J., Van Beek, B. and Van Der Molen, M. W. (2004). Heart rate and skin conductance analysis of antecendents and consequences of decision making. *Psychophysiology, 41*(4), 531–540. doi:10.1111/j.1469-8986.2004.00197.x

Crone, E. A. and van der Molen, M. W. (2004). Developmental changes in real life decision making: performance on a gambling task previously shown to depend on the ventromedial prefrontal cortex. *Dev Neuropsychol*, *25*(3), 251–279. doi:10.1207/s15326942dn 2503_2

Crone, E. A. and van der Molen, M. W. (2007). Development of decision making in school-aged children and adolescents: evidence from heart rate and skin conductance analysis. *Child Dev*, *78*(4), 1288–1301. doi:10.1111/j.1467-8624.2007.01066.x

Damasio, A. R. (1994). *Descartes' Error: Emotion, Reason and the Human Brain*. New York: Grosset/Putnam.

Damasio, H., Grabowski, T., Frank, R., Galaburda, A. M. and Damasio, A. R. (1994). The return of Phineas Gage: clues about the brain from the skull of a famous patient. *Science*, *264*(5162), 1102–1105. Retrieved from www.ncbi.nlm.nih.gov/pubmed/8178168

Ernst, M., Nelson, E. E., Jazbec, S., McClure, E. B., Monk, C. S., Leibenluft, E., Blair, J. and Pine, D. S. (2005). Amygdala and nucleus accumbens in responses to receipt and omission of gains in adults and adolescents. *NeuroImage*, *25*(4), 1279–1291. doi:10.1016/j.neuroimage.2004.12.038

Eshel, N., Nelson, E. E., Blair, R. J., Pine, D. S. and Ernst, M. (2007). Neural substrates of choice selection in adults and adolescents: development of the ventrolateral prefrontal and anterior cingulate cortices. *Neuropsychologia*, *45*(6), 1270–1279. doi:10.1016/j.neuro psychologia.2006.10.004

Fellows, L. K. and Farah, M. J. (2005). Different underlying impairments in decision-making following ventromedial and dorsolateral frontal lobe damage in humans. *Cereb Cortex*, *15*(1), 58–63. doi:10.1093/cercor/bhh108

Figner, B., Mackinlay, R. J., Wilkening, F. and Weber, E. U. (2009). Affective and deliberative processes in risky choice: age differences in risk taking in the Columbia Card Task. *J Exp Psychol Learn Mem Cogn*, *35*(3), 709–730. doi:10.1037/a0014983

Galvan, A., Hare, T., Voss, H., Glover, G. and Casey, B. J. (2007). Risk-taking and the adolescent brain: who is at risk? *Dev Sci*, *10*(2), F8–F14. doi:10.1111/j.1467-7687.2006.00579.x

Galvan, A., Hare, T. A., Davidson, M., Spicer, J., Glover, G. and Casey, B. J. (2005). The role of ventral frontostriatal circuitry in reward-based learning in humans. *J Neurosci*, *25*(38), 8650–8656. doi:10.1523/JNEUROSCI.2431-05.2005

Galvan, A., Hare, T. A., Parra, C. E., Penn, J., Voss, H., Glover, G. and Casey, B. J. (2006). Earlier development of the accumbens relative to orbitofrontal cortex might underlie risk-taking behavior in adolescents. *J Neurosci*, *26*(25), 6885–6892. doi:10.1523/JNEUROSCI. 1062-06.2006

Galvan, A. and McGlennen, K. M. (2013). Enhanced striatal sensitivity to aversive reinforcement in adolescents versus adults. *J Cogn Neurosci*, *25*(2), 284–296. doi:10.1162/jocn_a_00326

Gardner, M. and Steinberg, L. (2005). Peer influence on risk taking, risk preference, and risky decision making in adolescence and adulthood: an experimental study. *Dev Psychol*, *41*(4), 625–635. doi:10.1037/0012-1649.41.4.625

Geier, C. F., Terwilliger, R., Teslovich, T., Velanova, K. and Luna, B. (2010). Immaturities in reward processing and its influence on inhibitory control in adolescence. *Cereb Cortex*, *20*(7), 1613–1629. doi:10.1093/cercor/bhp225

Haber, S. N. and Knutson, B. (2010). The reward circuit: linking primate anatomy and human imaging. *Neuropsychopharmacology*, *35*(1), 4–26. doi:10.1038/npp.2009.129

Hoogendam, J. M., Kahn, R. S., Hillegers, M. H., van Buuren, M. and Vink, M. (2013). Different developmental trajectories for anticipation and receipt of reward during adolescence. *Dev Cogn Neurosci*, *6*, 113–124. doi:10.1016/j.dcn.2013.08.004

Hooper, C. J., Luciana, M., Conklin, H. M. and Yarger, R. S. (2004). Adolescents' performance on the Iowa Gambling Task: implications for the development of decision making and ventromedial prefrontal cortex. *Dev Psychol, 40*(6), 1148–1158. doi:10.1037/0012-1649.40.6.1148

Jahanshahi, M., Obeso, I., Rothwell, J. C. and Obeso, J. A. (2015). A fronto-striato-subthalamic-pallidal network for goal-directed and habitual inhibition. *Nat Rev Neurosci, 16*(12), 719–732. doi:10.1038/nrn4038

Jasinska, A. J., Stein, E. A., Kaiser, J., Naumer, M. J. and Yalachkov, Y. (2014). Factors modulating neural reactivity to drug cues in addiction: a survey of human neuroimaging studies. *Neurosci Biobehav Rev, 38*, 1–16. doi:10.1016/j.neubiorev.2013.10.013

Kahn, L. E., Peake, S. J., Dishion, T. J., Stormshak, E. A. and Pfeifer, J. H. (2015). Learning to play it safe (or not): stable and evolving neural responses during adolescent risky decision-making. *J Cogn Neurosci, 27*(1), 13–25. doi:10.1162/jocn_a_00694

Kokarovtseva, L., Jaciw-Zurakiwsky, T., Mendizabal Arbocco, R., Frantseva, M. V. and Perez Velazquez, J. L. (2009). Excitability and gap junction-mediated mechanisms in nucleus accumbens regulate self-stimulation reward in rats. *Neuroscience, 159*(4), 1257–1263. doi:10.1016/j.neuroscience.2009.01.065

Lamm, C., Benson, B. E., Guyer, A. E., Perez-Edgar, K., Fox, N. A., Pine, D. S. and Ernst, M. (2014). Longitudinal study of striatal activation to reward and loss anticipation from mid-adolescence into late adolescence/early adulthood. *Brain Cogn, 89*, 51–60. doi:10.1016/j.bandc.2013.12.003

Lieberman, M. D. and Eisenberger, N. I. (2009). Neuroscience. Pains and pleasures of social life. *Science, 323*(5916), 890–891. doi:10.1126/science.1170008

Longe, O., Senior, C. and Rippon, G. (2009). The lateral and ventromedial prefrontal cortex work as a dynamic integrated system: evidence from FMRI connectivity analysis. *J Cogn Neurosci, 21*(1), 141–154. doi:10.1162/jocn.2009.21012

McClure, S. M., Laibson, D. I., Loewenstein, G. and Cohen, J. D. (2004). Separate neural systems value immediate and delayed monetary rewards. *Science, 306*(5695), 503–507. doi:10.1126/science.1100907

O'Doherty, J. P. (2011). Contributions of the ventromedial prefrontal cortex to goal-directed action selection. *Ann N Y Acad Sci, 1239*, 118–129. doi:10.1111/j.1749-6632.2011.06290.x

Olson, E. A., Collins, P. F., Hooper, C. J., Muetzel, R., Lim, K. O. and Luciana, M. (2009). White matter integrity predicts delay discounting behavior in 9- to 23-year-olds: a diffusion tensor imaging study. *J Cogn Neurosci, 21*(7), 1406–1421. doi:10.1162/jocn.2009.21107

Op de Macks, Z. A., Gunther Moor, B., Overgaauw, S., Guroglu, B., Dahl, R. E. and Crone, E. A. (2011). Testosterone levels correspond with increased ventral striatum activation in response to monetary rewards in adolescents. *Dev Cogn Neurosci, 1*(4), 506–516. doi:10.1016/j.dcn.2011.06.003

Padmanabhan, A., Geier, C. F., Ordaz, S. J., Teslovich, T. and Luna, B. (2011). Developmental changes in brain function underlying the influence of reward processing on inhibitory control. *Dev Cogn Neurosci, 1*(4), 517–529. doi:10.1016/j.dcn.2011.06.004

Paulsen, D. J., Hallquist, M. N., Geier, C. F. and Luna, B. (2015). Effects of incentives, age, and behavior on brain activation during inhibitory control: a longitudinal fMRI study. *Dev Cogn Neurosci, 11*, 105–115. doi:10.1016/j.dcn.2014.09.003

Peper, J. S. and Dahl, R. E. (2013). Surging hormones: brain-behavior interactions during puberty. *Curr Dir Psychol Sci, 22*(2), 134–139. doi:10.1177/0963721412473755

Peper, J. S., Koolschijn, P. C. and Crone, E. A. (2013). Development of risk taking: contributions from adolescent testosterone and the orbito-frontal cortex. *J Cogn Neurosci, 25*(12), 2141–2150. doi:10.1162/jocn_a_00445

Peper, J. S., Mandl, R. C., Braams, B. R., de Water, E., Heijboer, A. C., Koolschijn, P. C. and Crone, E. A. (2013). Delay discounting and frontostriatal fiber tracts: a combined DTI and MTR study on impulsive choices in healthy young adults. *Cereb Cortex*, *23*(7), 1695–1702. doi:10.1093/cercor/bhs163

Pfeifer, J. H. and Allen, N. B. (2012). Arrested development? Reconsidering dual-systems models of brain function in adolescence and disorders. *Trends Cogn Sci*, *16*(6), 322–329. doi:10.1016/j.tics.2012.04.011

Richards, J. M., Plate, R. C. and Ernst, M. (2013). A systematic review of fMRI reward paradigms used in studies of adolescents vs. adults: the impact of task design and implications for understanding neurodevelopment. *Neurosci Biobehav Rev*, *37*(5), 976–991. doi:10.1016/j.neubiorev.2013.03.004

Satterthwaite, T. D., Ruparel, K., Loughead, J., Elliott, M. A., Gerraty, R. T., Calkins, M. E., Hakonarson, H., Gur, R. C., Gur, R. E. and Wolf, D. H. (2012). Being right is its own reward: Load and performance related ventral striatum activation to correct responses during a working memory task in youth. *NeuroImage*, *61*(3), 723–729. doi:10. 1016/j.neuroimage.2012.03.060

Schlottmann, A. and Anderson, N. H. (1994). Children's judgments of expected value. *Developmental Psychology*, *30*(1), 56–66.

Schultz, W. (1998). Predictive reward signal of dopamine neurons. *J Neurophysiol*, *80*(1), 1–27. Retrieved from www.ncbi.nlm.nih.gov/pubmed/9658025

Shulman, E. P., Smith, A. R., Silva, K., Icenogle, G., Duell, N., Chein, J. and Steinberg, L. (2016). The dual systems model: review, reappraisal and reaffirmation. *Dev Cogn Neurosci.*, *17*, 103–117

Silverman, M. H., Jedd, K. and Luciana, M. (2015). Neural networks involved in adolescent reward processing: an activation likelihood estimation meta-analysis of functional neuroimaging studies. *NeuroImage*, *122*, 427–439. doi:10.1016/j.neuroimage.2015.07.083

Smith, A. B., Halari, R., Giampetro, V., Brammer, M. and Rubia, K. (2011). Developmental effects of reward on sustained attention networks. *NeuroImage*, *56*(3), 1693–1704. doi:10.1016/j.neuroimage.2011.01.072

Smith, D. G., Xiao, L. and Bechara, A. (2012). Decision making in children and adolescents: impaired Iowa Gambling Task performance in early adolescence. *Dev Psychol*, *48*(4), 1180–1187. doi:10.1037/a0026342

Steinbeis, N., Haushofer, J., Fehr, E. and Singer, T. (2016). Development of behavioral control and associated vmPFC-DLPFC connectivity explains children's increased resistance to temptation in intertemporal choice. *Cereb Cortex*, *26*(1), 32–42. doi:10.1093/cercor/bhu167

Steinberg, L., Albert, D., Cauffman, E., Banich, M., Graham, S. and Woolard, J. (2008). Age differences in sensation seeking and impulsivity as indexed by behavior and self-report: evidence for a dual systems model. *Dev Psychol*, *44*(6), 1764–1778. doi:10.1037/a0012955

Strang, N. M., Chein, J. M. and Steinberg, L. (2013). The value of the dual systems model of adolescent risk-taking. *Front Hum Neurosci*, *7*, 223. doi:10.3389/fnhum.2013.00223

Teslovich, T., Mulder, M., Franklin, N. T., Ruberry, E. J., Millner, A., Somerville, L. H., Simen, P., Durston, S. and Casey, B. J. (2014). Adolescents let sufficient evidence accumulate before making a decision when large incentives are at stake. *Dev Sci*, *17*(1), 59–70. doi:10.1111/desc.12092

van den Bos, W., Rodriguez, C. A., Schweitzer, J. B. and McClure, S. M. (2014). Connectivity strength of dissociable striatal tracts predict individual differences in temporal discounting. *J Neurosci*, *34*(31), 10298–10310. doi:10.1523/JNEUROSCI.4105-13.2014

van den Bos, W., Rodriguez, C. A., Schweitzer, J. B. and McClure, S. M. (2015). Adolescent impatience decreases with increased frontostriatal connectivity. *Proc Natl Acad Sci USA*, *112*(29), E3765–3774. doi:10.1073/pnas.1423095112

Van Leijenhorst, L., Gunther Moor, B., Op de Macks, Z. A., Rombouts, S. A., Westenberg, P. M. and Crone, E. A. (2010). Adolescent risky decision-making: neurocognitive development of reward and control regions. *NeuroImage*, *51*(1), 345–355. doi:10.1016/j.neuroimage.2010.02.038

Van Leijenhorst, L., Westenberg, P. M. and Crone, E. A. (2008). A developmental study of risky decisions on the cake gambling task: age and gender analyses of probability estimation and reward evaluation. *Dev Neuropsychol*, *33*(2), 179–196. doi:10.1080/87565 640701884287

Van Leijenhorst, L., Zanolie, K., Van Meel, C. S., Westenberg, P. M., Rombouts, S. A. and Crone, E. A. (2010). What motivates the adolescent? Brain regions mediating reward sensitivity across adolescence. *Cereb Cortex*, *20*(1), 61–69. doi:10.1093/cercor/bhp078

4

YOU'RE NOT ANGRY, ARE YOU?

The importance of recognizing facial emotions

Despite seeing faces all around us all day long, we only need a few milliseconds to determine whether it belongs to a man or a woman, an older or a younger person, someone we know or don't know – even when faces appear to look very much alike. Even more remarkable is the speed at which we can tell from someone's face how they are feeling. We are able to very quickly recognize if someone is happy or angry, sad or relieved, confused or confident.

So, seeing a face – even for a very short time – provides us with information about the people around us, about social relations between them, and about our own relationship with them. You don't even have to hear what people are saying to each other in order to know how they are feeling. A facial expression often says it all: A man is sullenly walking behind a woman in a shop, the woman is shaking her head in incomprehension. A little girl is playing in the street when suddenly a motorcycle drives past. It almost hits her. With eyes wide, the girl rigidly stares at the motorcycle and then starts to cry. Her fear was immediately visible on her face.

We only need a fraction of a second to register all these emotions that can be read on people's faces. An adult needs less than 200 milliseconds to assess an emotion; often we can assess emotions from faces faster than our conscious perception (Niznikiewicz, 2013; Yovel, 2015). This assessment happens continuously, which is why we are constantly surrounded and (consciously or unconsciously) affected by the emotions of others. As a result, we are good at anticipating other people's feelings and empathizing with them. Whenever we see a face, we form an opinion about whether, for example, we think someone is attractive or trustworthy, and we also read faces to judge somebody's intentions. It is likely that assessing faces is the fastest and most basic way to take in social information (Todorov, Said, Engell and Oosterhof, 2008) and it alerts us as to what could be the next step in our social interactions.

The ability to recognize facial emotions develops at a very early age. There are even indications that shortly after birth, babies prefer seeing faces over other objects and facial recognition is clearly present from as early as two months after birth (Farroni *et al.*, 2005). Twelve-month-olds are already quite capable of distinguishing between happy and angry facial expressions.

Professor Paul Ekman (Ekman, Campos, Davidson and De Waal, 2003) extensively researched the recognizability and functioning of the six 'basic' emotions: happiness, sadness, anger, fear, surprise and disgust, which he believes are *universal*, meaning they can be found in all cultures. Even when children were born blind or deaf, they use these emotions to communicate their feelings (less accurate, to be sure, than children who are not blind or deaf, but still they know all these emotions).

Research in adolescents with regard to recognizing emotions on faces has resulted in three important findings. First, the ability to recognize emotions is still developing between the ages of 10 and 18 years. Some emotions can be easily recognized by 7-year-old children, such as happiness. Other emotions are not recognized very well by 7-year-olds yet, but they are recognized by 10-year-olds, such as anger and sadness. The most complex emotions aren't recognized very well until late-adolescence, such as surprise and fear (Herba, Landau, Russell, Ecker and Phillips, 2006). This does not mean that adolescents don't know or can't recognize these emotions, only that, compared to adults, adolescents confuse complex emotions more often. For example, they will categorize a face as surprised, while in reality it shows fear. A second important finding is that the ability to suppress or steer these emotions (i.e., emotion regulation) develops during childhood and adolescence (Tottenham, Hare and Casey, 2011). It is probable that this change in the way adolescents deal with emotions greatly influences the broad scope of changes that adolescents experience in the social relationships they maintain during this period. A third finding is that during all stages of development (during childhood, adolescence and adulthood), women are better at recognizing emotions on faces than men (Lewin and Herlitz, 2002).

In this chapter, we will focus on how exactly we recognize facial emotions, how our brain works in the process, and how we experience and register emotions. I will discuss the way young people look at faces, how faces change, which faces young people consider to be attractive and how young people deal with emotions on other people's faces. Here, too, the development of the brain plays an important, directive role. Based on patient studies and fMRI studies, we now know which areas of the brain are important for these developmental differences.

The Lady Gaga cell

Despite the extreme complexity of faces, they are processed in very specific areas of the brain. It so happens that there are areas in the brain that are specialized in recognizing important information about the environment, such as faces or familiar places.

One such area is sensitive to seeing faces: the *fusiform face area* (an area in the temporal lobe). In the near vicinity of this area, there are two areas that also have a very specific function: the *parahippocampal place area* (an area in the brain that specifically responds to seeing places, such as houses and landscapes), and the *extrastriate body area* (an area that is specifically sensitive to seeing body parts). For example, someone with damage to the fusiform face area will not be able to recognize faces, although this person will be able to describe what a face looks like, and will also be able to recognize body parts or objects. Similarly, damage to the parahippocampal area may result in someone being unable to recognize a room, despite being able to see and describe individual characteristics, such as the people present in the room and whether or not there is furniture in it. And when someone sees a hand or leg, this activates their extrastriate body area, which does not happen when they see a hammer or a broom. Such specializations are formed during early childhood, when the brain is still mouldable (Scherf, Behrmann and Dahl, 2012).

An interesting research question is the extent of the specialization in the brain. Researchers have examined whether there are specific cells in the brain that only respond to seeing a famous person. They placed about 100 sensors in the hippocampus (an important area for the formation of memories) of patients who were undergoing brain surgery for severe epilepsy. Subsequently, during their surgery, these people were shown photographs of both famous and unfamiliar people. One patient had a brain cell that specifically responded to seeing a photograph of Bill Clinton. Whenever a photograph of Bill Clinton was shown, this person's specific 'Bill Clinton cell' was activated. Similarly, a Halle Berry cell was discovered in another patient. Here, too, a single cell started firing as soon as a photograph of Halle Berry was shown, but not when another famous (or unfamiliar) person was shown (Quiroga, Reddy, Kreiman, Koch and Fried, 2005).

For several reasons, research into single brain cells is rare, but nevertheless the discovery of the Bill Clinton and Halle Berry cells forces us to ask some provocative questions about specialization in the brain: is there one single cell that responds to seeing your mother, your boyfriend, your granny or Lady Gaga? How are such cells formed? Will they be reserved for this one person for ever? These are questions we have yet to answer.

Let's go back to the area that specifically responds to seeing faces, the fusiform face area. This is not the only part of the brain that recognizes faces: the *occipital face area* and the (posterior) *superior temporal sulcus* are also active when we see faces. These three areas are situated close together. The two 'additional' areas (occipital face area and posterior superior temporal sulcus) play an important part in the recognition and interpretation of faces, but in addition to interpreting faces, these areas also have other functions.

We now know which three areas of the brain become active the moment we see a face. These are the basic areas, which are all necessary for face recognition; we are unable to recognize a face when, for example, the fusiform face area is damaged (Gainotti and Marra, 2011).

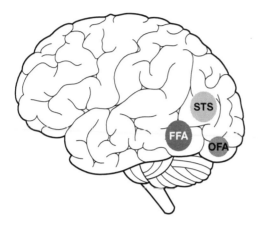

FIGURE 4.1 Brain regions involved in face processing. FFA = fusiform face area; OFA = occipital face areas; STS = superior temporal sulcus

In addition to these three basic areas, there are collaborating brain areas that are in charge of the emotional interpretation and the social processing of faces. It is the task of these areas to attribute social characteristics to a face, such as reading the emotions, interpreting intentions and making judgements about reliability, attractiveness, approachability and so on.

Collaborating brain areas: the role of emotions

A certain American patient has a very unusual abnormality. This patient is perfectly able to discern faces, indicate whether they are male or female and recognize the faces' identities. But when this patient is asked to describe an emotion, he gets into serious trouble. He has most difficulty with the emotion of fear, but surprise and anger are also often perceived incorrectly. When the patient is forced to choose an emotion when confronted with a fearful face, he chooses happiness just as often as disappointment; he simply cannot recognize the emotions. The remarkable thing is that this patient does know what fear is. He can describe a fearful situation and knows when fear is supposed to be felt. However, when asked to draw a face showing fear, he can't. This patient has a specific disability when it comes to categorizing negative and complex emotions. This is caused by damage to his amygdala, an almond-shaped, subcortical structure, meaning it is situated very deep inside the brain and is evolutionarily older than the cortex (Adolphs, Tranel, Damasio and Damasio, 1994).

The amygdala is part of the limbic system, a group of structures in the brain important for emotions and motivations. The amygdala is situated in the 'emotional brain', the deeper and evolutionary older areas of the brain that are able to quickly trigger (or elicit) an emotional experience and responds to different facial expressions, mainly to angry and fearful faces, but also to happy and sometimes to ambiguous faces that do not convey one single, explicit emotion. The amygdala mainly responds to the intensity of the emotion, and because fear and anger are usually the most intense, the amygdala is most sensitive to these emotions (Cunningham, Van Bavel and Johnsen, 2008).

The amygdala doesn't just respond to faces. In laboratory experiments, healthy participants were told they would possibly get an electric shock if a blue square appeared on the screen. In reality, the shocks were never administered, but the participants showed increased activity in the amygdala when the blue square was shown (Delgado, Jou, Ledoux and Phelps, 2009). So, the amygdala responds to emotionally important information in general, even when it is only supplied by way of instruction. For example, when someone tells you 'be careful, that dog may bite', your amygdala will become active, even if the dog hasn't done anything wrong yet.

A second area that is often involved in the emotional interpretation of faces is the insula. While the insula seems to be involved in a broad range of emotions, it has been linked mainly to seeing faces that show disgust. When, for example, during an experiment a video is shown of someone sniffing a glass and grimacing in disgust, it has been shown that the onlooker's insula becomes active – more so than when the observed person sniffs a glass and then pulls a happy or angry face (Chapman and Anderson, 2012).

So, the amygdala and insula respond most strongly when seeing a face expressing negative emotions, such as fear, anger and disgust. These ancient brain areas provide a fast response, for example to prepare you for a fight or for running away (*fight or flight*).

The third emotion area that is deep inside the evolutionary old brain areas and that is part of the emotional brain is the striatum. The striatum has proven to be a kind of pleasure area that responds to positive information, such as monetary

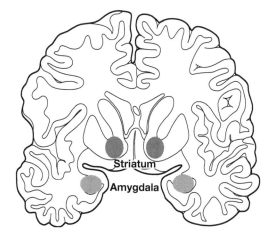

FIGURE 4.2 Display of ventral striatum and amygdala

rewards, sexually arousing pictures and chocolate (Lieberman and Eisenberger, 2009). Contrary to the other areas, this area responds to positive emotions, such as a smile or a happy face, and plays a role in approaching other people (Cunningham *et al.*, 2008). This approaching of others is very important to teenagers.

Collaborating brain areas: the role of intentions

Imagine you are being approached by an angry man, who is shouting the name of someone behind you. You see the man, you recognize him and you feel fear because he is angry, but subsequently you manage to suppress your fear, because you discover his anger is directed at someone else. Your own fear subsides, you try to imagine what is causing his anger, you may even try to help, because you empathize with the person the anger is directed at or with the man who is expressing his anger.

When we see emotions, it is important to recognize the identity of the person expressing the emotion and to be able to read what emotion we are dealing with – followed by the question what to do about this emotion. Other collaborating brain areas (other than the amygdala, insula and striatum) focus on assessing intentions and regulating fear. These interpretations and the assessment of such feelings call on the cortical brain areas that are on the outside, forming a shell around the deep emotional cores. These are evolutionary younger areas. The medial prefrontal cortex proves to be highly involved in thinking about the intentions of others (Tottenham, 2015). For example, the medial prefrontal cortex becomes active when we think about why somebody is fearful or angry.

Differences between men and women: a role for hormones

We don't know why exactly, but women outperform men in recognizing both the identity and the emotional expression of a face (Lewin and Herlitz, 2002).

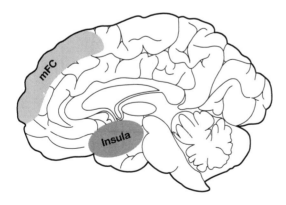

FIGURE 4.3 Display of mFC and insula. mFC = medial frontal cortex

This has been studied using recognition assignments, for which an experiment is conducted in two parts. During the first part, so many faces are shown that it becomes impossible to, for example, remember the order in which they were shown. During the second part, again a large number of faces is shown. Some of these were also shown during the first part, but others are new.

The participants are asked to indicate for every face whether it is 'new' or if they have seen it during the previous part of the experiment ('old'). In general, women perform better than men on this assignment. The difference between men and women specifically lies in facial recognition, for if the same assignment is carried out using objects (such as gardening tools, kitchen utensils or furniture), both men and women perform equally well.

In addition, research has been carried out using faces that express anger, fear, disappointment or surprise. The participants were asked to identify the emotions and here, too, women do slightly better than men. Incidentally, a better recognition of emotions by women/girls compared to men/boys is already evident in young children and remains unchanged over the entire age span (Rehnman and Herlitz, 2007).

During early adolescence, girls show a heightened response in the amygdala to negative faces compared to late-adolescence. This could mean that, in girls, the amygdala is hypersensitive during puberty and decreases in sensitivity later on. In boys, this hypersensitivity is observed all through adolescence. A possible explanation is that girls develop a little faster than boys, which may also cause their emotional system to mature faster (Killgore, Oki and Yurgelun-Todd, 2001).

Although there is some evidence for this idea, it is not conclusive. The fact is that a difference in the amygdala's response to negative faces remains in adult men and women: men show more amygdala activity than women (Killgore and Yurgelun-Todd, 2001). However, it is interesting that during development, girls show more activity in the frontal cortex upon seeing negative faces (Killgore *et al.*, 2001). This could mean that girls are better able to place the negative images in a context, allowing them to better control their emotional response.

It is known that the emotional brain areas in particular, such as the amygdala and the striatum, are sensitive to fluctuations in hormones. The hormone estrogen affects the amygdala particularly strongly (Engman, Linnman, Van Dijk and Milad, 2016; Pruis, Neiss, Leigland and Janowsky, 2009; Zeidan *et al.*, 2011).

An explanation for the better recognition of emotions by women could be that facial recognition is linked to specific female hormones that are already formed while the baby is still in the womb. This sex-specific development in the womb is also known as the first phase of sexual differentiation. Researchers owe the suspicion that estrogen plays a role in the recognition of facial emotions to the existence of Turner syndrome, a rare but very specific and striking disorder in which women miss an X-chromosome, meaning they do not produce estrogen. This syndrome results in specific problems with facial recognition, both of well-known and unfamiliar people. In addition, women with this syndrome have great difficulty with recognizing the emotions of fear and anger on faces (Lawrence *et al.*, 2008).

There is another indication that estrogen plays a role in facial recognition: the fluctuation of women's opinions during the menstrual cycle with regard to which men they find attractive. Upon reaching the highest estrogen levels during the menstrual cycle, women have an increased preference for symmetrical faces and for faces with strong masculine features (Little, DeBruine and Jones, 2011). Moreover, the same male faces will be considered more or less attractive, depending on which phase of the menstrual cycle a woman is currently in (Bobst and Lobmaier, 2014; Roney and Simmons, 2008; Rupp et al., 2009).

Incidentally, changes during the menstrual cycle (and also the natural fluctuation in testosterone levels in men (Welling et al., 2008)) are very small, compared to the hormonal fluctuations that occur as a result of changes during puberty.

Now that we know that even these minor fluctuations affect the interpretation of emotions, you can start to imagine what kind of pandemonium is taking place inside the adolescent brain, given the massive hormonal changes, and what consequences this has for the way teenagers read faces and emotions.

Puberty and faces

Adolescents have to deal with a great number of changes, including changes in their environment. As a result, recognizing faces becomes a challenge for them. As far as their appearance is concerned, the person they see in the mirror changes completely in just a year or two. First of all, the structure of their own face changes: from a child's face to that of an adult. Boys develop a more masculine face: the cheekbones become more prominent, the forehead changes, facial hair starts to appear, the Adam's apple becomes larger. Girls develop more feminine features, for example, their lips become fuller. Both boys and girls will develop pimples, to a greater or lesser extent. Of course, it's not just their own appearance that changes, but that of their peers as well. Because adolescents are becoming more focused on their social environment and the form and content of their friendships undergoes major changes, other aspects of their friends' faces are becoming important, such as attractiveness, trust and personality. In primary school, the boy with the snub nose and red curly hair may have been the darling of all the girls, but in secondary school, other aspects of appearance start playing a role in assessing who is considered attractive.

Who is attractive?

Computer programmes make it possible to 'blend' multiple faces together. The more different faces are blended together, the more average and perfectly symmetrical the faces become. It has been shown that faces that are most symmetrical (average) are considered the most attractive. When adult men and women are shown faces of adult women, there is a fairly large measure of agreement on who is considered attractive. When 12-year-old adolescents are asked to arrange adult women by attractiveness, the outcome is much the same. Remarkably, this preference for average, symmetrical faces was not found in 9-year-olds (pre-pubescents) (Cooper, Geldart, Mondloch and Maurer, 2006). Apparently, something happens between the ages of 9 and 12 that results in the preference for the average face.

But when you ask adolescents to assess the attractiveness of other adolescents' faces, they do not agree nearly as much. Some adolescents think a certain adolescent face is attractive, whereas other adolescents think another adolescent face is attractive. It seems that, over the course of adolescence, adolescents start to agree more on what they consider to be attractive faces. Given that adolescent faces change greatly and become more gender-specific, the assessment of attractiveness is continually changing as well.

Jon and Emma are both very popular at school. When Emma was only 13, she already had a group of devoted fans, and all the boys in her class thought she was pretty. All the girls in her class wanted to be friends with her and occasionally they were jealous of all the attention she was getting. When he was 13, Jon was fairly nondescript, but that quickly changed in 2-years' time. He grew into a cool, handsome guy. It was clear that Emma had her eye on him. First he didn't understand – she had never paid him any attention before, had she? But then he noticed that other girls were becoming interested in him and slowly he started to believe that he might stand a chance with Emma after all. When they were both 15 and in the third year of secondary school, Emma and Jon officially started dating. All the boys and girls secretly hoped they would break up and they all dreamed of dating their idols themselves. But the two best-looking classmates had found each other and it seemed that nobody could come between them.

It is remarkable that there are always one or two students in a class who are universally popular; it is probable that these adolescents also fit the image that most people find attractive at first sight, that is to say, symmetrical and gender-specific.

Who is recognized best? The own-age bias

There is a phenomenon in facial recognition research called 'own-age bias', which means that adults perform better at recognizing faces of people their own age than at recognizing older or younger faces (Rhodes and Anastasi, 2012). When a young woman has to recognize an older man, she will find this more difficult than recognizing a woman of her own age. Conversely, an older man will have more difficulty recognizing a young man or woman than a man or woman of his own age. This could have consequences for recognizing people in photographs or in a police line-up.

This own-age bias develops in adolescence: young children aren't better yet at recognizing children their own age. It's possible that this bias is simply a matter of experience (Anastasi and Rhodes, 2005). Young children may lack this experience because they still very much rely on their parents, teachers and other adults. It isn't until puberty that children start spending more time with their peers. Little is known about the emergence of the own-age bias during adolescence, but the fact that it develops during adolescence is yet another indication of the sheer scope of this transition phase for the formation of social relationships with peers.

Who is liked best? The own-gender bias

There is another interesting effect referred to as the cooties effect, which reflects people's preference towards individuals of their own gender, an effect which is especially prominent in young children. Eva Telzer and colleagues examined this effect by asking participants between ages 7 and 17 years to ascribe attributes to pictures of boys and girls (Telzer et al., 2015). Younger participants attributed more positive attributes to their own gender, an effect that was smaller in mid-teens and disappeared in older teens. With increasing age, adolescents also got better at identifying emotional expressions of opposite genders. Intruigingly, this effect was associated with a stronger amygdala response to oppositive genders in younger participants, and this effect also got smaller when adolescents turned older. These findings underline again that adolescence is an important time for social reorientation during which children start to value also the emotions of the opposite gender.

Dealing with other people's emotions and expressing your own emotions

The way people are recognized – based on faces – changes as children grow older. Earlier, we discussed the assignment with faces that have or have not been shown before, with which we can investigate whether or not a particular face has been remembered. Until the age of about 12 years, children still have difficulty recognizing faces that had already been shown before. From that age onward, they do much better. This is not simply a result of their memory getting better or worse. For example, young children are better at recognizing pictures of objects or landscapes than at recognizing faces. A possible explanation is that children do not have a specialized face-recognition system yet (Herba et al., 2006; Pascalis, de Haan and Nelson, 2002). This face-recognition system is possibly formed by interactive specialization, as described in Chapter 2.

It is not only facial recognition (of humans) that improves as children grow older. The recognition of emotions on faces also improves and puberty plays an important role in this process. Researchers have asked participants from multiple age groups to categorize pictures of faces, based on the emotion the faces were showing. It is well-known that young children are already very good at this task and adolescents are perfectly able to distinguish between the emotional extremes, such as anger and happiness. However, when it comes to discerning emotions that are similar, such as anger, fear and disgust, adolescents do not do quite as well as adults (Herba et al., 2006). The same goes for assignments in which they are asked to describe the emotion visible on the face.

It is only during adolescence that children learn how to recognize 'mixed emotions': the fact that someone may be angry and fearful at the same time, or sad and happy (for example, a girl who is put through to the second round of a dancing competition, but her best friend is not). Until the beginning of adolescence, children find these subtle, more ambiguous emotions hard to identify, but as they progress along the path to adulthood and gain more experience with complex social situations, adolescents get more experienced with this. During childhood, it's unambiguous: if your mother is angry with you, it probably means you should listen better. However, during adolescence, your mother being angry may also mean that she is disappointed in your actions and maybe also sad about what you did. As you get older, you learn to interpret your mother's anger in multiple ways. Combining all these emotional interpretations is a complex affair that needs a lot of practice.

Simultaneously, as they grow older, adolescents learn to use '*display rules*'. These are social norms that determine whether or not it is appropriate to express your emotions. It might be alright to feel sad and cry when your mother is angry with you, but it is less accepted to express those emotions when your teacher is angry with you (Begeer *et al.*, 2011).

Learning display rules is a process of trial and error, but these rules are quickly acquired during puberty. The acquisition of display rules and facial recognition do not just improve during the period of puberty. In fact, there are indications that suggest that the ability to recognize emotions on faces temporarily decreases upon the onset of puberty. One study, which looked at children between the ages of 8 and 16, has shown that the ability to recognize emotions deteriorated around the age of 12 (McGivern, Andersen, Byrd, Mutter and Reilly, 2002). These findings were more or less confirmed by other scientists, who found an increase in the ability to recognize emotions between the ages of 6 and 10. From then on, recognition reached a plateau between the ages of 10 and 13, meaning there was neither improvement nor deterioration. Subsequently, the ability improved again between the ages of 13 and 16, at which point an adult level was reached (Lawrence *et al.*, 2008). In this case, recognition was not found to deteriorate. However, improvement was found to have temporarily stopped, which is possibly connected to the hormonal changes that affect the brain during puberty (Scherf *et al.*, 2012). Scientists have yet to discover exactly how pubertal hormones affect the brain with regard to perceiving emotions on faces.

The emergence of the fusiform face area

Now, which areas of the brain ensure that adolescents get better and better at recognizing faces? Two processes are going on here: there is an early development of the basic areas for facial recognition, and a slower, later development of the collaborating areas that are able to recognize emotions.

Researchers designed an fMRI experiment to investigate the development of the basic areas that are important for recognizing faces and houses (Scherf, Luna, Avidan and Behrmann, 2011). Participants were children and adolescents ranging from 8 years old to adulthood. First, the faces and houses were presented in blocks, consisting for example of twenty faces, followed by twenty houses. When these blocks were presented, all participants – including the very youngest – showed activity in the fusiform area for faces, and in the parahippocampal cortex when seeing houses. In the second part of the experiment the houses and faces were mixed up and presented in a single block. Even though the 8-year-olds showed normal activity in the parahippocampal cortex when seeing houses, reduced activity was observed in the fusiform face area. In children of 11 years and older, both areas were shown to work just as well as they did in adults. It seems that the youngest children still have difficulty switching between quickly changing pictures, as a result of which they may find it harder to quickly recognize and contextualize faces. It is also possible that at this age, children are still more flexible with regard to seeing faces, and that, as such, this ability is not yet located in a single area.

Either way, it seems that between the ages of 8 and 11 years, a large specialization in the way faces are processed takes place. And even though 11-year-old children are able to respond to the faces to the same extent as adults, and the facial processing in the basic areas is quite specialized by then, there is still a lot going on in the emotional brain areas during this period, causing strong fluctuations in seeing, considering and experiencing emotions.

Hypersensitivity of the emotional brain

A number of studies tried to chart how the amygdala responds to emotional faces during different stages of development. These studies used fMRI and presented adolescents with neutral, positive and negative faces, that they only had to look at. In one of the earlier studies, a remarkable finding was reported. In young adolescents (10–12 years old), the amygdala was not only active when viewing fearful faces, but also active after being presented with a neutral face (Thomas et al., 2001). This was initially an unexpected finding, and researchers have long speculated what it could mean. One possible explanation is that neutral faces produce a lot of ambiguity. We immediately know the meaning of a happy or fearful face, but a neutral face can have any number of meanings. Often, parents even put on a neutral face when they are angry with their children. Therefore, the researchers concluded that young adolescents show more amygdala activity when they don't know what to make of the face they're confronted with. Possibly, this uncertainty is an emotionally significant situation for them, too.

Researchers have also addressed the question how adolescents process faces with an emotional valence. It is known that the amygdala reacts to faces with high intensity, such as angry or fearful faces. It is also known that the striatum responds to positive faces, such as happy and smiling faces. But in adolescents, the amygdala is especially active when seeing an angry face (Guyer et al., 2008b; Hare et al., 2008; Pfeifer et al., 2011), and the striatum is especially active when seeing a happy face (Somerville, Hare and Casey, 2011). The amygdala is also more active in adolescents compared to adults when *masked* sad faces are presented, suggesting that the heightened reactivity in the amygdala may work also for faces that are presented unconsciously (Killgore and Yurgelun-Todd, 2007).

You could say that adolescents are hypersensitive to faces that signal that it is better to stay out of the way, as well as to faces that indicate something nice is about to happen.

Regulating emotions becomes better across adolescence

Obviously, it is important to regulate emotions also, and this requires a broader set of communicating brain regions. Researchers have also observed that the medial prefrontal cortex, a region that works closely together with the amygdala, was more active in adolescent boys than in adult men, possibly reflecting an age-related reduction in attention demands (Deeley et al., 2008).

This was also found in research that examined how adolescents regulate feelings elicited by emotional stimuli. One study showed that when adolescents are instructed to press buttons to all kinds of emotional faces, except fearful faces, they have more difficulty inhibiting their responses, unlike children and adults. They also show more activation in the medial prefrontal cortex when fearful faces were presented, an effect that was stronger for boys than for girls (Dreyfuss et al., 2014). A similar finding was observed when adolescents had to reappraise emotions from pictures (making them less negative, for example), in these cases they also showed more activity in the medial prefrontal cortex (McRae et al., 2012). This was associated with less reappraisal success in adolescence, suggesting that emotional responses in the amygdala and the regions that support mental state attribution (such as medial prefrontal cortex) are possibly not yet well aligned.

Indeed, researchers have looked at how the amygdala is *connected* to other brain regions when adolescents need to react to or reappraise emotional social images. They observed that with increasing age, adolescents became better at reappraising, and that especially younger adolescents had stronger connectivity between the amygdala and other regions in the face-processing network, such as the fusiform face areas (Stephanou et al., 2015). Possibly, this stronger connectivity makes it more difficult to regulate the emotional responses elicited by the amygdala. During adolescence, the collaborating network of emotion areas is working overtime.

Not all adolescents are the same

Miriam was very shy in high school. She had always been a bit shy, but once she had started high school, it had become worse. She hardly dared to take part in the group assignments. Every morning when she arrived at school and parked her bike, there would be a group of older girls just staring at her in a nasty way. They were getting on her nerves. It's not that she was afraid that the girls would say anything to her, but just the way they stared made Miriam feel uncomfortable.

Not all adolescents are sensitive to angry looks from others. Some children don't let it worry them, but others may feel seriously bothered. So, among adolescents, there is a large difference in the extent to which they respond to the facial expressions of others, and in the extent to which their amygdalae respond to those faces. However, in individuals who happen to be sensitive to these social signals, this sensitivity is particularly heightened during adolescence (Hare et al., 2008).

Now let's consider the example of Sonia and Natasha. These two happy girls have been friends since their first year of high school and have been classmates for

3 years. At first, they were allowed to sit side by side, but now they have to sit separately in all of their classes. Fortunately, they can still talk to each other during breaks. And really, they don't even have to sit together any more − in class, they only have to look at each other and they burst out laughing. Their teachers get exasperated at times, but mostly, they just let it go.

Sonia and Natasha are almost the exact opposites of Miriam. No matter how many angry looks they get from their teachers and sometimes even their classmates, they simply can't help it. It is likely that their joy affects the striatum, the area of the brain that causes pleasure. Research has shown that adolescents who respond more strongly to seeing happy faces are less able to stop their behaviour when necessary (Somerville *et al.*, 2011). We all know the way some adolescents can get helpless with laughter, don't we? Apparently, the striatum plays a very important role in approaching other people. That is necessary, because you have to dare to take certain steps, but it also results in adolescents finding it difficult to switch back to behaving in class and paying attention.

The theory of reorganizing self-organized learning

So, does that mean that this temporary capriciousness during adolescence does nothing but cause embarrassment and inconvenience? Certainly not: these changes are necessary to make the transition from a child's brain to an adult brain. This is well explained by the model of Suzanne Scherf and colleagues (Scherf *et al.*, 2012). They argued that the brain is often considered to be an organ that is capable of self-organized learning. Children are active learners who always want to discover new things. Because of their brains' ability to engage in self-organized learning, connections that have been formed from a very young age get reinforced over and over. This can be compared to a path through high grass that gets walked on time and again, so that it eventually becomes a road on which you can walk better and faster.

Is it a good idea to walk along the same paths time and time again, so that they become faster? For many skills, it probably is, but certainly not for all of them. It is a good thing for learning how to walk, run, cycle and talk. But for social development, we need a transition, a change. If, as a young child, you have created the path in your brain to go and ask your parents every time you don't know something, then during adolescence, something will have to happen that will cause you to use that path less often and develop new paths. For example, a new path could be that you go and ask your friends for help.

So how do old paths get removed? And how do new paths get created? According to the self-organized learning model, pubertal hormones play an important part in temporarily playing havoc with the capacity for self-organized learning (Scherf *et al.*, 2012). Pubertal hormones influence the areas of the brain that amplify emotions and allow previously untrodden areas to form new pathways. This may be frustrating for parents at times, because rules and agreements they thought were normal and reasonable no longer seem to apply. But in the end, this temporary period of emotional instability has a purpose. During this period of confusion, old paths are used less, are re-routed or even closed off, so that new paths can be created and new connections can be formed. Eventually, these new connections see to it that adolescents step onto the road to adulthood.

What about social anxiety and depression?

There are several disorders that occur during adolescence, in which the hypersensitive period of facial and emotional recognition spins out of control. One of these disorders is anxiety, in which we see over-sensitivity to faces with a negative emotional charge. For example, adolescents with social anxiety will find it much harder than others to conduct a class presentation when they perceive negative feedback from the group, such as signs of disapproval or boredom (Blote, Kint, Miers and Westenberg, 2009).

Brain research in 12- to 14-year-old adolescents with social anxiety has shown that their amygdala and prefrontal cortex (especially important for curbing or steering emotions) are less connected. As a result, emotions that are processed by the amygdala are not regulated by the prefrontal cortex as much, causing adolescents with social anxiety to be more responsive or sensitive to emotional faces compared to adolescents without social anxiety (Guyer et al., 2008a).

Other disorders in which emotional faces are often assessed incorrectly are depression, schizophrenia and bipolar disorder. These disorders often emerge during adolescence. For adolescent bipolar disorder, there seems to be a problem in the collaboration between the basic network for facial recognition (including the fusiform face area) and the collaborating network for recognizing emotions (including the amygdala). So the issue is not that these teenagers 'miss' certain brain areas, or are unable to activate them. It is more likely that there is a disruption in the way these brain areas interact (Brotman et al., 2010).

Currently, researchers are trying to chart the specific sensitivities for angry and happy faces in adolescents with anxiety disorders and/or depression (Monk et al., 2006; van den Bulk et al., 2014). For this study, a computer shows faces that are angry, happy or neutral to adolescents while they are inside an MRI scanner. The participants are asked to indicate how happy or fearful it makes them to see these faces. Often, these adolescents are followed for a number of months, during which they receive therapy and participate in an fMRI-experiment multiple times (Maslowsky et al., 2010; van den Bulk et al., 2013).

The researchers are trying to answer the question whether the increased activity in the amygdala changes after the adolescents have undergone behavioural therapy. The next question is whether the therapy is effective in the long run (for example, after a few months). With this study, researchers are trying to bridge the gap between the search for the mechanisms behind these disorders, and the effects of treatment on these mechanisms. The ultimate goal is to ensure that future treatment provides the best possible fit for this group of young people.

References

Adolphs, R., Tranel, D., Damasio, H. and Damasio, A. (1994). Impaired recognition of emotion in facial expressions following bilateral damage to the human amygdala. *Nature, 372*(6507), 669–672. doi:10.1038/372669a0

Anastasi, J. S. and Rhodes, M. G. (2005). An own-age bias in face recognition for children and older adults. *Psychon Bull Rev, 12*(6), 1043–1047. Retrieved from www.ncbi.nlm.nih. gov/pubmed/16615326

Begeer, S., Banerjee, R., Rieffe, C., Terwogt, M. M., Potharst, E., Stegge, H. and Koot, H. M. (2011). The understanding and self-reported use of emotional display rules in children with autism spectrum disorders. *Cogn Emot, 25*(5), 947–956. doi:10.1080/0269 9931.2010.516924

Blote, A. W., Kint, M. J., Miers, A. C. and Westenberg, P. M. (2009). The relation between public speaking anxiety and social anxiety: a review. *J Anxiety Disord, 23*(3), 305–313. doi:10.1016/j.janxdis.2008.11.007

Bobst, C. and Lobmaier, J. S. (2014). Is preference for ovulatory female's faces associated with men's testosterone levels? *Horm Behav, 66*(3), 487–492. doi:10.1016/j.yhbeh.2014. 06.015

Brotman, M. A., Rich, B. A., Guyer, A. E., Lunsford, J. R., Horsey, S. E., Reising, M. M., Thomas, L. A., Fromm, S. J., Towbin, K., Pine, D. S. and Leibenluft, E. (2010). Amygdala activation during emotion processing of neutral faces in children with severe mood dysregulation versus ADHD or bipolar disorder. *Am J Psychiatry, 167*(1), 61–69. doi:10. 1176/appi.ajp.2009.09010043

Chapman, H. A. and Anderson, A. K. (2012). Understanding disgust. *Ann N Y Acad Sci, 1251*, 62–76. doi:10.1111/j.1749-6632.2011.06369.x

Cooper, P. A., Geldart, S. S., Mondloch, C. J. and Maurer, D. (2006). Developmental changes in perceptions of attractiveness: a role of experience? *Dev Sci, 9*(5), 530–543. doi:10.1111/ j.1467-7687.2006.00520.x

Cunningham, W. A., Van Bavel, J. J. and Johnsen, I. R. (2008). Affective flexibility: evaluative processing goals shape amygdala activity. *Psychol Sci, 19*(2), 152–160. doi:10.1111/j.1467-9280.2008.02061.x

Deeley, Q., Daly, E. M., Azuma, R., Surguladze, S., Giampietro, V., Brammer, M. J., Hallahan, B., Dunbar, R. I., Phillips, M. L. and Murphy, D. G. (2008). Changes in male brain responses to emotional faces from adolescence to middle age. *NeuroImage, 40*(1), 389–397. doi:10.1016/j.neuroimage.2007.11.023

Delgado, M. R., Jou, R. L., Ledoux, J. E. and Phelps, E. A. (2009). Avoiding negative outcomes: tracking the mechanisms of avoidance learning in humans during fear conditioning. *Front Behav Neurosci, 3*, 33. doi:10.3389/neuro.08.033.2009

Dreyfuss, M., Caudle, K., Drysdale, A. T., Johnston, N. E., Cohen, A. O., Somerville, L. H., Galván, A., Tottenham, N., Hare, T. A. and Casey, B. J. (2014). Teens impulsively react rather than retreat from threat. *Dev Neurosci, 36*(3–4), 220–227. doi:10.1159/ 000357755

Ekman, P., Campos, J., Davidson, R. J. and De Waal, F. (2003). *Emotions inside out.* New York: Annals of the New York Academy of Sciences.

Engman, J., Linnman, C., Van Dijk, K. R. and Milad, M. R. (2016). Amygdala subnuclei resting-state functional connectivity sex and estrogen differences. *Psychoneuroendocrinology, 63*, 34–42. doi:10.1016/j.psyneuen.2015.09.012

Farroni, T., Johnson, M. H., Menon, E., Zulian, L., Faraguna, D. and Csibra, G. (2005). Newborns' preference for face-relevant stimuli: effects of contrast polarity. *Proc Natl Acad Sci USA, 102*(47), 17245–17250. doi:10.1073/pnas.0502205102

Gainotti, G. and Marra, C. (2011). Differential contribution of right and left temporo-occipital and anterior temporal lesions to face recognition disorders. *Front Hum Neurosci, 5*, 55. doi:10.3389/fnhum.2011.00055

Guyer, A. E., Lau, J. Y., McClure-Tone, E. B., Parrish, J., Shiffrin, N. D., Reynolds, R. C., Chen, G., Blair, R. J., Leibenluft, E., Fox, N. A., Ernst, M., Pine, D. S. and Nelson, E. E. (2008a). Amygdala and ventrolateral prefrontal cortex function during anticipated peer evaluation in pediatric social anxiety. *Arch Gen Psychiatry, 65*(11), 1303–1312. doi:10.1001/archpsyc.65.11.1303

Guyer, A. E., Monk, C. S., McClure-Tone, E. B., Nelson, E. E., Roberson-Nay, R., Adler, A. D., Fromm, S. J., Leibenluft, E., Pine, D. S. and Ernst, M. (2008b). A developmental examination of amygdala response to facial expressions. *J Cogn Neurosci, 20*(9), 1565–1582. doi:10.1162/jocn.2008.20114

Hare, T. A., Tottenham, N., Galvan, A., Voss, H. U., Glover, G. H. and Casey, B. J. (2008). Biological substrates of emotional reactivity and regulation in adolescence during an emotional go-nogo task. *Biol Psychiatry, 63*(10), 927–934. doi:10.1016/j.biopsych.2008.03.015

Herba, C. M., Landau, S., Russell, T., Ecker, C. and Phillips, M. L. (2006). The development of emotion-processing in children: effects of age, emotion, and intensity. *J Child Psychol Psychiatry, 47*(11), 1098–1106. doi:10.1111/j.1469-7610.2006.01652.x

Killgore, W. D., Oki, M. and Yurgelun-Todd, D. A. (2001). Sex-specific developmental changes in amygdala responses to affective faces. *Neuroreport, 12*(2), 427–433. Retrieved from www.ncbi.nlm.nih.gov/pubmed/11209962

Killgore, W. D. and Yurgelun-Todd, D. A. (2001). Sex differences in amygdala activation during the perception of facial affect. *Neuroreport, 12*(11), 2543–2547. Retrieved from www.ncbi.nlm.nih.gov/pubmed/11496145

Killgore, W. D. and Yurgelun-Todd, D. A. (2007). Unconscious processing of facial affect in children and adolescents. *Soc Neurosci, 2*(1), 28–47. doi:10.1080/17470910701214186

Lawrence, K., Bernstein, D., Pearson, R., Mandy, W., Campbell, R. and Skuse, D. (2008). Changing abilities in recognition of unfamiliar face photographs through childhood and adolescence: performance on a test of non-verbal immediate memory (Warrington RMF) from 6 to 16 years. *J Neuropsychol, 2*(Pt 1), 27–45. Retrieved from www.ncbi.nlm.nih.gov/pubmed/19334303

Lewin, C. and Herlitz, A. (2002). Sex differences in face recognition—women's faces make the difference. *Brain Cogn, 50*(1), 121–128. Retrieved from www.ncbi.nlm.nih.gov/pubmed/12372357

Lieberman, M. D. and Eisenberger, N. I. (2009). Neuroscience. Pains and pleasures of social life. *Science, 323*(5916), 890–891. doi:10.1126/science.1170008

Little, A. C., DeBruine, L. M. and Jones, B. C. (2011). Exposure to visual cues of pathogen contagion changes preferences for masculinity and symmetry in opposite-sex faces. *Proc Biol Sci, 278*(1714), 2032–2039. doi:10.1098/rspb.2010.1925

Maslowsky, J., Mogg, K., Bradley, B. P., McClure-Tone, E., Ernst, M., Pine, D. S. and Monk, C. S. (2010). A preliminary investigation of neural correlates of treatment in adolescents with generalized anxiety disorder. *J Child Adolesc Psychopharmacol, 20*(2), 105–111. doi:10.1089/cap.2009.0049

McGivern, R. F., Andersen, J., Byrd, D., Mutter, K. L. and Reilly, J. (2002). Cognitive efficiency on a match to sample task decreases at the onset of puberty in children. *Brain Cogn, 50*(1), 73–89. Retrieved from www.ncbi.nlm.nih.gov/pubmed/12372353

McRae, K., Gross, J. J., Weber, J., Robertson, E. R., Sokol-Hessner, P., Ray, R. D., Gabrieli, J. D. E. and Ochsner, K. N. (2012). The development of emotion regulation: an fMRI study of cognitive reappraisal in children, adolescents and young adults. *Soc Cogn Affect Neurosci, 7*(1), 11–22. doi:10.1093/scan/nsr093

Monk, C. S., Nelson, E. E., McClure, E. B., Mogg, K., Bradley, B. P., Leibenluft, E., Blair, R. J., Chen, G., Charney, D. S., Ernst, M. and Pine, D. S. (2006). Ventrolateral prefrontal cortex activation and attentional bias in response to angry faces in adolescents with generalized anxiety disorder. *Am J Psychiatry, 163*(6), 1091–1097. doi:10.1176/ajp.2006. 163.6.1091

Niznikiewicz, M. A. (2013). The building blocks of social communication. *Adv Cogn Psychol, 9*(4), 173–183. doi:10.2478/v10053-008-0145-6

Pascalis, O., de Haan, M. and Nelson, C. A. (2002). Is face processing species-specific during the first year of life? *Science, 296*(5571), 1321–1323. doi:10.1126/science.1070223

Pfeifer, J. H., Masten, C. L., Moore, W. E., 3rd, Oswald, T. M., Mazziotta, J. C., Iacoboni, M. and Dapretto, M. (2011). Entering adolescence: resistance to peer influence, risky behavior, and neural changes in emotion reactivity. *Neuron, 69*(5), 1029–1036. doi:10. 1016/j.neuron.2011.02.019

Pruis, T. A., Neiss, M. B., Leigland, L. A. and Janowsky, J. S. (2009). Estrogen modifies arousal but not memory for emotional events in older women. *Neurobiol Aging, 30*(8), 1296–1304. doi:10.1016/j.neurobiolaging.2007.11.009

Quiroga, R. Q., Reddy, L., Kreiman, G., Koch, C. and Fried, I. (2005). Invariant visual representation by single neurons in the human brain. *Nature, 435*(7045), 1102–1107. doi:10.1038/nature03687

Rehnman, J. and Herlitz, A. (2007). Women remember more faces than men do. *Acta Psychol (Amst), 124*(3), 344–355. doi:10.1016/j.actpsy.2006.04.004

Rhodes, M. G. and Anastasi, J. S. (2012). The own-age bias in face recognition: a meta-analytic and theoretical review. *Psychol Bull, 138*(1), 146–174. doi:10.1037/a0025750

Roney, J. R. and Simmons, Z. L. (2008). Women's estradiol predicts preference for facial cues of men's testosterone. *Horm Behav, 53*(1), 14–19. doi:10.1016/j.yhbeh.2007.09.008

Rupp, H. A., James, T. W., Ketterson, E. D., Sengelaub, D. R., Janssen, E. and Heiman, J. R. (2009). Neural activation in the orbitofrontal cortex in response to male faces increases during the follicular phase. *Horm Behav, 56*(1), 66–72. doi:10.1016/j.yhbeh.2009.03.005

Scherf, K. S., Behrmann, M. and Dahl, R. E. (2012). Facing changes and changing faces in adolescence: a new model for investigating adolescent-specific interactions between pubertal, brain and behavioral development. *Dev Cogn Neurosci, 2*(2), 199–219. doi:10. 1016/j.dcn.2011.07.016

Scherf, K. S., Luna, B., Avidan, G. and Behrmann, M. (2011). 'What' precedes 'which': developmental neural tuning in face- and place-related cortex. *Cereb Cortex, 21*(9), 1963–1980. doi:10.1093/cercor/bhq269

Somerville, L. H., Hare, T. and Casey, B. J. (2011). Frontostriatal maturation predicts cognitive control failure to appetitive cues in adolescents. *J Cogn Neurosci, 23*(9), 2123–2134. doi:10.1162/jocn.2010.21572

Stephanou, K., Davey, C. G., Kerestes, R., Whittle, S., Pujol, J., Yucel, M., Fortino, A., Lopez-Sola, M. and Harrison, B. J. (2015). Brain functional correlates of emotion regulation across adolescence and young adulthood. *Hum Brain Mapp.* doi:10.1002/hbm.22905

Telzer, E. H., Flannery, J., Humphreys, K. L., Goff, B., Gabard-Durman, L., Gee, D. G. and Tottenham, N. (2015). 'The Cooties Effect': amygdala reactivity to opposite- versus same-sex faces declines from childhood to adolescence. *J Cogn Neurosci, 27*(9), 1685–1696. doi:10.1162/jocn_a_00813

Thomas, K. M., Drevets, W. C., Whalen, P. J., Eccard, C. H., Dahl, R. E., Ryan, N. D. and Casey, B. J. (2001). Amygdala response to facial expressions in children and adults. *Biol Psychiatry, 49*(4), 309–316. Retrieved from www.ncbi.nlm.nih.gov/pubmed/1123 9901

Todorov, A., Said, C. P., Engell, A. D. and Oosterhof, N. N. (2008). Understanding evaluation of faces on social dimensions. *Trends Cogn Sci*, *12*(12), 455–460. doi:10. 1016/j.tics.2008.10.001

Tottenham, N. (2015). Social scaffolding of human amygdala-mPFC circuit development. *Soc Neurosci*, *10*(5), 489–499. doi:10.1080/17470919.2015.1087424

Tottenham, N., Hare, T. A. and Casey, B. J. (2011). Behavioral assessment of emotion discrimination, emotion regulation, and cognitive control in childhood, adolescence, and adulthood. *Front Psychol*, *2*, 39. doi:10.3389/fpsyg.2011.00039

van den Bulk, B. G., Koolschijn, P. C., Meens, P. H., van Lang, N. D., van der Wee, N. J., Rombouts, S. A., Vermeiren, R. R. and Crone, E. A. (2013). How stable is activation in the amygdala and prefrontal cortex in adolescence? A study of emotional face processing across three measurements. *Dev Cogn Neurosci*, *4*, 65–76. doi:10.1016/j.dcn. 2012.09.005

van den Bulk, B. G., Meens, P. H., van Lang, N. D., de Voogd, E. L., van der Wee, N. J., Rombouts, S. A., Crone, E. A. and Vermeiren, R. R. (2014). Amygdala activation during emotional face processing in adolescents with affective disorders: the role of underlying depression and anxiety symptoms. *Front Hum Neurosci*, *8*, 393. doi:10.3389/fnhum.2014. 00393

Welling, L. L., Jones, B. C., DeBruine, L. M., Smith, F. G., Feinberg, D. R., Little, A. C. and Al-Dujaili, E. A. (2008). Men report stronger attraction to femininity in women's faces when their testosterone levels are high. *Horm Behav*, *54*(5), 703–708. doi:10.1016/ j.yhbeh.2008.07.012

Yovel, G. (2015). Neural and cognitive face-selective markers: an integrative review. *Neuropsychologia*. doi:10.1016/j.neuropsychologia.2015.09.026

Zeidan, M. A., Igoe, S. A., Linnman, C., Vitalo, A., Levine, J. B., Klibanski, A., Goldstein, J. M. and Milad, M. R. (2011). Estradiol modulates medial prefrontal cortex and amygdala activity during fear extinction in women and female rats. *Biol Psychiatry*, *70*(10), 920–927. doi:10.1016/j.biopsych.2011.05.016

5

DO I FIT IN, OR NOT?

Acceptance and rejection

We often think that we can manage on our own and are perfectly capable of looking after ourselves. But when push comes to shove, we can't do without other people. Our well-being very much depends on being accepted by others and belonging to certain groups or communities. When we are not part of a group, or think that we are part of a group but are then excluded from it, that can be a very painful experience, even when we are excluded by people we don't know.

Feeling excluded or accepted are very strong, primary emotions, which are present in people from a very young age. They may even be innate. Why is acceptance of such particular importance during adolescence? From the age of 5 until the age of around 18, children spend a lot of time with their peers. Likely, there is no other period during which children and teenagers spend so much time with people of their own age, and in which they are more focused on their peers than on, for example, their parents. The class compostition and the relationships between classmates play a crucial role during adolescence. Adolescents spend all their time in each other's company (at least in cultures where school classes are divided by age) and learn the 'social rules' of their group. They learn how groups are formed, who gets accepted and who is popular, and who is excluded. By trial and error, adolescents learn how to interact with each other.

Rejected and popular adolescents

Feeling rejected, or feeling like we don't fit in, occasionally happens to all of us, but some children are continuously rejected or bullied by their peers.

Marcel had been bullied since primary school. Outside of school, he had two friends he liked to play with: the boy next door and a cousin. But at school, everything was going wrong. Lars, the school's biggest bully, was all too happy to make fun of Marcel. It all started when he called Marcel 'smelly'. In no time, the other kids in his class had joined in. Marcel wasn't allowed to join in any of their games any more. At first, he had gone home crying and his mother had come to talk to the teacher, who subsequently discussed it in class. But this didn't help; the bullying continued. When Marcel had a new bike, his classmates said that the colour was all wrong and the brand was lame.

Not all children bullied him. Some left him alone, and very rarely a classmate even stood up for him, but he didn't have any real friends in school.

When he turned 11 years, he went to a new school, hoping he wouldn't be bullied there. The first week was promising but, soon after, things started to deteriorate. He did make a friend though, a 10-year-old boy, and he coped by spending as little time as possible on the school playground. Things finally improved when Marcel went to high school. He still wasn't very good at asserting himself in a group, but he had a few friends with whom he played computer games during breaks and his classmates at least left him alone.

In both primary schools and high schools, some children are consistently rejected by most of their peers (Peeters, Cillessen and Scholte, 2010). This rejection can manifest itself in a number of ways. Children may be completely excluded and ignored, or they may get bullied. Especially during adolescence, the impact of being bullied or excluded is huge. Children who are rejected do not want to go to school any more, feel lonely and even develop the same symptoms we see in people with depression (Rigby, 2000). In general, boys get bullied more than girls. In fact, girls often have a better quality of friendships during adolescence (Steinberg, 2008).

What determines whether someone is popular or not? Popular adolescents are often the ones who have a good grasp of social skills, but it isn't all that easy to predict who will be popular and who won't. This is because popularity can be described in several ways (Cillessen and Rose, 2005).

The first way to determine popularity is by looking at 'sociometric popularity'. This means that we determine the extent to which classmates *like* a particular person. The second way to determine popularity is based on perceived social status among peers, which depends on the group they belong to. Children and teenagers with a high sociometric popularity are usually friendly, funny and ready to help (they are generally prosocial). This opinion is usually shared by the majority of classmates. But the perceived popularity can vary strongly from person to person. One person might think that the arrogant boy has a high status, whereas the other may think the alternative girl with the dreads has a high status. In certain groups, a girl's status may increase if she has a boyfriend, while this may not be the case at all in other groups.

This is why perceived popularity very much depends on social environment. Some adolescents are very good at finding out what leads to being perceived as popular and find it easy to follow those rules. For example, when smoking leads to a high status, the girl from the popular group may be quick to join in, or the girl from the non-popular group may start smoking to fit in. This is why it is difficult for adolescents to abstain from bad habits such as smoking and drinking, because these are sometimes ways to increase their perceived status.

Popular adolescents are not just the 'nice' kids (such as adolescents who are athletic and friendly, verbally gifted, not shy but not aggressive either); there is another group of adolescents with a popular status. This group distinguishes itself by aggressive and 'tough' behaviour. These adolescents are physically strong and verbally gifted, but not particularly friendly. Often, they are cunningly aggressive (as opposed to more impulsive aggression). This division (friendly-popular and aggressive-popular) is found in both boys and girls (Puckett, Aikins and Cillessen, 2008). The latter group of aggressive-popular children often engage in bullying in order to attain or maintain a higher popularity status. This occurs at the expense of children who are the victims of bullying, who subsequently experience the psychological consequences such as loneliness and depression.

Being rejected has consequences for someone's well-being because it causes a great deal of stress. Researchers have proven this by measuring the stress hormone cortisol in adolescents who were or were not rejected in class (Peters, Riksen-Walraven, Cillessen and de Weerth, 2011). Cortisol is released in the body when a stressful situation is experienced and the body has to prepare itself for quick action (such as starting a fight or running away, the so-called fight-or-flight response). In the study, adolescents were asked to indicate whether or not they had friends and their classmates were asked to do the same. They also answered questions about who was excluded and who was being bullied. The adolescents who proved least popular had higher cortisol levels compared to those who were rejected less often. This did not apply to the adolescents who were being bullied; possibly, being completely excluded is even worse than being bullied. Considering that being part of a group is of almost vital importance for people, being completely ignored might lead to a lot more stress and eventually to feelings of depression.

The amount of stress that someone experiences depends on whether he or she has any friends. Often, children who are rejected by almost their entire class do have one or two friends in other environments (sports clubs or the neighbourhood, for example), just like Marcel from the example. The cortisol-level measurements showed that children who are rejected, but do have a few friends, recover from the stress of rejection more quickly. In the study described here, cortisol levels remained high during the research day in children who are rejected and do not have friends, but levels fell during the day in children who do have friends. This means that having friends can have a protective effect.

Exclusion results in social pain

Renowned psychologist Kipling Williams discovered that being excluded from a simple ball game has major consequences for our sense of well-being (Williams and Jarvis, 2006). Imagine someone is reading a book in a park, when suddenly a frisbee comes flying his way; two boys had accidentally thrown the frisbee in his direction. He gets up and throws the frisbee back to one of the boys with a splendid swing. The first boy then throws the frisbee to his friend, but the friend doesn't reciprocate, but instead throws the frisbee to the guy again. The guy may be surprised, but then throws the frisbee back at the boy, and they end up throwing the frisbee back and forth between the three of them for a while. However, at some point the boys go back to throwing the frisbee to one another. The guy who just joined in feels hopeful and waits for a while for the frisbee to come his way, but it doesn't.

Disappointed by being excluded, he sits back down. He doesn't know the boys and they hadn't explicitly agreed to include him in their game. And anyway, he doesn't even like playing frisbee, so it doesn't make sense that he feels so bad about being excluded from the game. But still he does.

Through this negative experience, Williams had stumbled upon an excellent way to study the psychological effects of exclusion. He designed a computer ball game for three players, in which one of the players is excluded. The effects of this computer-generated exclusion were comparable to the real-life experience of exclusion; it also led to a considerable drop in self-reported feelings of self-worth. It doesn't even matter whether we know the other players, or if the players have met before – the bad feeling is just as strong every time. Even when the participant knows he is playing with two computer-programmed 'others', and not with other people of flesh and blood, exclusion leads to a drop in the feeling of self-worth. There is a strong, primitive need to be included, even in a computer game, such as in virtual worlds like Second Life.

This way of exclusion, in which people are suddenly no longer allowed to join in, occurs frequently during adolescence. Adolescence is a time of continuously forming groups, which often change composition. Sometimes, it can be unpredictable whether a certain boy or girl will be included or not. Girl groups can sometimes be especially merciless with regard to criteria that decide whether somebody is included or not (Steinberg, 2008). The status of a girl who, earlier in a week, had been admitted to the group of girls who always hang out in the smokers' area may have been kicked out of the group the following week because she hung out with another group the day before who the girls didn't like, leading to her exclusion.

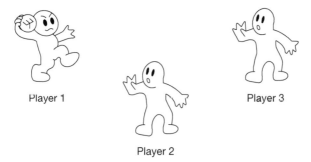

Player 1

Player 2

Player 3

FIGURE 5.1 Example of Cyberball Game

Since the composition of peer groups frequently changes, adolescents are often exposed to social acceptance and rejection. Is exclusion as painful for adolescents as it is for adults? This was studied by having adolescents and adults play the computer ball game. As it turned out, exclusion affects adolescents between the ages of 10 to 15 just as much as adults – or even more (Sebastian, Viding, Williams and Blakemore, 2010). Once more, this illustrates that the need for acceptance is developed very early on, and that adolescence might be a particularly painful period in development, as adolescents are subjected to rejection over and over again.

In order to investigate whether physical pain and social pain both stimulate the same areas of the brain, Naomi Eisenberger and colleagues had participants play the ball game while inside the MRI-scanner. First, three players played the game together and each of them was included in the game. Subsequently, the game was played once more, but now only two players were allowed to throw the ball to each other. The player in the scanner was excluded from playing. Afterwards, the participants filled in questionnaires in which they were asked to indicate their feelings of self-worth and how well they were able to cope with the situation. A comparison of brain activation showed that exclusion led to activity in both the anterior cingulate cortex and the insula, exactly those areas of the brain associated with experiencing physical pain (Eisenberger, Lieberman and Williams, 2003); for a meta-analysis, see Cacioppo *et al.*, 2013. This was clearest in participants who reported the largest drop in self-worth, which led researchers to conclude that exclusion literally causes pain (although some have argued that it is not literally the same region of the brain that responds to social pain and physical pain, but an adjacent area, see Woo *et al.*, 2014.

In adults, the ventral lateral prefrontal cortex was also activated, in addition to this pain network in the brain. Not only does the prefrontal cortex play an important role in suppressing unpleasant feelings, this brain area is also active when pain is being regulated. Activity in the prefrontal cortex was stronger for participants who indicated that they were better able to cope with rejection (Eisenberger *et al.*, 2003). Given that the prefrontal cortex develops during adolescence, adolescents might be less able than adults to engage in coping strategies.

Since this initial study many studies have used Cyberball to examine the neural correlates of social rejection. Some studies have shown that activity in the dorsal anterior cingulate cortex is dependent on personality characteristics, such as social distress and rumination (Cacioppo *et al.*, 2013). For example, the anterior cingulate cortex responds specifically strongly to social rejection in individuals who are anxiously attached (DeWall *et al.*, 2012), in indivduals with low self-esteem (Onoda *et al.*, 2010) and in individuals who had a history of child maltreatment (van Harmelen *et al.*, 2014). This is also the case for adolescents. Those adolescents who have a history of being excluded across the primary school period show more activity in the dorsal anterior cingulate cortex compared to popular adolescents when they are being excluded in the Cyberball game (Will, van Lier, Crone and Guroglu, 2015). Thus, the anterior cingulate cortex especially seems to be a strong indicator of *feelings* of social pain (Lieberman and Eisenberger, 2015).

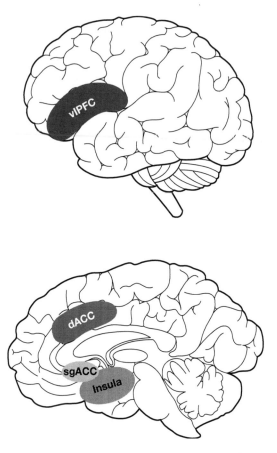

FIGURE 5.2 Brain regions from lateral and medial views. vlPFC = ventral lateral prefrontal cortex; dACC = dorsal anterior cingulate cortex; sgACC = subgenual anterior cingulate cortex

Earlier, we have seen that rejection is painful for adolescents, and that the pain network in the brain is active in adults when they are excluded. The question is now whether these pain areas work in the same way in adolescents. Results appear to confirm this. When they are excluded from the Cyberball game, the insula and dorsal anterior cingulate are just as active in children and adolescents as it is in adults (Masten *et al.*, 2009). The insula was especially active when adolescents were excluded. When the insula was more active, the drop in self-worth was also larger. In contrast, in adolescents who reported that they have many friends in daily life the insula response was less strong (Masten, Telzer, Fuligni, Lieberman and Eisenberger, 2012). Possibly, friends provide a social buffer that protect against the negative feelings of being rejected.

However, in teenagers between the ages of 9 and 13, an additional area was active that we haven't discussed before: the subgenual anterior cingulate cortex (Bolling *et al.*, 2011; Masten *et al.*, 2009; Moor *et al.*, 2012; Sebastian *et al.*, 2011). At the moment, it remains unknown whether this brain area is specifically sensitive to negative emotions. However, here too, we found that the more active the area was, the larger the drop in the feeling of self-worth was as well (Moor *et al.*, 2012). It may be due to the activity in this additional brain area that adolescents react even more emotionally to rejection than adults do.

However, adults differ from adolescents in the way they subsequently deal with the rejection or exclusion. As soon as adults hear that someone doesn't like them, they show stronger activity in the ventral lateral prefrontal cortex (Gunther Moor, van Leijenhorst, Rombouts, Crone and Van der Molen, 2010). Possibly, this helps them to deal with this unpleasant occurrence, for example by providing an explanation that is beyond their control. Or by thinking that, conversely, you don't like the other person much either, or that it's simply not possible for everyone to like you. So the prefrontal cortex helps us put our feelings into perspective and to make them less bad than they originally seemed to be. Activity in the prefrontal cortex for this type of rejection was only seen in adults and not yet in adolescents (Gunther Moor *et al.*, 2010). This means that adolescents temporarily find themselves between a rock and a hard place. They feel rejection just as strongly as adults do, but they have fewer options when it comes to dealing with it rationally.

Rejection in negiotiations

We see a different way of looking at social pain in a study which arranged for participants to negotiate. Participants were put in a situation in which money was being divided, and then asked to indicate whether they thought the proposed model of splitting the money was fair or not. While they were in the scanner, they were shown photographs of the other participants (who they had met before), together with the offer. Whenever the offer was unfair – for example when the participants making the offer wanted to keep a large share for themselves – this also led to activity in the anterior cingulate cortex and the insula (Sanfey, Rilling, Aronson, Nystrom and Cohen, 2003). This led the researchers to conclude that the offer induced disgust, seeing as the insula is also often active in cases of disgust. Another option is that the participants experienced the offer as painful.

Yet another example of ways in which social pain can be experienced is by coming off worst in a social comparison. People turn out to be very sensitive to social equality, and we quickly become jealous when we see certain victories or winnings going to a person who is better and more successful than we are. The girl who lives in a mansion, and always wins every sports competition and is very popular thanks to being extremely pretty, may not be the one we want to see winning the essay competition as well. We might prefer to see someone else win it – someone whose popularity status is not quite as high. When something is won by someone who we believe already has it all, this social comparison is accompanied by activity in the anterior cingulate cortex (Dvash, Gilam, Ben-Ze'ev, Hendler and Shamay-Tsoory, 2010). Also, we experience more activity in the anterior cingulate cortex when we make more mistakes than others when performing an assignment (Boksem, Kostermans and De Cremer, 2011). The lower our relative scores, the stronger the social pain we experience.

Inclusion is a reward

We now know that exclusion leads to social pain, a primary emotion that nearly everyone experiences at one time or another and which abounds during adolescence. But when we *do* feel included in a group, this can give us much pleasure. This, too, is the order of the day during adolescence because new friendships are always being formed and, moreover, existing friendships often become more intimate. The striatum, the area in the brain that is activated when we experience pleasure or reward, is also active when we feel socially accepted.

What does it feel like when someone you don't know likes you or treats you nicely? This question was studied by asking participants to send in a photograph of themselves, which was subsequently shown to people who didn't know the participant in the photograph (Gunther Moor *et al.*, 2010; Guyer, Choate, Pine and Nelson, 2012). These people (the rators) assessed the participant at first glance. Subsequently, the participants were placed in an MRI-scanner and shown photographs of the rators. The participants were asked to indicate whether they expected to be liked by the rators based on their photographs, after which they were shown the results. It was found that the striatum became very active when the participants thought somebody would like them, and that expectation was confirmed. So possibly, the feeling of being accepted works like a reward. This effect was strongest when people also had the expectation to be liked, indicating that it feels especially pleasurable when your expectations are confirmed.

The rewarding feeling of being accepted is just as strong in adolescents as it is in adults. In adults, too, the striatum becomes very active when someone else likes them at first glance (Gunther Moor *et al.*, 2010).

In this case, experience also matters. Those adolescents who have a better relationship with their mother (are more securely attached) show stronger reward responses when being accepted compared to adolescents who are insecurely attached (Tan *et al.*, 2014). So possibly the reward response we experience when we are being liked by others is dependent on the history of warm relationships with parents and peers.

Researchers also reported that even the prospect of interacting with someone you like can already activate the ventral striatum, but this effect was stronger in girls than in boys (Guyer *et al.*, 2012; Guyer, McClure-Tone, Shiffrin, Pine and Nelson, 2009). The two girlfriends who keep getting helpless with laughter as soon as they look at each other will experience a strong rewarding feeling as a result of the friendship they share together.

The rewarding feeling of sharing and cooperation

In another experiment, in which participants were asked to divide money, receipt of a fair offer (e.g., a fair share of 10 euros) resulted in activity in the striatum. This activity is unrelated to the size of the reward: an equal measure of activity was observed when a lower amount of money was divided fairly (e.g., when dividing 4 euros). It is the feeling of being treated fairly that causes the pleasure, more than the actual amount we stand to gain (Tabibnia, Satpute and Lieberman, 2008).

Furthermore, cooperation is rewarding. This has been studied using a game in which two participants can decide to work together, or not. Neither participant knows what choice the other will make: they make their decisions at the exact same moment and the outcome is not shown until afterwards. When they do not cooperate, that's the least profitable: they gain 3 euros each. Cooperation leads to the middle amount: 5 euros each. But now we get to the crux of this strategic game: when one person decides to cooperate, but the other does not, the one who does not cooperate gains the most money. The one who doesn't cooperate gains 9 euros; the one who does gains only 1 euro. This means it's a risk-based decision: you can make the most money by not cooperating, but when the other person makes the same decision, you both lose out. If money is rewarding, you'd expect the striatum to be most active in the situation in which you 'beat' the other person and walk away with 9 euros. On the contrary! The most striatum activity takes place when both participants are given the winnings caused by cooperation (Guroglu, Will and Crone, 2014; Rilling and Sanfey, 2011).

These findings go against all current economic theories, which assume that adults are always focused on maximizing their own personal gain. However, the results are in keeping with the way adolescents behave: they prefer being part of the group over having the nicest or most expensive scooter and being by themselves.

In this respect, the importance of social relationships is fairly complex. On the one hand, we love to obtain the highest collective gains. We find cooperation and pleasing more important than personal gain. But the striatum also becomes active the moment someone with a higher social status loses, for example, when the pretty girl who has it all doesn't win the essay competition in school. The pleasure an adolescent takes in the misfortune of someone with a higher status, the schadenfreude, is possibly connected to adolescents' (and probably adults') strong craving for fairness and equality – and their jealousy in situations when this is not the case (Braams, Peters, Peper, Guroglu and Crone, 2014).

In the cases described above, collective gains are experienced as pleasant. The rewarding feeling we experience in social contact goes even further, and can also occur when we have to sacrifice something or give something away. For example, giving money to charity also leads to a pleasant feeling and activity in the striatum (Harbaugh, Mayr and Burghart, 2007). Of course, you might wonder if we only give money to charity because it's the proper thing to do, or maybe out of guilt. Yet findings show that these are certainly not the only considerations: people actually enjoy giving money to charity, even if they suffer in their pocket.

So we can conclude that being accepted by others gives a rewarding feeling because the same areas that are activated by primary rewards are also activated by social acceptance. Also, we don't begrudge other people money or happiness; it makes us happier to share than to rake in as much as possible for ourselves. Not much is known yet about how adolescents experience these social rewards at the neural level, but these experiences may be highly important in developing long-term positive social relationships (Crone and Dahl, 2012; Guroglu, van den Bos and Crone, 2009).

Over-sensitivity to social rejection

Some adolescents are extremely sensitive to social contact. They are afraid of being rejected, don't dare go to school and worry about what other people think of them. When these feelings become so intense that they prevent adolescents from functioning normally, they might suffer from social-anxiety disorder.

Social anxiety is often coupled with multiple negative feelings, such as depression and psychosomatic complaints, and stomach aches or headaches. This disorder has a relatively high incidence during adolescence and usually develops during this period – in which friends and social networks are of particular importance. Now, how is this connected to the way the brain works, and to the changes in the brain that take place during adolescence?

This has been researched by Amanda Guyer and colleagues who had adolescents perform a chatroom task (Guyer et al., 2008). Adolescents were shown photographs of same-aged peers. For each of the photographs, they were asked to indicate whether they would want to chat with that person based on their first impression. The participants also had their photograph taken and were told that their picture would be shown to other participants in the study.

Two weeks later, the participants returned to do the chatroom task again, but this time inside the MRI-scanner. They were shown all photographs once more, but now they were asked to indicate whether they thought the person in the picture would want to chat with them or not. So now it didn't matter what their impression of the person in the picture was, but what they thought the other person would think about them (anticipation).

In adolescents with a social-anxiety disorder, the amygdala became active as soon as they saw a photograph of someone they themselves didn't want to chat with (analogous to the amygdala's activity upon seeing fearful and angry faces, and in other situations that cause an emotional reaction). This amygdala response was not found for adolescents without social-anxiety disorder. Possibly, a social-anxiety disorder is partially caused by over-sensitivity in emotional brain areas, especially when these are preparing for potentially negative interactions with same-aged peers.

References

Boksem, M. A., Kostermans, E. and De Cremer, D. (2011). Failing where others have succeeded: Medial Frontal Negativity tracks failure in a social context. *Psychophysiology*, *48*(7), 973–979. doi:10.1111/j.1469-8986.2010.01163.x

Bolling, D. Z., Pitskel, N. B., Deen, B., Crowley, M. J., Mayes, L. C. and Pelphrey, K. A. (2011). Development of neural systems for processing social exclusion from childhood to adolescence. *Dev Sci*, *14*(6), 1431–1444. doi:10.1111/j.1467-7687.2011.01087.x

Braams, B. R., Peters, S., Peper, J. S., Guroglu, B. and Crone, E. A. (2014). Gambling for self, friends, and antagonists: differential contributions of affective and social brain regions on adolescent reward processing. *NeuroImage*, *100*, 281–289. doi:10.1016/j.neuroimage.2014.06.020

Cacioppo, S., Frum, C., Asp, E., Weiss, R. M., Lewis, J. W. and Cacioppo, J. T. (2013). A quantitative meta-analysis of functional imaging studies of social rejection. *Sci Rep*, *3*, 2027. doi:10.1038/srep02027

Cillessen, A. H. and Rose, A. J. (2005). Understanding popularity in the peer system. *Current Directions in Psychological Science*, *14*, 102–105.

Crone, E. A. and Dahl, R. E. (2012). Understanding adolescence as a period of social-affective engagement and goal flexibility. *Nat Rev Neurosci*, *13*(9), 636–650. doi:10.1038/nrn3313

DeWall, C. N., Masten, C. L., Powell, C., Combs, D., Schurtz, D. R. and Eisenberger, N. I. (2012). Do neural responses to rejection depend on attachment style? An fMRI study. *Soc Cogn Affect Neurosci*, *7*(2), 184–192. doi:10.1093/scan/nsq107

Dvash, J., Gilam, G., Ben-Ze'ev, A., Hendler, T. and Shamay-Tsoory, S. G. (2010). The envious brain: the neural basis of social comparison. *Hum Brain Mapp*, *31*(11), 1741–1750. doi:10.1002/hbm.20972

Eisenberger, N. I., Lieberman, M. D. and Williams, K. D. (2003). Does rejection hurt? An fMRI study of social exclusion. *Science*, *302*(5643), 290–292. doi:10.1126/science.1089134

Gunther Moor, B., van Leijenhorst, L., Rombouts, S. A., Crone, E. A. and Van der Molen, M. W. (2010). Do you like me? Neural correlates of social evaluation and developmental trajectories. *Soc Neurosci*, *5*(5–6), 461–482. doi:10.1080/17470910903526155

Guroglu, B., van den Bos, W. and Crone, E. A. (2009). Neural correlates of social decision making and relationships: a developmental perspective. *Ann N Y Acad Sci*, *1167*, 197–206. doi:10.1111/j.1749-6632.2009.04502.x

Guroglu, B., Will, G. J. and Crone, E. A. (2014). Neural correlates of advantageous and disadvantageous inequity in sharing decisions. *PLoS One*, *9*(9), e107996. doi:10.1371/journal.pone.0107996

Guyer, A. E., Choate, V. R., Pine, D. S. and Nelson, E. E. (2012). Neural circuitry underlying affective response to peer feedback in adolescence. *Soc Cogn Affect Neurosci*, *7*(1), 81–92. doi:10.1093/scan/nsr043

Guyer, A. E., Lau, J. Y., McClure-Tone, E. B., Parrish, J., Shiffrin, N. D., Reynolds, R. C., Gabrieli, J. D. E. and Nelson, E. E. (2008). Amygdala and ventrolateral prefrontal cortex function during anticipated peer evaluation in pediatric social anxiety. *Arch Gen Psychiatry*, *65*(11), 1303–1312. doi:10.1001/archpsyc.65.11.1303

Guyer, A. E., McClure-Tone, E. B., Shiffrin, N. D., Pine, D. S. and Nelson, E. E. (2009). Probing the neural correlates of anticipated peer evaluation in adolescence. *Child Dev*, *80*(4), 1000–1015. doi:10.1111/j.1467-8624.2009.01313.x

Harbaugh, W. T., Mayr, U. and Burghart, D. R. (2007). Neural responses to taxation and voluntary giving reveal motives for charitable donations. *Science*, *316*(5831), 1622–1625. doi:10.1126/science.1140738

Lieberman, M. D. and Eisenberger, N. I. (2015). The dorsal anterior cingulate cortex is selective for pain: results from large-scale reverse inference. *Proc Natl Acad Sci USA*, *112*(49), 15250–15255. doi:10.1073/pnas.1515083112

Masten, C. L., Eisenberger, N. I., Borofsky, L. A., Pfeifer, J. H., McNealy, K., Mazziotta, J. C. and Dapretto, M. (2009). Neural correlates of social exclusion during adolescence: understanding the distress of peer rejection. *Soc Cogn Affect Neurosci*, *4*(2), 143–157. doi:10.1093/scan/nsp007

Masten, C. L., Telzer, E. H., Fuligni, A. J., Lieberman, M. D. and Eisenberger, N. I. (2012). Time spent with friends in adolescence relates to less neural sensitivity to later peer rejection. *Soc Cogn Affect Neurosci*, *7*(1), 106–114. doi:10.1093/scan/nsq098

Moor, B. G., Guroglu, B., Op de Macks, Z. A., Rombouts, S. A., Van der Molen, M. W. and Crone, E. A. (2012). Social exclusion and punishment of excluders: neural correlates and developmental trajectories. *NeuroImage*, *59*(1), 708–717. doi:10.1016/j.neuroimage.2011.07.028

Onoda, K., Okamoto, Y., Nakashima, K., Nittono, H., Yoshimura, S., Yamawaki, S., Yamaguchi, S. and Ura, M. (2010). Does low self-esteem enhance social pain? The relationship between trait self-esteem and anterior cingulate cortex activation induced by ostracism. *Soc Cogn Affect Neurosci*, *5*(4), 385–391. doi:10.1093/scan/nsq002

Peeters, M., Cillessen, A. H. and Scholte, R. H. (2010). Clueless or powerful? Identifying subtypes of bullies in adolescence. *J Youth Adolesc*, *39*(9), 1041–1052. doi:10.1007/s10964-009-9478-9

Peters, E., Riksen-Walraven, J. M., Cillessen, A. H. and de Weerth, C. (2011). Peer rejection and HPA activity in middle childhood: friendship makes a difference. *Child Dev*, *82*(6), 1906–1920. doi:10.1111/j.1467-8624.2011.01647.x

Puckett, M. B., Aikins, J. W. and Cillessen, A. H. (2008). Moderators of the association between relational aggression and perceived popularity. *Aggress Behav*, *34*(6), 563–576. doi:10.1002/ab.20280

Rigby, K. (2000). Effects of peer victimization in schools and perceived social support on adolescent well-being. *J Adolesc*, *23*(1), 57–68. doi:10.1006/jado.1999.0289

Rilling, J. K. and Sanfey, A. G. (2011). The neuroscience of social decision-making. *Annu Rev Psychol*, *62*, 23–48. doi:10.1146/annurev.psych.121208.131647

Sanfey, A. G., Rilling, J. K., Aronson, J. A., Nystrom, L. E. and Cohen, J. D. (2003). The neural basis of economic decision-making in the Ultimatum Game. *Science*, *300*(5626), 1755–1758. doi:10.1126/science.1082976

Sebastian, C., Viding, E., Williams, K. D. and Blakemore, S. J. (2010). Social brain development and the affective consequences of ostracism in adolescence. *Brain Cogn*, *72*(1), 134–145. doi:10.1016/j.bandc.2009.06.008

Sebastian, C. L., Tan, G. C., Roiser, J. P., Viding, E., Dumontheil, I. and Blakemore, S. J. (2011). Developmental influences on the neural bases of responses to social rejection: implications of social neuroscience for education. *NeuroImage*, *57*(3), 686–694. doi:10.1016/j.neuroimage.2010.09.063

Steinberg, L. (2008). A social neuroscience perspective on adolescent risk-taking. *Dev Rev*, *28*(1), 78–106. doi:10.1016/j.dr.2007.08.002

Tabibnia, G., Satpute, A. B. and Lieberman, M. D. (2008). The sunny side of fairness: preference for fairness activates reward circuitry (and disregarding unfairness activates self-control circuitry). *Psychol Sci*, *19*(4), 339–347. doi:10.1111/j.1467-9280.2008.02091.x

Tan, P. Z., Lee, K. H., Dahl, R. E., Nelson, E. E., Stroud, L. J., Siegle, G. J., Morgan, J. K. and Silk, J. S. (2014). Associations between maternal negative affect and adolescent's neural response to peer evaluation. *Dev Cogn Neurosci*, *8*, 28–39. doi:10.1016/j.dcn.2014.01.006

van Harmelen, A. L., Hauber, K., Gunther Moor, B., Spinhoven, P., Boon, A. E., Crone, E. A. and Elzinga, B. M. (2014). Childhood emotional maltreatment severity is associated with dorsal medial prefrontal cortex responsivity to social exclusion in young adults. *PLoS One*, *9*(1), e85107. doi:10.1371/journal.pone.0085107

Will, G. J., van Lier, P. A., Crone, E. A. and Guroglu, B. (2015). Chronic childhood peer rejection is associated with heightened neural responses to social exclusion during adolescence. *J Abnorm Child Psychol*. doi:10.1007/s10802-015-9983-0

Williams, K. D. and Jarvis, B. (2006). Cyberball: A program for use in research on interpersonal ostracism and acceptance. *Behav Res Methods*, *38*(1), 174–180. Retrieved from www.ncbi.nlm.nih.gov/pubmed/16817529

Woo, C. W., Koban, L., Kross, E., Lindquist, M. A., Banich, M. T., Ruzic, L., Andrews-Hanna, J. R. and Wager, T. D. (2014). Separate neural representations for physical pain and social rejection. *Nat Commun*, *5*, 5380. doi:10.1038/ncomms6380

6

IT'S ALL ABOUT ME

Self-concept

While it's perfectly normal for 3-year-olds to dance in front of a group of strangers without any embarrassment, this is not quite the case for teenagers and adults. This has all to do with the fact that our self-concept radically develops during adolescence: a relatively simple self-concept is replaced by a much more complex image which is more dependent on our environment. As a result, we become much more aware of the fact we may be 'judged' for our odd behaviour.

Self-knowledge and self-esteem

Many people are preoccupied with the fundamental question 'Who am I?' The way in which we think about ourselves is subject to change throughout our entire lives. In adolescence, this question focuses mainly on the development of our identity (Schwartz, Klimstra, Luyckx, Hale and Meeus, 2012).

The idea of being 'someone', the concept of having a 'self', develops very early on. At around the age of 12 months, children start discovering themselves in the mirror and when they are around 2 years old, children understand it's possible for them to want something that differs from what somebody else wants. But the complexity of the self-concept does not unfold until adolescence (Campbell, Assanand and Di Paula, 2003; Harter, 2012). The driving factor behind this change is an increase in the ability to take perspectives of others. Perspective taking allows adolescents to integrate perspectives of others in their perspective of self (Selman, 1980).

Boris (13 years) and Anna (6 years) are brother and sister, and despite the difference in their ages, they get along well. Boris truly is a big brother; he often babysits his sister, or they watch television together. Once, Anna had to describe herself for a school assignment. She didn't think that was very hard: 'I'm Anna, I'm 6 years old, and I'm a girl.' When she told her brother about this later on, he laughed a bit. He thought her answer was all too easy. So, Anna asked him how he would describe himself. This was his answer: 'I'm Boris, and I'm nice, because I look after my sister a lot. I'm good at swimming, but not very good at drawing.'

By the time children reach puberty, they become more and more capable of describing themselves in an abstract, complex way. Someone's self-concept is made up of several components, such as the distinction between self-knowledge and self-esteem (Harter, 2012).

The self-knowledge is made up of personality traits that you associate with your own identity: how good you think you are at something, and the way you think other people feel about you. In Anna's case, this description is still very basic; in Boris' case, this self-knowledge has become much more complex. He describes his traits, or skills, much more specifically: he is good at swimming, but not good at drawing. This means that he is capable of describing his strengths and his weaknesses. He also describes himself in a way in which he thinks other people see him, that is to say, as someone who is a nice person, because he often babysits.

Self-esteem, on the other hand, has to do with the value that you attribute to your self-knowledge, that is to say, how you think about a personality trait or skill that you have. Very low self-esteem often has a paralyzing effect because it makes you believe you are less worthy when, for example, you're not good at drawing. This wasn't much of a problem for Boris when he was in primary school; nobody in his class cared if you were good at drawing. But now that he is in year 7, the situation has changed completely. The arts teacher is one of the nicest, most popular teachers in the school, and as a result, all students wish to excel at drawing.

Boris has noticed that his classmates make fun of him because he can't even reproduce a simple figure from an example. Whenever he looks at his drawing assignments, he feels he is a hopeless failure. He believes he'll never learn and he wishes art class would just disappear. Thus, self-esteem refers to the subjective assessment of your own qualities and influences whether or not you feel that you can achieve something. Many studies have shown that low self-esteem is related to anxiety (Beck, Brown, Steer, Kuyken and Grisham, 2001; Muris, Meesters and Fijen, 2003) and depression (Mann, Hosman, Schaalma and de Vries, 2004). Low self-esteem is also sometimes related to externalizing problems, such as aggression (Donnellan, Trzesniewski, Robins, Moffitt and Caspi, 2005).

Our self-concept goes through a remarkable transition during adolescence. If you just think about how much small, subtle changes can influence the way we feel as adults (a new hairdo to show another side of yourself, a new outfit to boost your confidence for a job interview), it isn't hard to imagine how adolescents' self-concepts must be subject to huge shifts and changes, because in a very short period of time, they are going through a very large – maybe even the largest – change in the way they look. In addition, adolescents are also learning about the effects they have on others.

Mara (15 years) isn't quite sure how to behave towards boys she's trying to impress. When she goes out, she wears sexy clothes, like Beyoncé, and she also uses the same style of make-up as her idol. She is very flirtatious and dances exuberantly. But when she does, everybody gives her very weird looks and, suddenly, she no longer feels attractive – on the contrary, she feels like she's being stupid and extravagant. At that moment, she hates herself because she is extremely conscious of herself and no longer knows how to behave. Her main dilemma is that she doesn't really know who she is. She thinks she is extroverted, but when she behaves accordingly and it turns out others don't approve, all she wants to do is withdraw and be by herself.

Puberty is the first phase in which children not only feel different because of their changing appearance, but are also more able to anticipate the way they are perceived by others, and what these others will subsequently think of them (Dahl, 2004; Scherf, Behrmann and Dahl, 2012). As a result, they tend to see all sorts of situations in a more complex way. In other words, at this point, adolescents are able to think about the different ways of seeing themselves and the different identities they can adopt (Campbell *et al.*, 2003; Douvan, 1997). For example, Mara sees herself as extroverted and sexy, which impresses the boys, but at the same time, she realizes that this may make her seem outgoing and that it may come across as attention seeking.

Adolescents are also better able to think about their future selves. They consider the future consequences of their actions and their future development. They think about questions such as 'What kind of person will I be when I grow up?' and 'What am I really like?' Before children enter puberty, it is hard for them to realistically picture themselves as a different person, or as having different identities. But during adolescence, these concepts receive ample attention, as in the case of Mara, who is wondering whether she is introverted or extroverted, and who is trying to take all possible consequences of her behaviour, for herself and for her future, into account.

During the period of adolescence, questions concerning self-concept are becoming ever more important. Adolescents do not only show a tendency to think about themselves and their futures more, but they are also being forced to do so. During high school, adolescents face all sorts of choices, such as choosing their graduation subjects – a choice that will strongly affect their future career options. This choice is also strongly connected to their (lack of) dedication to their schoolwork. Questions about the future inevitably lead to questions about who you are, how you feel about yourself and how much self-confidence you have. The sum of these factors leads to the development of an identity: the feeling of who you are, where you come from and where you are going (Schwartz *et al.*, 2012). Because it would be overly simplistic to assume that a 14-year-old is capable of making 'adult' decisions about his future, it is of vital importance that teenagers should not have to make now-or-never decisions at that age. Instead, they should be able to make such choices at several different moments throughout adolescence.

Egocentricity

In order to develop a self-concept, we have to think about ourselves and who we are. This requires a certain amount of introspection and self-awareness. Whenever we engage in introspection, we think about our own thoughts and emotions; whenever we are self-aware, we think about the way other people think about us. For adolescents, introspection can sometimes cause them to become completely absorbed by their thoughts about themselves: the egocentricity of adolescence. This type of egocentricity manifests in two ways (Schwartz, Maynard and Uzelac, 2008; Steinberg, 2008).

The first way, the *imaginary audience*, is the conviction of adolescents that everybody is watching them and has an opinion about them. It is an extreme kind of self-awareness. For example, Mara can be so preoccupied with the way she looks that she thinks every single student in school will notice when her hair isn't styled perfectly. She imagines herself to be the centre of everyone's attention. Such feelings of self-awareness occur more often in girls than in boys, and are strongest around the age of 15, after which they subside – presumably because teenagers are starting to feel more confident socially around this time.

A second kind of egocentricity during adolescence is the *personal fable*. This amounts to the (unjust) conviction of adolescents that their experiences are unique. A girl who has broken up with her boyfriend will tell her mother she has no idea what it feels like to be abandoned. The mother may have some personal experience in this area, but nevertheless the girl is convinced her mother can't possibly imagine how bad she feels, and that's why she wants her mother to leave her alone. Scientists believe the personal fable may be a means of boosting adolescents' self-confidence, as it gives them the feeling they are unique (Steinberg, 2008). However, the personal fable can be deceiving when leading to the feeling of invulnerability (Greene *et al.*, 2000), for example in the case of the boy who believes he will not get into an accident and therefore rides his motorbike without wearing a helmet. Or the girl who is sure she will not get addicted, and therefore experiments freely with all kinds of drugs.

The imaginary audience and personal fable will slowly but surely be replaced by a more complex and realistic self-concept, which better fits the reality of their social environment (Harter, 2012). However, they will not completely disappear after adolescence – just think of the personal fable of many a smoking adult who believes he is not going to get lung cancer.

Development of self-concept

So, the development of the identity involves some experimenting. But how is the identity formed? Which steps have to be taken for this to happen? In order to understand this, we have to take a more detailed look at the development of the complex self-concept.

From the onset of adolescence, teenagers start evaluating themselves in more refined and more various ways. Adolescents will also describe themselves in more and more complex and abstract ways. Before the onset of adolescence, children may describe themselves more in ways such as: 'I'm nice,' whereas during adolescence, they will say something like: 'I'm nice when I'm around people I like,' or: 'My friends in my neighbourhood think I'm nice, but my classmates don't think I have anything interesting to say.' The fact that young people are able to indicate whether their personality traits depend on a certain situation or on who is describing them shows that they have started to think about who they are in a differentiated way (Harter, 2012; Pfeifer and Peake, 2012).

Adolescents are also becoming more aware of the possibility of having several conflicting personality traits. When teenagers are asked to describe these conflicting traits, 11–12-year-old adolescents will only consider one trait (e.g., 'playing outside makes me cheerful'), but they will not consider the other trait until the next day (e.g., 'I get angry when I have to do the washing up'). A 14–15-year-old could say: 'I'm a cheerful person and I'd prefer to be happy all the time, but it's hard not to get angry when my parents tell me to go and do my homework.' And finally, a 17–18-year-old will understand their conflicting emotions better and might say: 'I'm shy on a first date, but comfortable around my friends. I'm a different person in different situations, because you can't be the same all the time.' (Campbell et al., 2003; Harter, 2012).

The development of a more complex self-concept is accompanied by a slight overall decline in mood (Steinberg, 2008). When children and teenagers are asked to indicate how they feel during the day, young children more often indicate they are in a positive mood. This overall mood steadily declines during the final years of primary school until the age of about 12–14, after which the decline levels off and the mood stabilizes. However, researchers who have specifically investigated a possible connection between age and degree of self-esteem (so not overall mood) have consistently found that children between the ages of 10 and 14 more often experience swings in their self-esteem, both negatively and positively (Cote, 2009; Trzesniewski, Donnellan and Robins, 2003). So it's not necessarily that there is an increase or decrease in self-esteem in general, but the self-esteem of 10- to 14-year-olds undergoes more changes during the day compared to that of 16- to 18-year-olds. It's not only that there are more changes in how positively or negatively they think about themselves, but also in how frequently they worry about how they come across, and in how frequently they indicate a change in self-esteem during the day. A possible cause may be that puberty hormones, which fluctuate more during this period, affect their self-concept and feeling of self-esteem more strongly (Pfeifer and Peake, 2012). In order to understand these biological influences, we will now examine whether it is possible to retrace the self-concept to the brain.

Self-concept in the brain

For a long time, it was thought that it would not be possible to retrace something as complex as a self-concept to the brain, that is, to identify the neural basis of the self. While the question remains whether we will be able to find the entire self-concept in the brain, researchers have most certainly found an area in the brain that is specifically concerned with thinking about ourselves and our personality traits: the medial prefrontal cortex (Amodio and Frith, 2006; Denny, Kober, Wager and Ochsner, 2012).

The existence of a self-concept in the brain has been investigated in two ways (Pfeifer and Peake, 2012). First, by making use of autobiographical memories, that is to say, memories of specific moments in your life. These memories are both personal, because they concern a single individual's unique experiences (losing one's job, for example), and general, because they are formed over a certain period of time that is shared by others (e.g., the Olympics, the Football World Cup or the economic crisis). Autobiographical memories exist for different stages in our lives and strongly call upon the ability to picture something in our minds – such as clearing your desk on your last day at work, packing framed photographs into the box, colleagues dropping in to say goodbye and the weather that day.

When adult participants in an experiment are asked to think about their biographical memories, compared to a memory that isn't about them, two areas in the middle of the brain become active: the medial prefrontal cortex and the posterior cingulate cortex. Together, these two areas are called the cortical midline structures. The posterior cingulate cortex is thought to have a more general role in memory processes, given that the activity in this region varies depending on retrieval processes involved (Brewer, Garrison and Whitfield-Gabrieli, 2013). In that sense, the role of this brain area is more general compared to the medial prefrontal cortex, which is considered to be a 'true' self-concept area.

One way used for investigating the neural representation of self-concept is by asking participants to evaluate themselves on several different personality traits. So how is the self-concept captivated in these studies? This does not differ much from studies we discussed earlier, in which participants were asked to think about their personality traits. These brain studies also focused on the questions 'What am

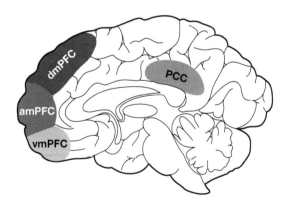

FIGURE 6.1 Brain regions from medial view. dmPFC = dorsal medial prefrontal cortex; amPFC = anterior medial prefrontal cortex; vmPFC = ventral medial prefrontal cortex; PCC = posterior cingulate cortex.

I like?' and 'What do other people think about me?' Participants were asked to indicate the extent to which several given personality traits applied to them, such as 'I am popular', 'I have many friends', 'I feel lonely in school' and 'my friends aren't popular'. These personality traits are mentioned within the context of several different domains, such as friendships ('I have many friends') or school performance ('I'm a fast reader', 'I make a lot of spelling mistakes'). Studies in adults have shown consistently that the dorsal part of the medial prefrontal cortex is active when we evaluate these traits (Flagan and Beer, 2013; Moran, Macrae, Heatherton, Wyland and Kelley, 2006). In a study that required participants to evaluate these traits for themselves or for a fictitious, but very well-known other (such as Harry Potter), it was found that the medial prefrontal cortex and the posterior cingulate cortex are more active when performing self-evaluations than when evaluating fictitious others (Pfeifer, Lieberman and Dapretto, 2007). Just like when we think of autobiographical memories, the two areas in the cortical midline we mentioned before become active when we evaluate our own personality traits.

In yet another study, participants were asked to answer these questions from their own perspective, and to answer questions about themselves from someone else's perspective. 'How good does your best friend think you are at maths?' or 'How does your mother feel about the number of friends you have?' It was found that the medial prefrontal cortex and the posterior cingulate cortex were most active in participants when they were thinking about themselves from the perspective of their best friend, mother or colleague/classmate (Pfeifer et al., 2009). Apparently, the medial prefrontal cortex and posterior cingulate cortex are more active in (most) people when they think about themselves than when they think about someone else, but even *more* active when they think about themselves from the perspective of how others feel about them.

It would be erroneous to presume that the self-concept is located in these two areas of the brain. It is unlikely that two areas of the brain would be completely responsible for the complex self-concept. Nevertheless, a more in-depth study of these brain areas may tell us something about the way in which these areas are sensitive to the evaluation of our own self-concept. The medial prefrontal cortex in particular appears to make an interesting distinction between parts of our brain that are important for a general aspect of our self-concept (the assessment whether or not something applies to someone), and parts of the brain that are important for the emotional aspect of our self-concept (such as how it feels to be popular or not). As it turns out, the general aspect involves a more dorsal (upper) area of the medial prefrontal cortex, whereas the emotional aspect involves a ventral (lower) area of the medial prefrontal cortex (Flagan and Beer, 2013; Ochsner et al., 2005).

And finally, an area of the medial prefrontal cortex that is situated more to the front of the brain (anterior) is mainly involved in thinking about ourselves in the future (Packer and Cunningham, 2009). Future research will have to prove how specific this distinction is, and whether or not it works the same for everyone – but several studies are providing more and more proof that the medial prefrontal cortex is important for several ways of thinking about our self-concept.

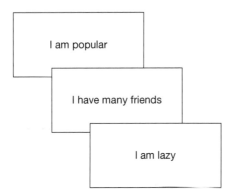

I am popular

I have many friends

I am lazy

FIGURE 6.2 Example of thinking about traits of self task

The medial prefrontal cortex is thought to be especially important for disconnecting ourselves from our environment, which allows us to think about ourselves, even though we continue to be a part of these thoughts (Frith and Frith, 2003). This is also known as metacognition, an ability that is likely unique to humans.

So indeed, there is an area in the brain – the medial prefrontal cortex – which is very important for thinking about ourselves and about how others feel about us. Subsequently, this leads to the question as to whether the medial prefrontal cortex works differently in children and adolescents than in adults.

Self-concept of adolescents in the brain

In order to better understand how the adolescent self-concept can be localized in the brain, we need to call to mind the characteristics of the adolescent period in the development of the self-concept. The first characteristic is that adolescents are often more extremely occupied with their self-concept than adults (egocentricity, imaginary audience, personal fable). A second characteristic is that adolescents' self-concept becomes more and more complex and differentiated as they grow older. So how does all of this present itself in the medial prefrontal cortex? Studies have shown a remarkably consistent pattern, even though they all used different research paradigms.

In the Harry Potter-study mentioned earlier, participants were asked to think about themselves using statements such as 'I am popular' or 'I am good at spelling'. The same questions were used when they were asked to consider whether these statements applied to a fictitious other, such as Harry Potter. It was also discussed earlier that adults show activity in the medial prefrontal cortex when they think about their own personality traits. As it turned out, this was also the case in young adolescents. However, the activity they showed in this area was much stronger (Pfeifer *et al.*, 2007). Possibly, the self-concept is much more dominant in adolescents than the image of the other, or they may have to put more effort into thinking about themselves.

In a second study, which used the same set-up, adolescents between 11 and 13 years old were asked to evaluate themselves, not just from their own perspective, but also from the perspective of their best friend, mother and classmate. We've already seen that the medial prefrontal cortex is active in adults when they think about themselves from someone else's perspective, which may indicate that the perspective of another person is important to them in forming their self-concept. This was not yet the case for the young adolescents. The 11- to 13-year-old adolescents showed a lot more activity in the medial prefrontal cortex when they were thinking about themselves from their own perspective, compared to somebody else's perspective (Pfeifer *et al.*, 2009).

This is not surprising, considering that we know that this age is characterized by a certain form of egocentricity. Apparently, the brains of 11- to 13-year-old adolescents work in such a way that the self-concept from their own perspective is the most dominant. This does not mean that the way other people think about them isn't important to them – on the contrary. But it does show that they mainly base the formation of their self-concept on who they are – that is to say, their own perspective – and not on the complexity that is necessary for the development of a multifaceted self-concept. By contrast, the self-concept in young adults is much more adjusted by the perspective of the way other people think about them.

Does that mean that it makes no difference to teenagers what their parents and friends think when it comes to their self-concept? That isn't quite true either. The medial prefrontal cortex distinguishes between the way friends think about them and the way parents think. You can imagine that parents are more important when adolescents think about themselves in relation to schoolwork, whereas friends are more important when thinking about themselves in their social environment. And this is exactly the distinction that is seen in the self-concept area of the brain. The medial prefrontal cortex is more active when adolescents think about their academic skills ('I'm good at English') from the perspective of their mother (but not when they think about *social* skills from the perspective of their mother). The exact opposite was found for friends. That is, adolescents' prefrontal cortices became more active when they were thinking about their own social skills ('I have a lot of friends') from the perspective of a friend (but not when they were thinking about *academic* skills from the perspective of a friend) (Pfeifer *et al.*, 2009). Intriguingly, adolescents also show more activity in the ventral striatum compared to adults when they think of what their friends think of them, especially in the social domain (Jankowski, Moore, Merchant, Kahn and Pfeifer, 2014). We have learned that the ventral striatum is very important for reward processing, so possibly the opinion of peers on social skills is most important for adolescents.

Apparently, the brain area that is so important for the formation of the self-concept is also sensitive to the way someone feels about you, and in which context. Mara, for example, wonders whether her friends like her when she is acting wild and extroverted, but she never really wonders what her friends will think when she hasn't done her homework, or fails her English test. However, she does worry about what her mother will think about the bad grade because she had promised her mother to work harder in school this year. This does not only apply to Mara. It is well known that teenagers worry more about what their parents will think of them where school performance is concerned ('I'm good at English'), but on the other hand, teenagers are more sensitive to their friends' opinion where social skills are concerned ('I have a lot of friends'). This distinction is also reflected in the activity in the medial prefrontal cortex. But most of all, this area is especially active when young people are thinking about themselves.

In a clever study with a relative simple set-up, Leah Somerville and colleagues examined self-conscious emotions in children, adolescents and adults (Somerville *et al.*, 2013). Participants were taking part in another study in the scanner and were asked to help with testing a camera that was installed inside the scanner. Sometimes the camera would be 'on', as indicated by a green light on the screen, and sometimes that camera would be 'off', as indicated by a red light. Participants were told that when the camera was 'on', that others in the scanner facility could see them. It turns out that having the feeling of being observed resulted in increased activity in the medial frontal cortex. But more intriguingly, this activity was stronger in adolescents than in children and adults, and correlated with self-reported embarrassment. Possibly, the medial frontal cortex reflects our self-conscious emotions, which are more dominant in adolescence.

Self-conscious social emotions

Social emotions are emotions in which the opinion of others plays a stronger role than in emotions such as disgust or anger, which can also be experienced without the judgement of others. Examples of social emotions are embarrassment, guilt or pride.

Misha (17 years) talks about Tim, her ex-boyfriend. They had been dating for 2 weeks and he had asked her to come to the pub for a drink. It was raining that evening and, unfortunately, her mascara proved to be less waterproof than advertised. When Misha came in, Tim was chatting in the corner with a few of his friends. They asked her if maybe she was a fan of Dracula, but Misha didn't understand what they were talking about. The boys were laughing at her and Tim just stood there grinning stupidly, and hardly paid her any attention. A girlfriend of Misha's who arrived a little later suggested she should go and fix her eye make-up. Misha was absolutely mortified and felt she could never show her face in that pub again. She hasn't spoken to Tim since, but she's assuming they've broken up.

Such complex emotions can be intense during adolescence, especially because their self-concept is still developing. Who we are and how we feel in uncomfortable situations is still mainly controlled by other people's reactions during adolescence. That's why it was so devastating for Misha to be laughed at in this way.

The effect of these social emotions on our self-concept has been investigated in a British study (Burnett, Bird, Moll, Frith and Blakemore, 2009). Adolescents between 11 and 18 years and adults were presented with certain scenarios and asked to imagine themselves in that situation. Some stories described situations of fear or disgust, such as 'your friend is screaming because a wasp got in your shirt' or 'your friend who's sitting next to you throws up, and the smell makes your stomach turn'. Other stories described situations in which social emotions like shame or guilt play a part, such as 'your friend tells you you've had a wet stain on your trousers all through lunch break, right on your behind' or 'you laughed when your friend told you he was feeling bad'.

When participants were reading the stories about social emotions, the medial prefrontal cortex became active when compared to the stories about basic emotions. However, here too the activity in the medial prefrontal cortex was much higher in adolescents than it was in adults (Burnett *et al.*, 2009; Goddings, Burnett Heyes, Bird, Viner and Blakemore, 2012).

The shame that Misha felt possibly had a greater influence on her self-concept than it would have had in an adult. It is possible that, in this stage of brain development, the medial prefrontal cortex plays an extra-large part in adjusting the self-concept, with a multifaceted self-concept as its objective. This will allow us to put things into perspective and come to the conclusion that it's only human if you don't always look your best.

The advantages of a more complex self-concept

So, adolescence is a necessary stage in the development of the self-concept. However, very little is known about the differences among young people when it comes to this sensitivity. Does it have any advantages to have a more complex self-concept? By now, we know that the self-concept of adolescents is not necessarily more negative than that of adults, but that it does fluctuate more during early adolescence, both in a negative and a positive sense (Cote, 2009). This can be a risk factor. Teenagers between the ages of 10 and 14 years who indicate that they experience more fluctuations in their self-concept and who worry more about how other people feel about them, more often suffer from anxiety and tensions, and will remain more sensitive to stress throughout their lives (Steinberg, 2008).

It can be confusing when adolescents discover that their self-concept is so diverse that it depends on how they are feeling ('I'm very quiet when I'm with my parents, but active and lively when I'm with my friends'), and that it can be extremely variable, depending on the day or situation ('yesterday I was very cheerful and the life of the party, but today I'm worried about my schoolwork'). But in the long run, a more differentiated self-concept seems beneficial to our well-being. While it may cause us to discover that we have weaknesses, it enables us to better deal with these weaknesses. For example, if an adult has lost his temper with someone and is sorry about it, a more differentiated self-concept will allow the adult to deal with this better. For example, you could tell yourself: 'I'm basically not a nasty person, but when people pester me, I can't stand it and I fly off the handle sometimes.' Research shows that adolescents with a more differentiated self-concept less often suffer from depression (Jordan and Cole, 1996).

Another advantage is that people with a more complex self-concept are better able to distinguish between their true self (the way you see yourself at a given moment), their ideal self (the way you would want to be) and their feared self (the way you absolutely do not want to be). When you are capable of making this distinction, you are better able to think about who you would like to become and/or avoid who you wouldn't want to become. When your self-concept is healthy, your ideal self and your feared self balance each other out. A study of underage offenders proved that these young people do have a feared self (they don't want to relapse back into their criminal ways) but they do not have a clear ideal self (something they want to aspire to) (Oyserman and Markus, 1990). This means that they lack the advantages of a more complex self-concept. One of the challenges for teenagers, therefore, is to develop a stable and complex self-concept, which will allow them to see that their behaviour depends on the situation but which also gives them the opportunity to aspire to a realistic ideal self.

The studies mentioned in this chapter convincingly show that the brain area that is very important to the self-concept in adults is especially active in adolescents when they think about themselves. Although we often think that the development of academic skills takes centre stage during adolescence, these studies consistently show that the development of a complex and diverse self-concept, predominantly formed by social interactions, is at least as big of a task for the adolescent.

References

Amodio, D. M. and Frith, C. D. (2006). Meeting of minds: the medial frontal cortex and social cognition. *Nat Rev Neurosci*, 7(4), 268–277. doi:10.1038/nrn1884

Beck, A. T., Brown, G. K., Steer, R. A., Kuyken, W. and Grisham, J. (2001). Psychometric properties of the Beck Self-Esteem Scales. *Behav Res Ther*, 39(1), 115–124. Retrieved from www.ncbi.nlm.nih.gov/pubmed/11125720

Brewer, J. A., Garrison, K. A. and Whitfield-Gabrieli, S. (2013). What about the 'Self' is processed in the Posterior Cingulate Cortex? *Front Hum Neurosci*, 7, 647. doi:10.3389/fnhum.2013.00647

Burnett, S., Bird, G., Moll, J., Frith, C. and Blakemore, S. J. (2009). Development during adolescence of the neural processing of social emotion. *J Cogn Neurosci*, 21(9), 1736–1750. doi:10.1162/jocn.2009.21121

Campbell, J. D., Assanand, S. and Di Paula, A. (2003). The structure of the self-concept and its relation to psychological adjustment. *J Pers*, 71(1), 115–140. Retrieved from www.ncbi.nlm.nih.gov/pubmed/12597239

Cote, J. E. (2009). Identity formation and self-development. In R. Lerner and L. Steinberg (eds), *Handbook of Adolescent Psychology, Vol 1.: Individual Bases of Adolescent Development* (pp. 266–304). Hoboken, NJ: Wiley.

Dahl, R. E. (2004). Adolescent brain development: a period of vulnerabilities and opportunities. Keynote address. *Ann N Y Acad Sci*, 1021, 1–22. doi:10.1196/annals.1308.001

Denny, B. T., Kober, H., Wager, T. D. and Ochsner, K. N. (2012). A meta-analysis of functional neuroimaging studies of self- and other judgments reveals a spatial gradient for mentalizing in medial prefrontal cortex. *J Cogn Neurosci*, 24(8), 1742–1752. doi:10.1162/jocn_a_00233

Donnellan, M. B., Trzesniewski, K. H., Robins, R. W., Moffitt, T. E. and Caspi, A. (2005). Low self-esteem is related to aggression, antisocial behavior and delinquency. *Psychol Sci, 16*(4), 328–335. doi:10.1111/j.0956-7976.2005.01535.x

Douvan, E. (1997). Erik Erikson: critical times, critical theory. *Child Psychiatry Hum Dev, 28*(1), 15–21. Retrieved from www.ncbi.nlm.nih.gov/pubmed/9256525

Flagan, T. and Beer, J. S. (2013). Three ways in which midline regions contribute to self-evaluation. *Front Hum Neurosci, 7*, 450. doi:10.3389/fnhum.2013.00450

Frith, U. and Frith, C. D. (2003). Development and neurophysiology of mentalizing. *Philos Trans R Soc Lond B Biol Sci, 358*(1431), 459–473. doi:10.1098/rstb.2002.1218

Goddings, A. L., Burnett Heyes, S., Bird, G., Viner, R. M. and Blakemore, S. J. (2012). The relationship between puberty and social emotion processing. *Dev Sci, 15*(6), 801–811. doi:10.1111/j.1467-7687.2012.01174.x

Greene, K., Krcmar, M., Walters, L. H., Rubin, D. L., Jerold and Hale, L. (2000). Targeting adolescent risk-taking behaviors: the contributions of egocentrism and sensation-seeking. *J Adolesc, 23*(4), 439–461. doi:10.1006/jado.2000.0330

Harter, S. (2012). *The Construction of the Self: Second Edition: Developmental and Sociocultural Foundations*. New York: The Guilford Press.

Jankowski, K. F., Moore, W. E., Merchant, J. S., Kahn, L. E. and Pfeifer, J. H. (2014). But do you think I'm cool? Developmental differences in striatal recruitment during direct and reflected social self-evaluations. *Dev Cogn Neurosci, 8*, 40–54. doi:10.1016/j.dcn.2014.01.003

Jordan, A. and Cole, D. A. (1996). Relation of depressive symptoms to the structure of self-knowledge in childhood. *J Abnorm Psychol, 105*(4), 530–540. Retrieved from www.ncbi.nlm.nih.gov/pubmed/8952186

Mann, M., Hosman, C. M., Schaalma, H. P. and de Vries, N. K. (2004). Self-esteem in a broad-spectrum approach for mental health promotion. *Health Educ Res, 19*(4), 357–372. doi:10.1093/her/cyg041

Moran, J. M., Macrae, C. N., Heatherton, T. F., Wyland, C. L. and Kelley, W. M. (2006). Neuroanatomical evidence for distinct cognitive and affective components of self. *J Cogn Neurosci, 18*(9), 1586–1594. doi:10.1162/jocn.2006.18.9.1586

Muris, M., Meesters, C. and Fijen, P. (2003). The self-perception profile for children: further evidence for its factor structure, reliability and validity. *Personality and Individual Differences, 35*, 1791–1802.

Ochsner, K. N., Beer, J. S., Robertson, E. R., Cooper, J. C., Gabrieli, J. D., Kihsltrom, J. F. and D'Esposito, M. (2005). The neural correlates of direct and reflected self-knowledge. *NeuroImage, 28*(4), 797–814. doi:10.1016/j.neuroimage.2005.06.069

Oyserman, D. and Markus, H. R. (1990). Possible selves and delinquency. *J Pers Soc Psychol, 59*(1), 112–125. Retrieved from www.ncbi.nlm.nih.gov/pubmed/2213484

Packer, D. J. and Cunningham, W. A. (2009). Neural correlates of reflection on goal states: the role of regulatory focus and temporal distance. *Soc Neurosci, 4*(5), 412–425. doi:10.1080/17470910902750186

Pfeifer, J. H., Lieberman, M. D. and Dapretto, M. (2007). 'I know you are but what am I?!': neural bases of self- and social knowledge retrieval in children and adults. *J Cogn Neurosci, 19*(8), 1323–1337. doi:10.1162/jocn.2007.19.8.1323

Pfeifer, J. H., Masten, C. L., Borofsky, L. A., Dapretto, M., Fuligni, A. J. and Lieberman, M. D. (2009). Neural correlates of direct and reflected self-appraisals in adolescents and adults: when social perspective-taking informs self-perception. *Child Dev, 80*(4), 1016–1038. doi:10.1111/j.1467-8624.2009.01314.x

Pfeifer, J. H. and Peake, S. J. (2012). Self-development: integrating cognitive, socioemotional, and neuroimaging perspectives. *Dev Cogn Neurosci, 2*(1), 55–69. doi:10.1016/j.dcn.2011.07.012

Scherf, K. S., Behrmann, M. and Dahl, R. E. (2012). Facing changes and changing faces in adolescence: a new model for investigating adolescent-specific interactions between pubertal, brain and behavioral development. *Dev Cogn Neurosci*, 2(2), 199–219. doi:10. 1016/j.dcn.2011.07.016

Schwartz, P. D., Maynard, A. M. and Uzelac, S. M. (2008). Adolescent egocentrism: a contemporary view. *Adolescence*, 43(171), 441–448. Retrieved from www.ncbi.nlm.nih. gov/pubmed/19086662

Schwartz, S. J., Klimstra, T. A., Luyckx, K., Hale, W. W., 3rd and Meeus, W. H. (2012). Characterizing the self-system over time in adolescence: internal structure and associations with internalizing symptoms. *J Youth Adolesc*, 41(9), 1208–1225. doi:10.1007/s10964-012-9751-1

Selman, R. L. (1980). *The Growth of Interpersonal Understanding*. New York: Academic Press.

Somerville, L. H., Jones, R. M., Ruberry, E. J., Dyke, J. P., Glover, G. and Casey, B. J. (2013). The medial prefrontal cortex and the emergence of self-conscious emotion in adolescence. *Psychol Sci*, 24(8), 1554–1562. doi:10.1177/0956797613475633

Steinberg, L. (2008). *Adolescence*. New York: McGraw-Hill.

Trzesniewski, K. H., Donnellan, M. B. and Robins, R. W. (2003). Stability of self-esteem across the life span. *J Pers Soc Psychol*, 84(1), 205–220. Retrieved from www.ncbi.nlm.nih. gov/pubmed/12518980

7

WHAT WILL OTHER PEOPLE THINK?

Perspective-taking

Once they've entered adolescence, teenagers get better and better at retaining information in their minds, and they are able to process increasingly large amounts of information in their minds, too. This increase in their abilities to retain, process and organize information in mind is not only important for their academic performance – these skills play a part in all kinds of social situations, too.

In order to be able to fathom other people's thoughts and intentions, it is essential that you are able to understand intentions and motives, to consider different options, and to think about the consequences of your actions for yourself and your social environment, like your circle of friends or your family. So, in addition to offering all sorts of possibilities for academic learning, the increase in cognitive abilities is also important at this stage in life for being able to take the perspective of others. We refer to these specific kinds of abilities as social-cognitive abilities.

Thinking about possibilities

American psychologist Laurence Steinberg (Steinberg, 2008) has described a number of cognitive abilities at which adolescents perform better than children. These cognitive abilities ensure that they are better equipped to learn in school and are able to enter into more complex, advanced social relationships:

1   Adolescents are more capable of thinking about future possibilities and will not be held back by the present situation. Adolescents can systematically switch between concrete (the present moment) and abstract (the future) ideas. As a result, they think more about who they are, now *and* in the future.
2   Adolescents learn to think on an abstract level. As a result, they develop an interest in politics, ideals, religion and spirituality during later adolescence. In addition, they are able to grasp abstract concepts (such as democracy or justice)

and think about the meaning of life more frequently as a result of their increased abstract thinking skills.

3   Another skill developed by adolescents is metacognition (which we mentioned before); that is, being able to evaluate one's own thoughts as part of the thought process itself. This is a very valuable skill for adolescents and has a very important social function, because it allows adolescents to think about someone else's possible thoughts.

4   Adolescents are able to consider multiple dimensions of a problem. They are able to approach questions from several different angles, and they will be able to consider different perspectives in their answers. Because adolescents no longer look at a situation from a single perspective, they will build up more diverse social relationships.

5   A final form of cognitive ability mastered by adolescents is the ability to think critically. Adolescents no longer automatically accept 'facts' as true, but think about them from different perspectives as well. Some scientists believe that this phase of extreme scepticism towards the world is necessary in order to subsequently come to a balanced attitude towards rules and agreements.

Being able to better think about possibilities and your own thoughts, as well as to take different perspectives, will lead adolescents to think in a more complex way about all kinds of social situations and other people's thoughts and intentions. We will now take a closer look at what this means in a number of social situations and how this is connected to the development of the brain.

The social brain

Neuroscientists have investigated how the brain works while you're thinking about someone else's thoughts and points of view (taking a social perspective). We have already seen that the medial prefrontal cortex becomes active when someone thinks about himself. But when you focus your thoughts on imagining yourself in someone else's situation instead, other brain areas become active – areas which are also part of our social brain. These areas are situated at crossroads of several brain regions – areas where many structures and information pathways come together. It will come as no surprise that many different brain areas are involved in imagining ourselves in someone else's thoughts, such as areas that are important for attention, memory and emotions, and these areas all have to cooperate to give rise to social behaviours, such as perspective-taking. Below, we will discuss the areas that ensure that all this information comes together: the areas at the crossroads of several regions of the brain (also referred to as association cortices).

The first area that becomes active when we empathize with other people's thoughts is an area of the temporal cortex that is situated towards the back and in a groove (sulcus). For this reason, the area is known as the posterior superior temporal sulcus (or pSTS). This area is especially important when people are thinking about the consequences of a particular action (such as following someone's eye

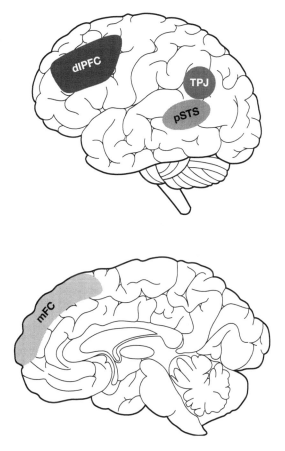

FIGURE 7.1 Brain regions from lateral and medial views. dlPFC = dorsal lateral
prefrontal cortex; TPJ = temporal parietal junction; pSTS = posterior
superior temporal sulcus; mFC = medial frontal cortex

movements to find out what they are looking at) (Mosconi, Mack, McCarthy and
Pelphrey, 2005). The second area is located where two lobes of the brain meet:
the parietal cortex and temporal cortex. Therefore, this area is called the
temporoparietal junction (or TPJ). This area is mainly active when people are asked
to think about other people's intentions (such as when you consider what someone
might be thinking when they are looking at something) (Saxe and Kanwisher, 2003).

Posterior superior temporal sulcus (pSTS): understanding movements and reasoning about intentions

When we are talking to someone, we follow their movements and predict what
they are about to do. For example, when someone reaches for the coffeepot, you

will probably deduce that they are about to pour out the coffee. When we see a movement like that, we don't think of it as a random act, but simultaneously consider its consequences. Researchers have discovered this by showing short films to participants who were lying in a scanner (Pelphrey *et al.*, 2003).

The first film only showed a stick moving in different directions, but it was difficult to predict in which direction the stick would move. The second film showed a ticking grandfather clock, its pendulum moving from side to side. In this case, the motion is meaningful and you will be able to predict the pendulum's movement – however, it's impossible to think about the clock's intentions. The third film showed an animation of a person walking. His legs were moving at the same pace as the clock's pendulum, so the movement was the same in that respect. However, this animation does allow you to think about the person's movements, for example where he came from or where he's going. The posterior superior temporal sulcus only becomes active in the case of the film that shows the moving person. Apparently, the movement has to be performed by a person for this area to become active.

Let's look at the way the posterior superior temporal sulcus develops during adolescence. Do children and teenagers get better at predicting and tracking movement as they grow older?

This has been researched in children and young adults aged between 6 and 11 years (Saxe, 2009) and adolescents between the ages of 9 and 16 years (Moriguchi, 2007). There was discernible activity in the posterior superior temporal sulcus of all of these participants, even the very youngest, while watching the movements of people. Compared to adults, this activity was the same in young children. Apparently, the brains of young children are already well-equipped for predicting intentions in movements. This is hardly surprising, because predicting other people's movements is important for (outdoor) play and other activities that we do together – things that children are good at from a very young age.

But what about more 'difficult' intentions, for example what can be read from someone's face? This has been studied using an experiment in which participants were shown photographs of faces which clearly showed a certain intention (Moor *et al.*, 2012; Overgaauw, van Duijvenvoorde, Gunther Moor and Crone, 2015). For example, the participants were shown a photograph of a woman and then asked to indicate whether the look in her eyes was surprised, happy, funny or confident. So the question was not whether participants were able to discern general emotions on a face, instead, the photographs had been selected especially to represent the intentions in the eyes. Young adolescents (10 to 12 years old), older adolescents (14 and 15 years old) and adults were all able to discern the intentions. In addition, all three age groups showed activity in the posterior superior temporal sulcus while reading the intentions.

These studies show that from very early on, we are equipped with a brain that enables us to discern the direction of other people's movements and the intentions expressed in other people's eyes – both skills that involve the posterior superior temporal sulcus.

Yet, when participants need to make decisions about intentions, this is when developmental differences start to appear. In a study where participants had to make choices that involved social scenario's (such as you are going to the movies and a tall person sits in front of you, will you change seats?) versus physical scenario's (such as a tree falls down in a forest, will it make a loud noise?), it was found that for social scenario's both the medial frontal cortex and the superior temporal sulcus were activated. However, in adolescents, activity was larger in the medial frontal cortex, whereas in adults, activity was larger in the superior temporal sulcus (Blakemore, den Ouden Choudhury and Frith, 2007). We already saw in the previous chapters that medial prefrontal cortex is often more active in adolescence. This was the first study to show that superior temporal sulcus was more active in adults, suggesting prolonged development of the social-brain network.

Temporoparietal junction (TPJ): theory of mind and perspective-taking

So, it appears that the posterior superior temporal sulcus is able early on to discern intentions in movement, but still develops when it comes to making choices about social intentions. It's a different story when we ask teenagers to look at a situation from someone else's perspective, an ability referred to as *theory of mind* or *perspective-taking*. Young people go through several stages of perspective-taking before they reach a balanced way of taking other people's perspective.

Somewhere between the ages of 3 and 5 years, children realize for the first time that other people perceive, believe or think different things from what they themselves perceive, believe or think. The first signs of a *theory of mind* are observed around this age. This form of perspective-taking is limited to the understanding that you can perceive different things from the other end of the room than you can perceive when looking into the room from the kitchen. Although this form of situational empathy will also continue to improve into adolescence, it is social perspective-taking in particular that will develop by leaps and bounds after childhood and during adolescence (Burnett, Sebastian, Cohen Kadosh and Blakemore, 2011).

Before children enter adolescence, they have trouble empathizing with other people's thoughts and feelings. But once they have entered adolescence, they learn to empathize with the feelings and thoughts of others, and even to take a third person's perspective. This means that they understand that the feelings and thoughts of Person A influence the feelings and thoughts of Person B.

Older adolescents do still improve at perspective-taking, because they are able to take a more layered form of perspective, in which they understand that a certain person's perspective is related to someone else's perspective in a complex way. This form of perspective-taking, in which you imagine yourself in the position of another person, requires strong involvement of the temporoparietal junction.

The temporoparietal junction often becomes active at the same time as the posterior superior temporal sulcus. Nevertheless, this area has a different function with regard to empathizing with others. This area is mainly activated when we think about someone else's intentions, that is, when we take someone else's perspective (Carter and Huettel, 2013; Saxe and Kanwisher, 2003). For example, when you are wondering why someone is being nasty to you when you've just helped them carry their heavy groceries, or why the popular boy in your class has asked you to work with him on an assignment, even though you're not part of the popular group at all.

The role the temporoparietal junction plays in this process has been investigated in several ways. For example, by getting participants to read stories in which the main character is making a plan, such as a story about two boys who are going treasure-hunting in the garden (you need to think about intentions and imagine yourself in their position for this). In addition, participants read a story that explained how old the boys were and where they lived (facts about people), or a story about a falling tree in a garden, which doesn't mention people (there is some action, but it doesn't involve people). The temporoparietal junction only becomes active during the story that requires you to empathize with the boys who go treasure-hunting (Saxe, Whitfield-Gabrieli, Scholz and Pelphrey, 2009). That indicates that this area is specifically sensitive to thinking about other people's intentions. Two studies used theory of mind tasks to examine activity in the social brain regions across age groups. The first study compared children (ages 8–12 years) to adults (ages 18–40) (Kobayashi, Glover and Temple, 2007), and the second study compared adolescents (ages 11–16-years) to adults (ages 24–40 years) (Sebastian *et al.*, 2012). Interestingly, both studies found activity in the classic theory of mind network (including activity in the temporal parietal junction) and this activity was similar across age groups, confirming that children are already capable of performing simple theory of mind tasks. The latter study also reported that adolescents activated the ventral medial prefrontal cortex more than adults, but only when the theory of mind tasks involved an affective component (in these cases participants had to make inferences about an emotional state of others) (Sebastian *et al.*, 2012).

Even though it is well known that basic theory of mind develops early on, an interesting set of studies by Iroise Dumontheil and colleagues showed that more advanced forms of perspective-taking continue to develop across adolescence. These studies made use of the Director Game, which is a task where someone needs to move objects on open and closed shelves from the viewpoint of themselves or from the viewpoint of a 'director', who is standing on the other side of the cabinet (and therefore has a different viewpoint on open and closed shelves). Thus, participants need to literally imagine putting themselves in the shoes of the director. It turns out that the ability to take the perspective of the director continues to increase over the course of adolescence. These findings indicate that cognitive perspective-taking develops much longer than what was previously thought (Dumontheil, Apperly and Blakemore, 2010).

In a subsequent study, the Director task was performed in the scanner. The study included adolescents (ages 11 to 16 years) and adults (ages 21 to 30 years). The findings showed that when more objects had to be moved, this resulted in stronger activity in the lateral prefrontal cortex and intraparietal cortex, and these activities were more pronounced for adults than for adolescents. This effect was expected; activity in this network probably scales with the difficulty of the task. However, when the researchers made the comparison between the director perspective (perspective-taking) and the control condition, they found a very interesting effect. When taking the perspective of the director, this resulted in stronger activity in the superior temporal sulcus and temporal parietal junction. This activity was present in adolescents independent of the number of objects that had to be moved, whereas adults activated these regions exclusively for perspective-taking that involved a larger number of objects (Dumontheil, Hillebrandt, Apperly and Blakemore, 2012). Thus, with increasing age, adults use a more specialized network for perspective-taking than adolescents.

Switching between perspectives: what's good for someone else can be disadvantageous for you

So far, we've seen that there are different stages of complexity when empathizing. Young people get progressively better at dealing with varying perspectives of different people. But what if someone else's perspective clashes with your own? What if you're willing to consider what is good for someone else, when this may be disadvantageous to you?

Many of the choices we make when we do something for someone else require that we give up something of our own. When you have to take a detour to drop someone else off at home, it will take you longer to get home yourself, which may make you late for your favourite television show. And if you give your best friend a hand with her homework during lunch break, you won't be able to go outside to talk to your boyfriend. It's a question of how much we are willing to give up and under which circumstances.

Scientists have studied this with the use of social dilemma games, where children and teenagers may share money between themselves and someone else. Let's start with one of the most basic games, the Dictator Game, which works as follows. You are given an amount, 10 euros for example, to divide between yourself and someone else. Let's say the other person is someone you've met online. You only know his/her first name and you will never meet him/her in real life. As it turns out, most people will give money to the other person, even though it's someone they do not really know. They don't give them half, but usually 2 to 3 euros and keep the rest of the money for themselves. Children aged 8–10 years already do this; they are inherently social from a young age, and they also care about what other people get (Guroglu, van den Bos and Crone, 2009).

Now, let's say the other person can divide the money and you're at the receiving end. We're going to change the game a little, so that you get to decide whether or not you accept the offer. If you do, the money will be divided between you in the way the other person suggested. However, if you don't accept the offer, both of you will get nothing. This game is referred to as the Ultimatum Game.

Would you accept an offer of 2 euros if this means the other person gets 8 euros? As it turns out, most people turn this offer down. They'd rather have nothing than get 2 euros while someone else gets 8. This just seems too unfair and leaves you feeling worse than walking off with 2 euros in your pocket. In that case, you'd prefer that neither of you gets anything at all. This, too, is seen in young children – it seems that the sense of fairness is ingrained very early on (Guroglu et al., 2009). However, the intentions of the person making the offer make a difference.

Let's make a few more changes to the game. Now, the person dividing the money is given a choice of two options: 8 euros for himself and 2 for you, or 5 for himself and 5 for you. You would think, of course, it very unfair if the person dividing the money would choose the 8–2 option. After all, he could have gone with 5–5, which would have been a much fairer way to split the money. In this case, children, adolescents and adults will reject the 8–2 offer.

But now, the person dividing the money is given the following two options: 8 for himself and 2 for you, or 8 for himself and 2 for you (that is to say: two identical options). Here, we see an important change that occurs during adolescence. Young adolescents will still refuse this offer, whereas adults will tend to accept it more often. Adults understand that the person dividing the money had no other options and could only propose an unfair division. This does not yet make a difference to young adolescents, who cannot yet take the perspective of the person dividing the money. Older adolescents are often right in the middle. They accept this offer more often than the young adolescents, but less often than adults. This means that the skill of empathizing with someone else's perspective develops during adolescence (Guroglu et al., 2009).

Researchers also had this game played inside an MRI-scanner by young adolescents, older adolescents and adults (Guroglu, van den Bos, van Dijk, Rombouts and Crone, 2011). The adults activated the lateral prefrontal cortex and the temporoparietal junction if the dividing player had no other option; however, young adolescents did not yet activate these brain areas. Adolescents are taking the other person's perspective more and more during this game, which requires you to consider what is good for you and what is good for someone else. Also, they

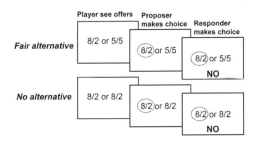

FIGURE 7.2 Example of the Ultimatum Game with alternatives.

make more and more use of the prefrontal cortex, the area of the brain that is important in directing behaviour. You could say that it is a part of proper social behaviour to empathize with someone else's perspective from time to time. Adolescents get progressively better at this as they get older.

Interestingly, when a comparison is made between receiving an unfair offer and a fair offer in a classic Ultimatum Game, young children show stronger activity in the insula and dorsal anterior cingulate cortex (Steinmann *et al.*, 2014). These regions are often associated with norm violations, suggesting that children may experience an unfair offer as more unacceptable. This is indeed also often seen in their rejection rates of unfair offers (Guroglu *et al.*, 2009). In contrast, in this same study adolescents and adults showed stronger activity in the lateral prefrontal cortex when receiving unfair offers.

Possibly, the older participants were better able to inhibit initial impulses to reject, and they may have thought more about the intentions why someone made an unfair offer (Steinmann *et al.*, 2014).

Another study examined the development of fairness behaviour from the proposer perspective. In this study, children and adolescents between ages 6 to 13 years played both the Dictator Game and the Ultimatum Game as a proposer. Given that the Ultimatum Game requires participants to think about possible rejections by the receiver (whereas this is not the case for the Dictator Game), the differences between offers in the Ultimatum Game and the Dictator Game was seen as an index of strategic behaviour. The researchers reported that when entering adolescence (between ages 6 and 13 years), participants more often made strategic choices. Moreover, an increase in strategic offers was associated with more activity in the dorsal lateral prefrontal cortex (Steinbeis, Bernhardt and Singer, 2012). The researchers interpreted this as that the dorsal lateral prefrontal cortex is important for the control of our impulse to be self-centred.

Handling trust

We frequently put our trust in others in the hope this will be reciprocated, for example when we lend someone money or when someone tells you a secret. Sometimes, the choice between honouring someone's trust (e.g., by keeping their secret) or betraying it for your own benefit (e.g., bolstering your popularity in class by passing on a secret) can be a difficult one.

Another social dilemma game was used to study the way young people handle trust and being trusted. This game is referred to as the Trust Game. Let's say, you're playing an online game again. You've been partnered, just for a single game, with someone you'll never meet in real life. You only know his first name: Danny. Danny has some money to divide between himself and you, for example he has 6 euros. But Danny is given the option to entrust you with the money. In that case, the amount in the game is tripled – now, there's 18 euros in the kitty instead of 6.

If Danny chooses to trust you, he is in fact taking a risk; after all, he could easily have pocketed the 6 euros. Instead, he decided to put his trust in you, hoping that this will leave you both better off in the end. Now, it's up to you: you get to decide how you want to divide the money. You get to choose between two scenarios: either you split the money fairly, so that you both profit. Or you take the other option and give 2 euros to Danny and keep the other 16 for yourself; a division that betrays Danny's trust, but comes off well for you.

In this game, it turns out that adults repay the trust by sharing the money fairly in about half of the cases, and in the other half they betray the trust and keep most of the money for themselves. These percentages fluctuate somewhat based on context (the situation isn't quite the same when you're not playing online, but with someone in the same room as you). However, in the case of playing online and anonymously with a stranger they've never met (and will never meet), about half of adults honour the trust placed in them. Economists would have predicted that people never repay trust, because you stand to gain nothing at all if you do. Nevertheless, people do it often, because they believe that being honest is important, and they appreciate the trust that was placed in them.

Adolescents repaid the trust a little less frequently than adults. Children may do it in about 30 per cent of cases, adolescents in 40 per cent of cases. The percentage only stabilizes at around 50 per cent during early adulthood. This means that as adolescents get older, they more often take the perspective of the person dividing the money, and they become more prosocial – that is to say, more concerned about others (van den Bos, Westenberg, Van Dijk and Crone, 2010).

Does their brain work differently for this form of perspective-taking? When individuals give trust this is associated with increased activity in the temporal parietal junction, possibly reflecting the perspective-taking required when you think of whether someone else is trustworthy. This activation, however, increases over the course of adolescence (between ages 13 years and adulthood) (Fett, Gromann, Giampietro, Shergill and Krabbendam, 2014).

The question then arises if similar perspective-taking occurs when you receive trust from someone else. This has been studied in young adolescents, older adolescents and adults while they were playing the game in an MRI-scanner as a receiver of trust (van den Bos, van Dijk, Westenberg, Rombouts and Crone, 2011). In adults, the prefrontal cortex and the temporoparietal junction became active the moment someone placed their trust in them. Apparently, being given someone's trust automatically made them take that person's perspective. Older adolescents also activated these areas, but not as strongly. In young adolescents, the prefrontal cortex and the temporoparietal junction were activated even less when someone placed their trust in them.

So, as adolescents grow older, it becomes more automatic for them to take the perspective of another person who puts his trust in them. The brain area involved in this process becomes more and more active as adolescents grow older. The moment a friend tells you a secret and asks you to keep it, older adolescents will more often take the perspective of the other person.

So why is it still so hard to stop yourself from telling a secret? Possibly you can get a higher status in your peer group when you do tell the secret. How do you balance between profit for yourself and repaying trust? To better understand this, we have to look at the brain areas that become active when you take the profit for yourself. What happens in the brain the moment you keep money for yourself? An area in the frontal cortex, the medial prefrontal cortex, becomes active then – the area that is important for your self-image. It is this area that becomes active when you think about yourself (van den Bos, van Dijk, Westenberg, Rombouts and Crone, 2009).

When making decisions about betraying or repaying trust, this area is more active in young adolescents than in older adolescents and adults (van den Bos et al., 2011). This shows that the self-area is possibly more dominant in young adolescents. This again may explain why younger adolescents are sometimes self-centred. We already recognized this when early adolescence was described as a period of temporary egocentricity. So, during adolescence, we see a gradual transition from dominance by the self-area (medial prefrontal cortex; thinking about yourself) to dominance by the other-area (the temporoparietal junction; taking the perspective of the other).

Understanding irony

Perspective-taking is also necessary for understanding humour. Much adult humour uses a kind of irony or sarcasm that children only learn to understand during adolescence. When your neighbour winks at you and says 'This really was the most interesting performance I've ever seen in my life' – his opinion on a long-winded play, made worse by actors who kept forgetting their lines – you'll immediately understand that in fact he thought it was incredibly boring and uninteresting. This kind of irony requires perspective-taking, because you have to enter into someone else's way of thinking and the context in which they made their remark.

Neuroscientists have tried to locate this kind of irony-understanding in the brain, and have studied whether this works differently in adolescents than in adults (Wang, Lee, Sigman and Dapretto, 2006). Participants were shown cartoons accompanied by a voice-over, which concluded with a remark that could be considered ironic, or not. For example, they were shown a cartoon of two young people blowing up balloons. The balloon of one of them bursts, to which the other responds by saying: 'Nice going.' Participants were asked to indicate whether they thought the speaker was being ironic or serious.

Adolescents between 9 and 14 years of age had a little more difficulty than adults at judging whether irony had been used or not. Both adults and adolescents activated areas in the temporal cortex that we know to be important to social interactions. In addition, however, adolescents also activated the medial prefrontal cortex more than adults in this study (Wang et al., 2006). This is the brain area that is important for thinking about yourself in relation to others, which becomes active when you think about your own personality traits and your own gain (Blakemore, 2008; Pfeifer and Peake, 2012). This same area, then, is also more active in adolescents when they think about irony in cartoons.

According to the researchers, adolescents were probably better than young children at empathizing with the cartoon figures, because the cartoons depicted everyday situations they experienced often or could easily imagine themselves in. But it is also possible that adults understand irony so automatically they no longer have to try especially hard to empathize with the story. Little research has been done on the understanding of humour in the brain. However, this study shows that age really does play a part in the way humour is processed.

Theoretical perspectives: the social information processing network model

How does the network important for thinking about others emerge? This has been captured elegantly in the social information processing network model (Nelson, Jarcho and Guyer, 2016). According to this model, social information processing occurs through maturation and interaction of different social 'nodes' in the brain. The detection node, which relies on the superior temporal sulcus, fusiform face area and occipital regions, is important for the early detection of social stimuli. This network develops already at the early age, which is evident from the studies showing that young children are already successful at detecting biological motion.

The second node involves subcortical regions in the brain, such as the amygdala and the ventral striatum. These regions are thought to be important for detecting emotional value or significance to social stimuli in the environment. It is thought that this social-affective node is highly sensitive during adolescence, possibly related to the release of pubertal hormones. This is also described in the Triadic Model, which assumes that both the ventral striatum and amygdala are not yet in tune with prefrontal cortex regulation during adolescence (Ernst, 2014).

Finally, the third node involves regions, which have previously been described as social brain regions, such as the medial frontal cortex and the temporal parietal junction. This network of regions is thought to have the most protracted development, and most likely underlies complex social-cognitive functions, although medial frontal cortex and temporal parietal junction probably have different roles in perspective-taking and theory of mind.

One of the challenging questions is how these regions develop in relation to the social-cultural context in which adolescents grow up. Some studies have suggested that adolescence may be a sensitive window for social experiences, which suggests that brain maturation is also dependent on the experiences that adolescents have when growing up (Blakemore and Mills, 2014).

Autonomy

We have learned that perspective-taking develops in stages during adolescence. This skill increases more and more, which is closely linked to the increasing skills for projecting situations into the future, abstract thinking, seeing different angles and putting things into perspective. In their turn, these skills are connected to the development of a number of 'social' areas in the brain.

The development of perspective-taking is incredibly important for the development of autonomy, the state of adulthood that adolescents reach over the years. Autonomy allows a person to take independent decisions and to take care of himself. Perspective-taking plays such a large role in this process, because it allows adolescents' decisions to be influenced by different people and situations. When adolescents have to choose between studying for an exam or going to their best friend's party, they are able to take two different perspectives. If they take the perspective of their parents or teacher, they will possibly understand that this is an important exam that they will not be able to retake, so the better choice at this moment is to invest time in preparing for the exam. But if they take the perspective of their best friend, they will possibly understand that they should be there for his birthday, because he will be counting on seeing his best friends at his party.

In order to make a decision, the adolescent will have to weigh the perspective of his parents or teacher and that of his best friend against each other. Towards the end of adolescence, young people become able to consider both perspectives, to weigh the pros and cons against each other, and to form a representation of the future consequences of their choices, until they eventually reach an intellectual stage that allows them to make independent choices.

The development of this type of autonomy goes hand in hand with a complicated, continuously improving cooperation between certain brain areas. The brain areas for self-focus (such as the medial prefrontal cortex) are becoming relatively less important, whereas the brain areas for other-focus (such as the lateral prefrontal cortex and the temporoparietal junction) are becoming relatively more important (Crone, 2013). Of course, young people vary greatly in how swiftly they reach this finishing point, and some will achieve a more balanced form of perspective-taking than others. But in the end, all adolescents reach a more or less advanced form of perspective-taking and autonomy.

References

Blakemore, S. J. (2008). The social brain in adolescence. *Nat Rev Neurosci, 9*(4), 267–277. doi:10.1038/nrn2353

Blakemore, S. J., den Ouden, H., Choudhury, S. and Frith, C. (2007). Adolescent development of the neural circuitry for thinking about intentions. *Soc Cogn Affect Neurosci, 2*(2), 130–139. doi:10.1093/scan/nsm009

Blakemore, S. J. and Mills, K. L. (2014). Is adolescence a sensitive period for sociocultural processing? *Annu Rev Psychol, 65*, 187–207. doi:10.1146/annurev-psych-010213-115202

Burnett, S., Sebastian, C., Cohen Kadosh, K. and Blakemore, S. J. (2011). The social brain in adolescence: evidence from functional magnetic resonance imaging and behavioural studies. *Neurosci Biobehav Rev, 35*(8), 1654–1664. doi:10.1016/j.neubiorev.2010.10.011

Carter, R. M. and Huettel, S. A. (2013). A nexus model of the temporal-parietal junction. *Trends Cogn Sci, 17*(7), 328–336. doi:10.1016/j.tics.2013.05.007

Crone, E. A. (2013). Considerations of fairness in the adolescent brain. *Child Development Perspectives*, 7(2), 97–103.

Dumontheil, I., Apperly, I. A. and Blakemore, S. J. (2010). Online usage of theory of mind continues to develop in late adolescence. *Dev Sci*, 13(2), 331–338. doi:10.1111/j.1467-7687.2009.00888.x

Dumontheil, I., Hillebrandt, H., Apperly, I. A. and Blakemore, S. J. (2012). Developmental differences in the control of action selection by social information. *J Cogn Neurosci*, 24(10), 2080–2095. doi:10.1162/jocn_a_00268

Ernst, M. (2014). The triadic model perspective for the study of adolescent motivated behavior. *Brain Cogn*, 89, 104–111. doi:10.1016/j.bandc.2014.01.006

Fett, A. K., Gromann, P. M., Giampietro, V., Shergill, S. S. and Krabbendam, L. (2014). Default distrust? An fMRI investigation of the neural development of trust and cooperation. *Soc Cogn Affect Neurosci*, 9(4), 395–402. doi:10.1093/scan/nss144

Guroglu, B., van den Bos, W. and Crone, E. A. (2009). Fairness considerations: increasing understanding of intentionality during adolescence. *J Exp Child Psychol*, 104(4), 398–409. doi:10.1016/j.jecp.2009.07.002

Guroglu, B., van den Bos, W., van Dijk, E., Rombouts, S. A. and Crone, E. A. (2011). Dissociable brain networks involved in development of fairness considerations: understanding intentionality behind unfairness. *NeuroImage*, 57(2), 634–641. doi:10.1016/j.neuroimage.2011.04.032

Kobayashi, C., Glover, G. H. and Temple, E. (2007). Children's and adults' neural bases of verbal and nonverbal 'theory of mind'. *Neuropsychologia*, 45(7), 1522–1532. doi:10.1016/j.neuropsychologia.2006.11.017

Moor, B. G., Macks, Z. A., Guroglu, B., Rombouts, S. A., Molen, M. W. and Crone, E. A. (2012). Neurodevelopmental changes of reading the mind in the eyes. *Soc Cogn Affect Neurosci*, 7(1), 44–52. doi:10.1093/scan/nsr020

Mosconi, M. W., Mack, P. B., McCarthy, G. and Pelphrey, K. A. (2005). Taking an 'intentional stance' on eye-gaze shifts: a functional neuroimaging study of social perception in children. *NeuroImage*, 27(1), 247–252. doi:10.1016/j.neuroimage.2005.03.027

Nelson, E. E., Jarcho, J. M. and Guyer, A. E. (2016). Social re-orientation and brain development: an expanded and updated review. *Dev Cogn Neurosci* 17, 118–127.

Overgaauw, S., van Duijvenvoorde, A. C., Gunther Moor, B. and Crone, E. A. (2015). A longitudinal analysis of neural regions involved in reading the mind in the eyes. *Soc Cogn Affect Neurosci*, 10(5), 619–627. doi:10.1093/scan/nsu095

Pelphrey, K. A., Mitchell, T. V., McKeown, M. J., Goldstein, J., Allison, T. and McCarthy, G. (2003). Brain activity evoked by the perception of human walking: controlling for meaningful coherent motion. *J Neurosci*, 23(17), 6819–6825. Retrieved from www.ncbi.nlm.nih.gov/pubmed/12890776

Pfeifer, J. H. and Peake, S. J. (2012). Self-development: integrating cognitive, socioemotional, and neuroimaging perspectives. *Dev Cogn Neurosci*, 2(1), 55–69. doi:10.1016/j.dcn.2011.07.012

Saxe, R. and Kanwisher, N. (2003). People thinking about thinking people. The role of the temporo-parietal junction in 'theory of mind'. *NeuroImage*, 19(4), 1835–1842. Retrieved from www.ncbi.nlm.nih.gov/pubmed/12948738

Saxe, R. R., Whitfield-Gabrieli, S., Scholz, J. and Pelphrey, K. A. (2009). Brain regions for perceiving and reasoning about other people in school-aged children. *Child Dev*, 80(4), 1197–1209. doi:10.1111/j.1467-8624.2009.01325.x

Sebastian, C. L., Fontaine, N. M., Bird, G., Blakemore, S. J., Brito, S. A., McCrory, E. J. and Viding, E. (2012). Neural processing associated with cognitive and affective theory of mind in adolescents and adults. *Soc Cogn Affect Neurosci*, 7(1), 53–63. doi:10.1093/scan/nsr023

Steinbeis, N., Bernhardt, B. C. and Singer, T. (2012). Impulse control and underlying functions of the left DLPFC mediate age-related and age-independent individual differences in strategic social behavior. *Neuron, 73*(5), 1040–1051. doi:10.1016/j.neuron.2011.12.027

Steinberg, L. (2008). *Adolescence.* New York: McGraw-Hill.

Steinmann, E., Schmalor, A., Prehn-Kristensen, A., Wolff, S., Galka, A., Mohring, J., Gerber, W-D., Petermann, F., Stephani, U. and Siniatchkin, M. (2014). Developmental changes of neuronal networks associated with strategic social decision-making. *Neuropsychologia, 56*, 37–46. doi:10.1016/j.neuropsychologia.2013.12.025

van den Bos, W., van Dijk, E., Westenberg, M., Rombouts, S. A. and Crone, E. A. (2009). What motivates repayment? Neural correlates of reciprocity in the Trust Game. *Soc Cogn Affect Neurosci, 4*(3), 294–304. doi:10.1093/scan/nsp009

van den Bos, W., van Dijk, E., Westenberg, M., Rombouts, S. A. and Crone, E. A. (2011). Changing brains, changing perspectives: the neurocognitive development of reciprocity. *Psychol Sci, 22*(1), 60–70. doi:10.1177/0956797610391102

van den Bos, W., Westenberg, M., Van Dijk, E. and Crone, E. A. (2010). Development of trust and reciprocity in adolescence. *Cognitive Development, 25*, 90–102.

Wang, A. T., Lee, S. S., Sigman, M. and Dapretto, M. (2006). Neural basis of irony comprehension in children with autism: the role of prosody and context. *Brain, 129*(Pt 4), 932–943. doi:10.1093/brain/awl032

8

WHAT SHOULD I DO WITHOUT FRIENDS?

Friendships and relationships

Susie and Nathalie are best friends and go to the same high school. Though they're not in the same class, they frequently meet during breaks at their agreed spot near the bicycle shed. They've known each other since their first year in high school and this is their final year. They know each other through and through. After school, they either go to Nathalie's or Susie's house, until it's time for dinner. In the evening, they often call or text each other. They also want to go to the same university after their exams, although they haven't yet decided where.

From childhood on, friendships with other children are an important part of the social world. Just visit a random school playground, and you'll see that children love to be together. This is true during primary school, but something happens during adolescence that changes the form of friendship. This has a lot to do with a change in the things children share with each other – a change in the level of intimacy experienced in a friendship (Bukowski, Hoza and Boivin, 1993; Bukowski and Sippola, 2005).

For example, children start spending relatively more time with their peers and less with their parents. Of course, adolescents spend the entire school day with their peers, but they also spend a lot of time together once they come home, whereas their parents may be out until dinner time, or in another room. This also applies to Nathalie and Susie, who call and text a lot also after dinner.

The transformation that friendships undergo goes hand in hand with changes brought about by pubertal hormones, as well as with the development of the brain. At the same time as puberty starts, children distance themselves somewhat from their parents and want to spend more time with their peers. The changes in brain development possibly allow young people to start looking for their own identity (Guroglu, van den Bos and Crone, 2009). They are able to consider problems in more varied ways and are better able to empathize with someone else's life. Possibly, they start creating or joining groups that match their identity and interests as a result.

The friend group

Friend groups are often made up of adolescents who have something in common, such as a shared interest or hobby. Alternatively, they can be made up of adolescents who grew up together. These friend groups are the most important context in which adolescents form social relationships (Bukowski and Adams, 2005; Bukowski et al., 1993; Guroglu et al., 2009; Newcomb, Bukowski and Pattee, 1993).

Often, the members of these friend groups share a certain attitude towards school (hard-working or not) and an appreciation of particular styles of music, clothes or sports. Young adolescents often form groups that consist of only boys or only girls, primarily because the interests of boys and girls still differ widely at this age. But approximately halfway through adolescence, around the age of 14 or 15, this changes and groups start to include both boys and girls. Some scientists believe this is a safe way of 'discovering' the opposite sex (or in some cases the same sex), in a manner that is still innocent but allows the first steps down that road to be taken (Steinberg, 2008).

Towards the end of adolescence, the groups often break up and adolescents begin doing things in pairs rather than in groups. This runs parallel to the development of romantic relationships; possibly the security of the friend group is no longer necessary.

Some friend groups are open to others, other groups tend towards being cliquish or exclusive, but the friend groups are always small enough for all members to know each other well. Not all adolescents are part of a friend group, though. About half of all adolescents are not part of a fixed group, but switch between groups instead. Boys and girls who belong to a friend group often stay part of it for a long period of time (Ennett and Bauman, 1996; Urberg, Degirmencioglu, Tolson and Halliday-Scher, 1995), which could indicate that some adolescents feel a stronger need to belong to a group than others.

How brain development relates to changing friendships

How does a changing brain lead to changing friendships? In the previous chapters, we've learned a few things about this subject. Let me summarize what we've learned so far:

1   Many things change during puberty, not just in children's bodies (raging hormones), but also in the way they look. We have seen that this is connected to the way the facial network (the fusiform face area and parts of the occipital cortex) cooperates with the emotional network in the brain (such as the amygdala) (Chapter 4).

2   In addition, pubertal hormones greatly influence the areas of the brain that are sensitive to basic emotions, such as feeling happy when your friends play a good joke on someone, or feeling sad when you are excluded from the group. The areas that steer these emotions are located deep inside the brain, and are

old from an evolutionary point of view. This means that these are basic areas, which already played a major part in human interaction very early on in evolution. The reward area (ventral striatum/nucleus accumbens) in the brain becomes especially active when teenagers are admitted into a group. This means that this area is incredibly important for the formation of friendships because it confirms the pleasant feeling of being part of a group (Chapters 3 and 5).

3   However, the most prominent changes in the brain, which make adolescent friendships so different from children's friendships, probably have to do with the development in the cortex – the outer layer of the brain, which is much younger from an evolutionary point of view. This means that these areas were formed later on during evolution. The social-cognitive brain areas especially go through some major changes (Chapters 6 and 7).

Within the cortex, the medial prefrontal cortex plays a crucial role in being able to think about our own thoughts (metacognition). So people can think ('How do I feel') about their thoughts ('about the fact that she abandoned me yesterday') in relation to what they felt before ('when I believed she was my best friend?'). It's not a surprise to learn that this area of the brain plays an important role in our self-concept. And adolescents think about themselves a lot, and are relatively more self-absorbed during early adolescence. This is accompanied by increased activity in the medial prefrontal cortex (Chapter 6).

Second, there are the social brain areas that are involved in the ability to think about someone else's intentions, and the ability to think in more abstract ways about what someone else thinks or says. Two of these brain areas, the lateral prefrontal cortex and the temporoparietal junction, become increasingly more important between early adolescence and late adolescence. As a result, the perspective of others is considered in ever more advanced ways within friendships (Chapter 7).

These changes most likely play a part in the friendship changes during adolescence, such as spending more time with peers, forming friend groups and the need to be part of a group with a particular identity. There are several studies that have looked into specifically these processes.

Social influence

As adolescents start spending more time with friends and start attaching more importance to their friends' opinions, they will automatically start to experience more social pressure from their friend group. For example, when a 16-year-old girl goes shopping for new clothes, she'll prefer her friend's advice over her mother's – or at the very least, she will closely observe her popular classmates' dress style before she goes shopping. When considering future career choices, she will not only ask her parents' advice, but that of her age peers from her friend group as well. If these opinions clash, she will weigh them against each other and try to come to an independent choice.

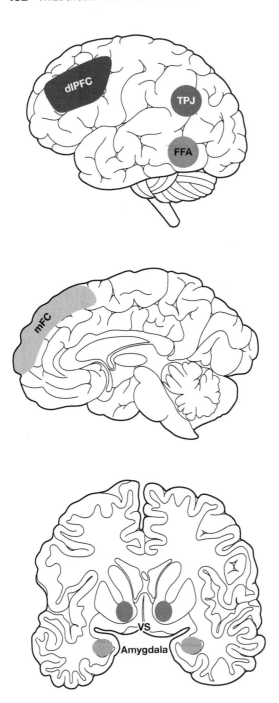

FIGURE 8.1 Brain regions from lateral and medial views. dlPFC = dorsal lateral prefrontal cortex; TPJ = temporal parietal junction; FFA = fusiform face area; mFC = medial prefrontal cortex; VS= ventral striatum

Researchers have examined which areas of the brain are particularly sensitive to social influence in adolescence. For example, what is the role of peer or parental advice when making risky choices? One study examined the role of expert advice on risky choices by showing participants what choice an expert would take. They found that adolescents were more influenced by the advice from the expert than adults, suggesting that they are more susceptible to social pressure. Interestingly, in adolescents this was associated with stronger correlation strength between the non-risky choice and activity in dorsolateral prefrontal cortex (a region of the brain important for controlling our thoughts and actions [Casey, 2015]). In contrast, adults showed, under conditions of social influence, less correlation strength between non-risky choices and activity in the ventromedial prefrontal cortex, a region often associated with reward valuation (O'Doherty, 2011). Possibly, adolescents rely more on cognitive assessment when they listen to expert advice, whereas for adults this actually leads to a change in how they value rewards (Engelmann, Moore, Monica Capra and Berns, 2012).

Social influence on risk taking was also examined in a study that hypothesized that being excluded possibly leads to more risk taking in adolescence, for example by impressing your friends and hoping to regain status. Researchers had adolescents play the Cyberball Game, which we know leads to the strong feeling of being socially excluded (Williams and Jarvis, 2006). When they subsequently played a risk-taking task, adolescents indeed showed more risk taking after social exclusion, but this was only true for adolescents who report that they were more susceptible to peer influences. These participants also showed stronger activity in the temporal parietal junction when taking risks, a region often implicated in perspective-taking (Carter and Huettel, 2013). This result possibly suggests that adolescents engaged in more perspective-taking when they want to retain their status after social exclusion (Peake, Dishion, Stormshak, Moore and Pfeifer, 2013).

These effects of social influence were not only observed in the risk-taking domain, but also when making more abstract choices, such as what is a good piece of artwork. This was examined in a study that included 16–18-year-old adolescents. It was discovered that advice of both adolescents and adults influenced the behaviour of adolescents, and this was associated with increased activation in regions that have previously been associated with social reasoning, such as the medial prefrontal cortex and temporoparietal junction (Blakemore, 2008), but also regions that are associated with self-control, such as the lateral prefrontal cortex (Steinbeis, Bernhardt and Singer, 2012). Interestingly, these effects were similar for advice from peers and adults, suggesting that there is susceptibility from multiple sources in adolescence (Welborn et al., 2016).

One study asked the question whether positive peer influence also results in different patterns of brain activity in adolescents compared to children and adults. The researchers asked participants to learn rules during which they received positive or negative social feedback from peers. All participants of all age groups showed stronger activity in the ventral striatum and ventromedial prefrontal cortex after positive feedback. These regions have previously been implicated in reward processing (Haber and Knutson, 2010). However, unique for adolescents was stronger activity in the putamen (part of the ventral striatum) and reduced activity in motor areas of the brain when receiving positive peer feedback, relative to children and adults (Jones *et al.*, 2014). Possibly, peer influence can lead to stronger approach behaviour, specifically in adolescence.

Thus, there seems to be evidence that in adolescents, social influence plays an important role in the decisions that they take. This again leads to multiple questions regarding how this influences their choices in daily life, such as in the case of participating in traffic.

Driving under the influence of friends

Psychologists Laurence Steinberg and Jason Chein used a computer game in which the participant drives a car in a simulated computer task to investigate the susceptibility to peer pressure (Gardner and Steinberg, 2005). In this computer game, participants are driving a car on a deserted road in the direction of a crossing with traffic lights. As the participants approach the crossing, the traffic light may turn yellow.

Now, the participants have to make a choice. If they accelerate, they can clear the crossing quickly and arrive at their destination faster. The faster they arrive at their destination, the more points they earn. However, it is possible for the traffic light to turn red and for a car to come from the left or right. In that case, they risk a crash in which they wreck their car and lose points. This means that every time they approach the crossing, they have to make a choice: drive on quickly and risk a crash, or stop and lose time.

Adolescents and adults playing this game take approximately equal amounts of risk. But the researchers then refined the study. You see, the participants had been playing by themselves for part of the time, but for another part, they had been playing with their friends who were in the same room with them. The friends were allowed to give advice and cheer them on. Both adolescents and adults took more risks with their friends in the room. However, the adolescents were influenced more strongly than the adults, taking risks more frequently when their friends were in the room (Gardner and Steinberg, 2005). The study also investigated whether the outcome could be recognized in the brain, by having the participants play the game inside an MRI-scanner (Chein, Albert, O'Brien, Uckert and Steinberg, 2011). Although they couldn't see their friends, they were able to use the intercom to communicate with them. Did the effect of the friend group show up in the brain? Many studies have shown that when people take risks and subsequently win money, the striatum area in the brain becomes active – the deeper pleasure area of the brain, which is especially active during adolescence. This is connected to the onset of puberty, when hormones such as testosterone start to have a large influence on the striatum (Braams, van Duijvenvoorde, Peper and Crone, 2015; Op de Macks *et al.*, 2011). Because a lot of points can be won by taking risks, it was expected that the striatum would also become active as soon as the participants started taking risks.

And this is exactly what the study found: the reward centre in the brain becomes active when the participant takes a large risk in this game. But here comes the most striking finding: this activity was much larger in adolescents when their age peers were present. The presence of age peers possibly has a rewarding effect on adolescents, much more so than on adults. This may potentially explain why adolescents also take more risks when their friends are present. They may no longer recognize the danger as a result of experiencing the pleasurable or exciting feeling of having their friends with them (Chein *et al.*, 2011; Smith, Steinberg, Strang and Chein, 2015).

The presence of age peers affected the brains of adults differently in still another way. In contrast to adolescents, adults showed more activity in the prefrontal cortex when they take risks with peers present. This activity was situated in the ventral lateral prefrontal cortex, an area of the brain we use for suppressing behaviour (Chein *et al.*, 2011). This area is also active when, for example, we want to suppress an unpleasant thought or when we want to stop ourselves from performing certain actions (Casey, 2015). It is interesting to see that adults activate this particular area while they are taking risks in the presence of their friends. Possibly, they are more actively trying to suppress their friends' influence and ignore their encouragement. Or they may want to suppress their actions first, so that they can better consider whether or not they should take a risk.

It had been previously found that in adolescents, the reward centre in the brain is more active when risks are involved, whereas in adults, the prefrontal cortex is more active, especially in the case of considered choices. This has been described in detail in the dual-processing model of adolescent brain development (Shulman *et al.*, 2016). This has given rise to the idea that there is a temporary imbalance in the cooperation between these areas. However, this does not only have to lead to negative consequences. This is possibly a *necessary* imbalance; it may be beneficial to adolescents to be temporarily more focused on actively going out and discovering things without being held back by risks (Peper and Dahl, 2013; Peper, Koolschijn and Crone, 2013). Moreover, it has been suggested that some risk taking is necessary for social development, such as when seeking out and valuing new relationships (Telzer, 2016).

The traffic risk study was the first to prove that this imbalance also occurs in the presence of age peers. It is known that in the United States, where driving is allowed from the age of 16, teenagers are most frequently involved in accidents when they are in a car with their friends (Williams, 2003). Possibly, this is connected to the stronger activity in adolescents' striatum when their friends are present, causing them to take more risks.

The empathic brain

Let's go back to the question how adolescents develop the capacity to form close social bonds. Why do friendships become more intimate when we get older? Jean Decety and colleagues examined the question how empathic responses to emotional states of others changes during adolescence. One study included participants between ages 7 years and 40 years who observed short movies of people in pain. In some of these movies, the pain was accidental, and in other movies the pain was intentionally inflicted on the person in the movie. The results of the study showed that with increasing age, participants showed stronger activity in dorsolateral prefrontal cortex and ventromedial prefrontal cortex when observing the intentionally inflicted pain movies, suggesting that over the course of adolescence and into adulthood, participants may provide more effort into analysing the intentions behind the pain inflicted (Decety and Michalska, 2010). Similar results were found in a subsequent study that used similar types of stimuli and that included participants between 4 and 37 years of age. Again, with increasing age there was more activity in ventromedial prefrontal cortex, and this was associated with increased functional connectivity between the ventromedial prefrontal cortex and the amygdala (Decety, Michalska and Kinzler, 2012). Possibly, these connections allowed participants to regulate and evaluate emotions and intentions behind the harm better when they got older.

The studies described above showed pictures or movies to the participants, which quite explicitly focused on pain, and that did not show a lot of social context. Therefore, the researchers performed another study in which they found the following. When the images that are presented are *social* scenarios of harm rather than only pain stimuli, it was found that regions within the social brain network become active, especially for stimuli that represent a moral violation (such as people fighting). It was found that activity in the temporoparietal junction increased with age (ages 13 to 53 years) when participants had to judge moral severity (Harenski, Harenski, Shane and Kiehl, 2012). Thus, possibly this indicated that perspective-taking is an important developing skill to evaluate moral violations.

We also know that not all adolescents are the same and some may respond with more empathy towards harm inflicted on people than others. This question was addressed in a study that included only adolescents between ages 12 and 19 years. It was found that moral violations were associated with increased activity in the posterior superior temporal sulcus, a region we previously learned was also related to understanding social emotions (Blakemore, 2008). Interestingly, the extent of activity depended on the level of empathy people reported in daily life (Overgaauw, Guroglu, Rieffe and Crone, 2014). Thus, there are indications that the brain regions that are important for understanding moral violations are changing during adolescence and that there are important individual differences as well. In the next sections we'll look into how the social brain regions are involved when interacting with friends.

Brain regions responding to friends

Are there areas of the brain that are specifically sensitive to being with one's friends? In a study of young adult members of an orchestra, the participants were asked who in the orchestra was their best friend (Guroglu *et al.*, 2008). They were also asked to indicate any people they particularly disliked, but there were very few cases of people disliking others in this particular student orchestra. As a result, the researchers could only distinguish between friends within the orchestra, and people the participants had a neutral opinion of.

The participants were then placed in a scanner and shown photographs of their friends. They were asked to indicate whether or not they would like to approach the person in the picture. When the participants saw their friends, all kinds of areas in the social neural network became active (such as areas in the medial prefrontal cortex, posterior cingulate cortex and temporal cortex). This activity was much stronger when they saw their friends than when they saw people they had a neutral opinion of. Presumably, the photograph of their friend reminded participants of the things they had in common, their own self-image within the friendship, the memories they shared, how the friend felt about having their picture shown here, etcetera.

Researchers thought this might be caused by the fact that participants simply preferred looking at their friends. In order to investigate this, they also showed participants photographs of film stars they liked, did not like and felt neutral about. The favourite film stars also caused some activity in the social brain, but not nearly as much as the photographs of the friends. One brain area was particularly active when participants were looking at their friends. This was a brain area in the ventral medial prefrontal cortex, which is also frequently activated when you empathize with someone (Decety and Meyer, 2008). This means that there is something special about seeing our friends.

Several studies have shown that feelings or friends align more with our own feelings compared to feelings of strangers. For example, one study had participants experience and observe social exclusion using a version of Cyberball (Williams and Jarvis, 2006). It turned out that observing a friend being excluded from the Cyberball game was associated with activity in the same brain areas as when we are being excluded ourselves (such as the insula and the anterior cingulate cortex). In contrast, observing the exclusion of a stranger was associated with increased activity in several regions in the social brain network (such as the dorsal medial prefrontal cortex, precuneus and temporal regions) (Meyer et al., 2013). Moreover, the same brain regions that respond to observed social exclusion of friends (anterior cingulate, insula) are also more active during vicarious embarrassment of a friend's failure (Muller-Pinzler, Rademacher, Paulus and Krach, 2015). Thus, there is probably a shared affective state associated with feelings of exclusion or failure between friends (Guroglu et al., 2008).

There is also evidence that sharing feelings with friends or winning money for friends is associated with a strong rewarding feeling. For example, adults show stronger activity in the ventral striatum when they win money for their friend compared to when they win money for a stranger (Braams et al., 2014; Fareri, Niznikiewicz, Lee and Delgado, 2012). Interestingly, this effect is stronger after having read a story where sharing feelings are primed. In fact, after reading such a story there is actually no difference anymore between winning for your friend and winning for yourself, it feels the same (Varnum, Shi, Chen, Qiu and Han, 2014). There is also more activity in the ventral striatum when we see emotional pictures simultaneously with a friend relative to alone (Wagner *et al.*, 2015), and reading warm, friendly messages from a friend (social warmth) even results in similar brain activity as holding a warm pack (physical warmth) (Inagaki and Eisenberger, 2013). Finally, this same region of the brain is also more active when we are attending to pictures of our loved ones (Langeslag, van der Veen and Roder, 2014).

Researchers were then interested in testing the question whether this rewarding friend response is also present in adolescence. Interestingly, the reward response related to winning money for a friend was the same across the whole age range of 8–25 years. Thus, apparently, we feel connected to friends already from an early age on. However, those adolescents who reported a higher friendship quality also showed larger activity in the ventral striatum when winning money for their friend, a finding that was especially true for girls (Braams *et al.*, 2014).

The relationships adolescents have with their friends also affect how they process rewards for themselves. For example, a longitudinal study that followed forty-six adolescents across 2 years showed that peer conflict and low peer report was associated with more risk taking and stronger activity in the ventral striatum when receiving rewards for oneself. In contrast, high peer support buffered this effect (Telzer, Fuligni, Lieberman, Miernicki and Galvan, 2015). Interestingly, not only friends but also family members have an influence on experiencing rewards. For example, adolescents who report strong family obligations show reduced ventral striatum activity when receiving monetary rewards in a balloon analogue risk-taking task, whereas they show stronger activity in the dorsolateral prefrontal cortex when they inhibit actions (Telzer, Fuligni, Lieberman and Galvan, 2013a). In addition, in an elegant within-person design study it was found that in the same adolescents, less reward activity during risk-taking was observed when they heard through the intercom that their mother was watching them compared to when they were playing alone (Telzer, Ichien and Qu, 2015).

It seems like the activity in the ventral striatum is a good indicator of the subjective reward value we attach to winning money for ourselves and for friends or others.

Distinguishing between friends

A study done on U.S. summer camp participants has shown that there are differences in the way in which adolescents experience friendships (Sharp, Burton and Ha, 2011). Two groups were formed in this study based on how they were rated by others. The adolescents in the first group were accepted by almost everyone and had a lot of friends; the adolescents in the second group often displayed hyperactive and aggressive behaviour, and as a result they were less liked and had fewer friends.

The participants were asked to indicate whom they liked and whom they didn't like, and subsequently they played a Trust Game in the scanner. They played this game with a person they liked, a person they didn't like and someone they didn't know. The participants indicated that they wanted to entrust the people they didn't like with less money, and the people they did like with more money. The unknown person was somewhere in between.

During the game, both the well-liked, nice adolescents and the unfriendly, aggressive adolescents activated several areas of the social neural network, such as the insula and the anterior cingulate cortex, when playing the Trust Game. However, the popular adolescents made a stronger distinction between participants they knew (and that they liked or disliked) and participants they didn't know. The aggressive, less popular adolescents did not make this distinction. Apparently, not everybody experiences friendship in the same way. Just as we saw in the social rejection and exclusion study in which having friends attenuated the brain response, this study also shows that having friends affects the way the brain works. Young people who have many friends are probably better able to distinguish between age peers that they like and those they don't like, possibly because they are more experienced at it.

Prosocial development

One of the most important predictors for high quality friendships is prosocial behaviour. Prosocial behaviour is described as voluntary behaviour to benefit others, and has a major role in strengthening social ties between individuals, which is crucial for the formation and continuation of friendships. Given that adolescence is the period in life when individuals develop more intimate friendships, important changes in prosocial development is expected as well. This stands in sharp contrast with the traditional views in which adolescents are often renowned for being rebellious and risk taking. Yet, even though these numbers indeed rise in adolescence, not all adolescents develop problems like delinquency or substance abuse (Willoughby, Good, Adachi, Hamza and Tavernier, 2014). In fact, most adolescents develop into socially responsible and caring adults with mature personal and social goals. Important questions therefore concern: how and when do adolescents learn to care for others, how do they develop in prosocial individuals, and given that adolescence is a period of increased sensitivity to social influence, are there ways to foster positive social development? (Telzer, 2016).

Researchers have examined these questions using a variety of tasks to measure prosocial development. For example, some studies that have made use of social dilemma paradigms (where individuals can divide goods between self and others). In some cases the donations were costly, and individuals had to give up something to give to the other, and in other cases the donations were non-costly. The results show that, in general, adolescents become more sharing when they get older (Meuwese, Crone, de Rooij and Guroglu, 2015). There were some interesting differences between boys and girls in this study, showing that with increasing age girls developed a preference for equity (an equal division where neither self nor the other person benefits), whereas boys developed a preference for the optimal outcomes, where they would give more to self if this was not harming the other, but also gave more to the other if this was not harming themselves. However, a subsequent study examined these patterns in social interactions with friends, disliked others and unknown others (based on sociometric assessments). This study showed that the developmental progression towards becoming more prosocial with age was especially true for friends, but not for disliked others (where prosocial behaviour actually decreased with age). Possibly, this indicates that adolescents become especially more prosocial towards their ingroup (Guroglu, van den Bos and Crone, 2014).

Finally, a study that used another type of division game, referred to as the Public Goods Game, found that adolescents were highly sensitive to peer opinions when making decisions about distribution to goods. That is to say, when peers showed stronger approval for prosocial behaviour (illustrated with thumbs up), adolescents increased their prosocial choices. However when peers showed stronger approval for anti-social behaviour (illustrated with thumbs down for prosocial behaviour), this decreased prosocial choices (Van Hoorn, Van Dijk, Meuwese, Rieffe and Crone, 2016).

Taken together, even though there is a general tendency to become more prosocial with age, it is not yet well understood how this is dependent on the interaction partner and the influence of the environment. Possibly, we can learn more about this by understanding the brain regions that become active when we are being prosocial. Which regions in the brain support prosocial development?

It has been found in several studies that the reward centre of the brain, the ventral striatum, becomes active not only when we win money for ourselves, but also when we provide financial support to charity (Harbaugh, Mayr and Burghart, 2007; Moll *et al.*, 2006) or when we share with others (Guroglu, Will and Crone, 2014). This has been interpreted as a warm glow effect, suggesting that it feels good to be prosocial. But this does not yet tell us who is more likely to be prosocial in daily life. Two studies addressed this question in the following ways.

In the first study, researchers examined this question by showing adult participants' pictures of positive (happy), negative (anxiety) and neutral events, and related this to how often participants reported daily helping over a period of 2 weeks. It turned out that one area in the brain, the septal area, was positively associated with viewing emotional pictures (independent of whether these were positive and negative). Thus, possibly this stronger affective state also leads people to show more daily life helping (Morelli, Rameson and Lieberman, 2014). Another study examined the neural responses to observing someone being excluded from a Cyberball game and emails that participants wrote afterwards to victims of the exclusion. Participants showed activity in the dorsal medial frontal cortex and insula when they observed exclusion, but those participants who showed stronger medial frontal activity also wrote more prosocial emails (helping and comforting the victim of exclusion). This again was also related to how empathic participants were in daily life (Masten, Morelli and Eisenberger, 2011).

A similar approach was used by Eva Telzer and colleagues, who examined the relations between neural responses to rewards and prosocial behaviour in adolescents. In her studies, adolescents played a donating game in which they could earn money for themselves or donate money to their family. Interestingly, participants who had stronger family obligation preferences and who derived greater fulfilment from helping their family, showed increased reward-system activation when donating (Telzer, Masten, Berkman, Lieberman and Fuligni, 2010). They also showed increased activation in lateral prefrontal cortex and the temporal parietal junction when contributing to their family (Telzer, Masten, Berkman, Lieberman and Fuligni, 2011). The ventral striatum was also more strongly connected to the dorsolateral prefrontal cortex when making costly family donations in participants with stronger family obligation preferences. Possibly, the reward responses to prosocial donations have protective functions, given that those adolescents who show stronger ventral striatum activity to rewards when donating to their family, also reported less risk-taking behaviour one year later (Telzer, Fuligni, Lieberman and Galvan, 2013b) and lower depressive symptoms (Telzer, Fuligni, Lieberman and Galvan, 2014).

It is currently not known how brain development supports prosocial behaviour across adolescent development, but it is likely that our brain is also shaped by prosocial experiences, given the massive changes that go on in the social brain areas and the emotional responsiveness to rewards in adolescence.

Differential susceptibility and interactive specialization

The changes in friendship are probably related to the dynamic development of the brain and the influence of pubertal hormones on these brain changes. It is difficult to say whether the rise of these brain areas really is the cause of changing friendships, because it could also be the case that the brain adapts to the changes in young people's social environment. After all, their environment begins to have different expectations of adolescents, to which they will start to adapt.

Within this process there are also individual differences between adolescents in how, and to what extent, the environment influences their development. This idea has been captured in the theory of differential susceptibility (Belsky and de Haan, 2011; Schriber and Guyer, 2015). According to this theory, there is differential susceptibility between adolescents to their environment. This means that adolescents who are more susceptible to environment influences may be more sensitive to bad outcomes in non-supportive environments and more sensitive to good outcomes in supportive environment, relative to less susceptible adolescents. Adolescents who are less susceptible may therefore be less affected to the changes in the environment. Some researchers have suggested that these susceptibility factors can be related to certain genetic profiles, resulting in gene x environment interactions (Bakermans-Kranenburg and Van IJzendoorn, 2015). Thus, the same adolescents may grow up for better or for worse, depending on their social relationships.

In this case, as in many other domains of brain research, it is difficult to differentiate between the biological basis and environmental influences because these two elements have been interwoven since birth. The brain processes that we measure are the products of nature as well as nurture. That is to say that on the one hand, young people's brains develop according to a fixed pattern, which is analogous for different individuals (nature), but on the other hand, everybody has their own unique experiences, and the shared environment (such as a particular educational system) also influences the way in which the brain develops (nurture).

It is likely that the formation of friendships is the most complex type of social behaviour. It requires all the skills and capabilities that we have discussed so far: recognizing emotions in others, finding your own place within a group and being able to deal with feelings of rejection and acceptance, forming a self-image and an identity and learning to consider the perspective of others (Nelson, Jarcho and Guyer, 2016). We already know quite a lot about all these separate skills, but the way these aspects come together during friendship development has not yet been extensively studied. How do brain regions become tuned towards developing complex social behaviour in a constantly changing environment?

One way we can try to understand this dynamic process is by taking the theoretical viewpoint of interactive specialization. This theory was already introduced in Chapter 2, where it was explained how interactive specialization may account for changes in cognitive development. The idea behind this theory is that the role of certain cortical brain regions, and the way they respond to stimuli in the environment, is the result of interaction and competition with between these regions to acquire their roles. According to Mark Johnson, who developed the theory, the same principles may account for developing social behaviour. Some brain regions may early on in development have broad functionality and are partially activated in a wide range of functions (Johnson, Grossmann and Cohen Kadosh, 2009). During development, activity-dependent interactions make cortical regions become more specialized with development. This may be especially important during social development, when adolescents develop the capacities to reason about intentions of others and take their perspectives, and would thereby also explain the prolonged development of brain regions that support these social functions (Blakemore, 2008; Mills, Lalonde, Clasen, Giedd and Blakemore, 2014).

The current theoretical models remain largely descriptive and have focused on the 'what' and 'when' question, but not the 'how' and 'why' questions. This is not surprising in a relatively young field where only recently meta-analyses are confirming consistent patterns in brain activity differences over the course of development. To answer the 'how' and 'why' questions, it will be important to follow the same individuals over time and to study the consequences of interventions on the developing brain. Many of these studies are currently ongoing in several labs across the world. It is to be expected that in the upcoming years, we'll learn much more of how brain development in adolescence provides not only risks, but also opportunities for healthy, prosocial development. The complex interplay between different social-affective and social-control functions will ultimately prove very important for developing high quality friendships (Guroglu et al., 2009).

References

Bakermans-Kranenburg, M. J. and Van IJzendoorn, M. H. (2015). The hidden efficacy of interventions: genexenvironment experiments from a differential susceptibility perspective. *Annu Rev Psychol, 66*, 381–409. doi:10.1146/annurev–psych–010814-015407

Belsky, J. and de Haan, M. (2011). Annual research review: parenting and children's brain development: the end of the beginning. *J Child Psychol Psychiatry, 52*(4), 409–428. doi:10.1111/j.1469-7610.2010.02281.x

Blakemore, S. J. (2008). The social brain in adolescence. *Nat Rev Neurosci, 9*(4), 267–277. doi:10.1038/nrn2353

Braams, B. R., Guroglu, B., de Water, E., Meuwese, R., Koolschijn, P. C., Peper, J. S. and Crone, E. A. (2014). Reward-related neural responses are dependent on the beneficiary. *Soc Cogn Affect Neurosci, 9*(7), 1030–1037. doi:10.1093/scan/nst077

Braams, B. R., Peters, S., Peper, J. S., Guroglu, B. and Crone, E. A. (2014). Gambling for self, friends and antagonists: differential contributions of affective and social brain regions on adolescent reward processing. *NeuroImage, 100*, 281–289. doi:10.1016/j.neuroimage.2014.06.020

Braams, B. R., van Duijvenvoorde, A. C., Peper, J. S. and Crone, E. A. (2015). Longitudinal changes in adolescent risk-taking: a comprehensive study of neural responses to rewards, pubertal development and risk-taking behavior. *J Neurosci, 35*(18), 7226–7238. doi:10.1523/JNEUROSCI.4764-14.2015

Bukowski, W. M. and Adams, R. (2005). Peer relationships and psychopathology: markers, moderators, mediators, mechanisms, and meanings. *J Clin Child Adolesc Psychol, 34*(1), 3–10. doi:10.1207/s15374424jccp3401_1

Bukowski, W. M., Hoza, B. and Boivin, M. (1993). Popularity, friendship, and emotional adjustment during early adolescence. In B. Laursen (ed.), *Close Friendships in Adolescence* (pp. 23–37). San Francisco: Jossey-Bass.

Bukowski, W. M. and Sippola, L. K. (2005). Friendship and development: putting the most human relationship in its place. *New Dir Child Adolesc Dev*(109), 91–98. Retrieved from www.ncbi.nlm.nih.gov/pubmed/16342897

Carter, R. M. and Huettel, S. A. (2013). A nexus model of the temporal-parietal junction. *Trends Cogn Sci, 17*(7), 328–336. doi:10.1016/j.tics.2013.05.007

Casey, B. J. (2015). Beyond simple models of self-control to circuit-based accounts of adolescent behavior. *Annu Rev Psychol, 66*, 295–319. doi:10.1146/annurev-psych-010814-015156

Chein, J., Albert, D., O'Brien, L., Uckert, K. and Steinberg, L. (2011). Peers increase adolescent risk taking by enhancing activity in the brain's reward circuitry. *Dev Sci, 14*(2), F1–10. doi:10.1111/j.1467-7687.2010.01035.x

Decety, J. and Meyer, M. (2008). From emotion resonance to empathic understanding: a social developmental neuroscience account. *Dev Psychopathol, 20*(4), 1053–1080. doi:10.1017/S0954579408000503

Decety, J. and Michalska, K. J. (2010). Neurodevelopmental changes in the circuits underlying empathy and sympathy from childhood to adulthood. *Dev Sci, 13*(6), 886–899. doi:10.1111/j.1467-7687.2009.00940.x

Decety, J., Michalska, K. J. and Kinzler, K. D. (2012). The contribution of emotion and cognition to moral sensitivity: a neurodevelopmental study. *Cereb Cortex, 22*(1), 209–220. doi:10.1093/cercor/bhr111

Engelmann, J. B., Moore, S., Monica Capra, C. and Berns, G. S. (2012). Differential neurobiological effects of expert advice on risky choice in adolescents and adults. *Soc Cogn Affect Neurosci, 7*(5), 557–567. doi:10.1093/scan/nss050

Ennett, S. and Bauman, K. (1996). Adolescent social networks: school, demongraphic, and longitudinal considerations. *Journal of Adolescent Research, 11*, 194–215.

Fareri, D. S., Niznikiewicz, M. A., Lee, V. K. and Delgado, M. R. (2012). Social network modulation of reward-related signals. *J Neurosci, 32*(26), 9045–9052. doi:10.1523/JNEUROSCI.0610-12.2012

Gardner, M. and Steinberg, L. (2005). Peer influence on risk taking, risk preference, and risky decision making in adolescence and adulthood: an experimental study. *Dev Psychol, 41*(4), 625–635. doi:10.1037/0012-1649.41.4.625

Guroglu, B., Haselager, G. J., van Lieshout, C. F., Takashima, A., Rijpkema, M. and Fernandez, G. (2008). Why are friends special? Implementing a social interaction simulation task to probe the neural correlates of friendship. *NeuroImage, 39*(2), 903–910. doi:10.1016/j.neuroimage.2007.09.007

Guroglu, B., van den Bos, W. and Crone, E. A. (2009). Neural correlates of social decision making and relationships: a developmental perspective. *Ann N Y Acad Sci, 1167*, 197–206. doi:10.1111/j.1749-6632.2009.04502.x

Guroglu, B., van den Bos, W. and Crone, E. A. (2014). Sharing and giving across adolescence: an experimental study examining the development of prosocial behavior. *Front Psychol, 5*, 291. doi:10.3389/fpsyg.2014.00291

Guroglu, B., Will, G. J. and Crone, E. A. (2014). Neural correlates of advantageous and disadvantageous inequity in sharing decisions. *PLoS One, 9*(9), e107996. doi:10.1371/journal.pone.0107996

Haber, S. N. and Knutson, B. (2010). The reward circuit: linking primate anatomy and human imaging. *Neuropsychopharmacology, 35*(1), 4–26. doi:10.1038/npp.2009.129

Harbaugh, W. T., Mayr, U. and Burghart, D. R. (2007). Neural responses to taxation and voluntary giving reveal motives for charitable donations. *Science, 316*(5831), 1622–1625. doi:10.1126/science.1140738

Harenski, C. L., Harenski, K. A., Shane, M. S. and Kiehl, K. A. (2012). Neural development of mentalizing in moral judgment from adolescence to adulthood. *Dev Cogn Neurosci, 2*(1), 162–173. doi:10.1016/j.dcn.2011.09.002

Inagaki, T. K. and Eisenberger, N. I. (2013). Shared neural mechanisms underlying social warmth and physical warmth. *Psychol Sci, 24*(11), 2272–2280. doi:10.1177/0956797613492773

Johnson, M. H., Grossmann, T. and Cohen Kadosh, K. (2009). Mapping functional brain development: building a social brain through interactive specialization. *Dev Psychol, 45*(1), 151–159. doi:10.1037/a0014548

Jones, R. M., Somerville, L. H., Li, J., Ruberry, E. J., Powers, A., Mehta, N. and Casey, B. J. (2014). Adolescent-specific patterns of behavior and neural activity during social reinforcement learning. *Cogn Affect Behav Neurosci, 14*(2), 683–697. doi:10.3758/s13415-014-0257-z

Langeslag, S. J., van der Veen, F. M. and Roder, C. H. (2014). Attention modulates the dorsal striatum response to love stimuli. *Hum Brain Mapp, 35*(2), 503–512. doi:10.1002/hbm.22197

Masten, C. L., Morelli, S. A. and Eisenberger, N. I. (2011). An fMRI investigation of empathy for 'social pain' and subsequent prosocial behavior. *NeuroImage, 55*(1), 381–388. doi:10.1016/j.neuroimage.2010.11.060

Meuwese, R., Crone, E. A., de Rooij, M. and Guroglu, B. (2015). Development of equity preferences in boys and girls across adolescence. *Child Dev, 86*(1), 145–158. doi:10.1111/cdev.12290

Meyer, M. L., Masten, C. L., Ma, Y., Wang, C., Shi, Z., Eisenberger, N. I. and Han, S. (2013). Empathy for the social suffering of friends and strangers recruits distinct patterns of brain activation. *Soc Cogn Affect Neurosci, 8*(4), 446–454. doi:10.1093/scan/nss019

Mills, K. L., Lalonde, F., Clasen, L. S., Giedd, J. N. and Blakemore, S. J. (2014). Developmental changes in the structure of the social brain in late childhood and adolescence. *Soc Cogn Affect Neurosci, 9*(1), 123–131. doi:10.1093/scan/nss113

Moll, J., Krueger, F., Zahn, R., Pardini, M., de Oliveira-Souza, R. and Grafman, J. (2006). Human fronto-mesolimbic networks guide decisions about charitable donation. *Proc Natl Acad Sci USA, 103*(42), 15623–15628. doi:10.1073/pnas.0604475103

Morelli, S. A., Rameson, L. T. and Lieberman, M. D. (2014). The neural components of empathy: predicting daily prosocial behavior. *Soc Cogn Affect Neurosci, 9*(1), 39–47. doi:10.1093/scan/nss088

Muller-Pinzler, L., Rademacher, L., Paulus, F. M. and Krach, S. (2015). When your friends make you cringe: social closeness modulates vicarious embarrassment-related neural activity. *Soc Cogn Affect Neurosci.* doi:10.1093/scan/nsv130

Nelson, E. E., Jarcho, J. M. and Guyer, A. E. (2016). Social re-orientation and brain development: an expanded and update review. *Dev Cogn Neurosci, 17*, 118–127.

Newcomb, A. F., Bukowski, W. M. and Pattee, L. (1993). Children's peer relations: a meta-analytic review of popular, rejected, neglected, controversial, and average sociometric status. *Psychol Bull, 113*(1), 99–128. Retrieved from www.ncbi.nlm.nih.gov/pubmed/8426876

O'Doherty, J. P. (2011). Contributions of the ventromedial prefrontal cortex to goal-directed action selection. *Ann N Y Acad Sci, 1239*, 118–129. doi:10.1111/j.1749-6632.2011.06290.x

Op de Macks, Z. A., Gunther Moor, B., Overgaauw, S., Guroglu, B., Dahl, R. E. and Crone, E. A. (2011). Testosterone levels correspond with increased ventral striatum activation in response to monetary rewards in adolescents. *Dev Cogn Neurosci, 1*(4), 506–516. doi:10.1016/j.dcn.2011.06.003

Overgaauw, S., Guroglu, B., Rieffe, C. and Crone, E. A. (2014). Behavior and neural correlates of empathy in adolescents. *Dev Neurosci, 36*(3–4), 210–219. doi:10.1159/000363318

Peake, S. J., Dishion, T. J., Stormshak, E. A., Moore, W. E. and Pfeifer, J. H. (2013). Risk-taking and social exclusion in adolescence: neural mechanisms underlying peer influences on decision-making. *NeuroImage, 82*, 23–34. doi:10.1016/j.neuroimage.2013.05.061

Peper, J. S. and Dahl, R. E. (2013). Surging hormones: brain-behavior interactions during puberty. *Curr Dir Psychol Sci, 22*(2), 134–139. doi:10.1177/0963721412473755

Peper, J. S., Koolschijn, P. C. and Crone, E. A. (2013). Development of risk taking: contributions from adolescent testosterone and the orbito-frontal cortex. *J Cogn Neurosci, 25*(12), 2141–2150. doi:10.1162/jocn_a_00445

Schriber, R. A. and Guyer, A. E. (2015). Adolescent neurobiological susceptibility to social context. *Dev Cogn Neurosci, 19*, 1–18. doi:10.1016/j.dcn.2015.12.009

Sharp, C., Burton, P. C. and Ha, C. (2011). 'Better the devil you know': a preliminary study of the differential modulating effects of reputation on reward processing for boys with and without externalizing behavior problems. *Eur Child Adolesc Psychiatry, 20*(11–12), 581–592. doi:10.1007/s00787-011-0225-x

Shulman, E. P., Smith, A. R., Silva, K., Icenogle, G., Duell, N., Chein, J. and Steinberg, L. (2016). The dual systems model: review, reappraisal and reaffirmation. *Dev Cogn Neurosci, 17*, 103–117.

Smith, A. R., Steinberg, L., Strang, N. and Chein, J. (2015). Age differences in the impact of peers on adolescents' and adults' neural response to reward. *Dev Cogn Neurosci, 11*, 75–82. doi:10.1016/j.dcn.2014.08.010

Steinbeis, N., Bernhardt, B. C. and Singer, T. (2012). Impulse control and underlying functions of the left DLPFC mediate age-related and age-independent individual differences in strategic social behavior. *Neuron, 73*(5), 1040–1051. doi:10.1016/j.neuron. 2011.12.027

Steinberg, L. (2008). *Adolescence.* New York: McGraw-Hill.

Telzer, E. H. (2016). Dopaminergic reward sensitivity can promote adolescent health: a new perspective on the mechanism of ventral striatum activation. *Dev Cogn Neurosci, 17,* 57–67.

Telzer, E. H., Fuligni, A. J., Lieberman, M. D. and Galvan, A. (2013a). Meaningful family relationships: neurocognitive buffers of adolescent risk taking. *J Cogn Neurosci, 25*(3), 374–387. doi:10.1162/jocn_a_00331

Telzer, E. H., Fuligni, A. J., Lieberman, M. D. and Galvan, A. (2013b). Ventral striatum activation to prosocial rewards predicts longitudinal declines in adolescent risk taking. *Dev Cogn Neurosci, 3,* 45–52. doi:10.1016/j.dcn.2012.08.004

Telzer, E. H., Fuligni, A. J., Lieberman, M. D. and Galvan, A. (2014). Neural sensitivity to eudaimonic and hedonic rewards differentially predict adolescent depressive symptoms over time. *Proc Natl Acad Sci U S A, 111*(18), 6600–6605. doi:10.1073/pnas.1323014111

Telzer, E. H., Fuligni, A. J., Lieberman, M. D., Miernicki, M. E. and Galvan, A. (2015). The quality of adolescents' peer relationships modulates neural sensitivity to risk taking. *Soc Cogn Affect Neurosci, 10*(3), 389–398. doi:10.1093/scan/nsu064

Telzer, E. H., Ichien, N. T. and Qu, Y. (2015). Mothers know best: redirecting adolescent reward sensitivity toward safe behavior during risk taking. *Soc Cogn Affect Neurosci, 10*(10), 1383–1391. doi:10.1093/scan/nsv026

Telzer, E. H., Masten, C. L., Berkman, E. T., Lieberman, M. D. and Fuligni, A. J. (2010). Gaining while giving: an fMRI study of the rewards of family assistance among white and Latino youth. *Soc Neurosci, 5*(5–6), 508–518. doi:10.1080/17470911003687913

Telzer, E. H., Masten, C. L., Berkman, E. T., Lieberman, M. D. and Fuligni, A. J. (2011). Neural regions associated with self control and mentalizing are recruited during prosocial behaviors towards the family. *NeuroImage, 58*(1), 242–249. doi:10.1016/j.neuroimage. 2011.06.013

Urberg, K., Degirmencioglu, S., Tolson, J. and Halliday-Scher, K. (1995). The structure of adolescent peer networks. *Developmental Psychology, 31,* 540–547.

Van Hoorn, J., Van Dijk, E., Meuwese, R., Rieffe, C. and Crone, E. A. (2016). Peer influence on prosocial behavior in adolescence. *Journal of Research on Adolescence.* Epub ahead of print.

Varnum, M. E., Shi, Z., Chen, A., Qiu, J. and Han, S. (2014). When 'Your' reward is the same as 'My' reward: self-construal priming shifts neural responses to own vs. friends' rewards. *NeuroImage, 87,* 164–169. doi:10.1016/j.neuroimage.2013.10.042

Wagner, U., Galli, L., Schott, B. H., Wold, A., van der Schalk, J., Manstead, A. S., Scherer, K. and Walter, H. (2015). Beautiful friendship: social sharing of emotions improves subjective feelings and activates the neural reward circuitry. *Soc Cogn Affect Neurosci, 10*(6), 801–808. doi:10.1093/scan/nsu121

Welborn, B. L., Lieberman, M. D., Goldenberg, D., Fuligni, A. J., Galvan, A. and Telzer, E. H. (2016). Neural mechanisms of social influence in adolescence. *Soc Cogn Affect Neurosci, 11*(1), 100–109. doi:10.1093/scan/nsv095

Williams, A. F. (2003). Teenage drivers: patterns of risk. *J Safety Res, 34*(1), 5–15. Retrieved from www.ncbi.nlm.nih.gov/pubmed/12535901

Williams, K. D. and Jarvis, B. (2006). Cyberball: a program for use in research on inter-personal ostracism and acceptance. *Behav Res Methods, 38*(1), 174–180. Retrieved from www.ncbi.nlm.nih.gov/pubmed/16817529

Willoughby, T., Good, M., Adachi, P. J., Hamza, C. and Tavernier, R. (2014). Examining the link between adolescent brain development and risk taking from a social-develop-mental perspective (reprinted). *Brain Cogn, 89,* 70–78. doi:10.1016/j.bandc.2014.07.006

INDEX